SPANISH BALLADS

PYRENEES

GALICIA
• Oviedo
ASTURIAS
• Santiago de
  Compostela
• León

The Pass of
Roncesvalles
• Pamplona
NAVARRE

• Burgos
• Palencia
• Salas de los
  Infantes

Arlanzón

LEÓN

Douro

CASTILLE

Ebro

• Zaragoza

ARAGON

CATALONIA

• Zamora

SPAIN

• Ávila

Tagus

EXTREMADURA

• Toledo

NEW CASTILLE

VALENCIA

• Valencia

BALEARIC I.

• Córdoba
• Baeza
Jaén
• Lorca
ANDALUSIA
• Alcalá
  la Real
• Cartagena
Guadalquivir
• Seville
• Cabra
• Granada
• Guadix
• Antequera
• Álora
• Alhama
• Jerez
• Málaga
• Almería

MEDITERRANEAN SEA

PORTUGAL

ATLANTIC
OCEAN

• Gibraltar
• Ceuta

MEDITERRANEAN

0   Km   200

HISPANIC CLASSICS

SPANISH BALLADS

Roger Wright

Aris & Phillips Ltd — Warminster — England

ISBN 0 85668 339 6 (cloth)
     0 85668 340 X (limp)

Printed and published by Aris & Phillips Ltd, Teddington House, Warminster, Wiltshire, England .

CONTENTS

PREFACE

I would like to thank the following, who have helped me in the preparation of this book: Brian Tate, Colin Smith, Angus Mackay, Derek Lomax, Lucinda Phillips, Barry Henry, Christy MacHale, and librarians of Liverpool University, The British Library, The Taylorian Institute, La Biblioteca Nacional in Madrid, and the Herzog August Bibliothek in Wolfenbüttel.

If this book has any value, it lies in the translations; and if these show any talent, that has been inherited from my mother, authoress Elinor Lyon. This book is dedicated to her.

Liverpool, December 1986

INTRODUCTION

There is an ancient ballad-singing tradition in the Hispanic world. Social anthropologists and literary specialists still regularly discover ballads all over the Iberian peninsula, Latin America and the Sephardic communities around the Mediterranean, in every Hispanic language and dialect. Most of the themes are old, although new ballads are occasionally composed. The genre is essentially oral, which means that the invention of the tape-recorder has suddenly made their existence and documentation more visible; in earlier ages the genre was in essence undocumented. Fortunately there have at times been fashions for collecting and printing ballads. Although it seems certain that Spanish ballads have been sung since the fourteenth century, and likely that the genre was in existence much earlier than that, the first texts we have in any number are from the sixteenth century. Most of the 71 ballads included in this present collection are transcribed from those early printed versions. The others come from ballads documented for the first time from rural singers by nineteenth-century collectors, but which seem certain to have existed in much earlier times also. There is no fixed text to a ballad, and different performed versions can vary quite widely in details from each other; even so, it has seemed sensible to transcribe exactly, when possible, early printed versions rather than modern recreations. Since Castilian has been the official written language of Spain since the fifteenth century, all these texts are in Castilian, but the genre is in no sense peculiar to Castille, and can be discovered in any Hispanic community. It now largely survives in the mouths of aged country people, but was once more widely known, often, it seems, performed for an audience.

The Spanish ballad (in Castilian, "romance") is simple in form. It can be of any length. Texts in this collection range from 12 to 412 lines, but the average is 50 to 60. Most lines are octosyllabic: that is, they have eight syllables, since such regularity fits the simple tunes they are sung to. The ends of all the even-numbered lines are in assonance: that is, all the vowels from the last stressed vowel onwards are the same at the end of each even line within a ballad, whatever the consonants may be. This simple structure is enough to give an aesthetically pleasing form without cramping the style of the composer or performers, since Spanish only has five vowels and the arsenal of available assonating words is consequently large.

The themes of the ballads that are most appreciated nowadays deal with universally interesting emotions such as love, sex, duty, honour, horror and poetic justice. In the sixteenth century many of the plots, although still depending for their appeal on universal human feelings, were ultimately based on and set in great events of Mediaeval history. As general knowledge of that history has now receded, so has the appeal of most of these tales for modern singers, but they are of great interest to a literary historian, and form about 60 per cent of the texts selected in this collection. In this series, the texts are meant to be Mediaeval; an intentionally modern collection would now include fewer historically-based and more of the general "adventure" ballads. All those included here, however, are anonymous, likely to be or to have been genuinely "oral", in the repertoire of at least some singers. Since 1600 the genre has been used by many self-conscious erudite poets (including Lope de Vega, the Duque de Rivas, Lorca, etc.), but only those that seem at some time to have been part of an unlettered tradition are eligible here.

For the present collection, many of the best-known ones have been selected, plus some that are less well known but which I like. The most notable omissions are those concerned with Early Mediaeval History. Rather than choosing a few on each of the main topics, as most selective anthologies do, I have included many on El Cid and compensated by omitting all those on Fernán González, the Infantes de Lara, and on twelfth to fourteenth century history other than Pedro the Cruel. The point of this collection, however, lies not in the Spanish texts selected but in the English translations. The texts have been anthologized many times, by scholars well qualified to do so, but English translations hitherto attempted have not usually succeeded in being simultaneously accurate and appealing, often being tainted by the most unattractive kind of Romantic patronization of the past. These new translations have been prepared without any reference at all to previous attempts, and are meant to be both accurate renditions of the original sense, tone and spirit, and versions that could actually be performed by a modern folk-singer (I hope some might be inspired to try). It seems necessary, therefore, to explain in detail the techniques adopted in the English translations.

STRUCTURE AND RHYME

As explained above, the Spanish ballads are structured into couplets, with assonance at the end of each couplet. This sounds natural to a Spanish ear, being unobtrusive, easy to manage, but demanding enough to stop poets from simply rambling on. In English such a structure would not work. We have over 50 vowel phonemes (including diphthongs), and such regularity in a long poem would sound obtrusive, awkward and unnatural. What we are used to, including in native ballad verse, is rhyme: that is, identity or near identity of all the sounds, consonants as well as vowels, from the last stressed vowel in each couplet onwards. This is more demanding than assonance – that is, the number of available words in the vocabulary is much fewer for each pattern – but it sounds more natural. So it has been chosen. To compensate for the extra demands created by the decision to use rhyme rather than assonance, the gap between changes in the rhyme pattern is drastically shortened. Most Spanish ballads have the same vowels in assonance all the way through, but it would be unacceptable to have the same rhyme-pattern for as long as that in English. As well as being very difficult to do, the accidental exigencies of the words available within a particular rhyme-pattern would in effect direct what the author would be able to say, and the result would be similar to that produced by the last stanza of Lewis Carroll's *Aged Aged Man* (the White Knight's song in *Alice through the Looking-Glass*, which is intentionally absurd). The normal ballad arrangement in English is to have the same rhyme either two times (as in many traditional Scots ballads) or three times (as in the main part of the *Aged Aged Man*) and then change the pattern. This makes a ballad in English seem more like a series of stanzas than a continuous text, a structure which is reinforced in performance by the usual British tendency to organize the music into four-line units. The Spanish music accompanying ballads, however, is usually arranged into two-line units, and it has seemed preferable to maintain some kind of parallel between the two by presenting the versions in English also as a continuous series of couplets rather than as a sequence of stanzas with blank space between. This arrangement has the great advantage that it is possible to choose in the translation whether to have the same rhyme pattern continuing for two couplets or for three couplets (or more). Since it makes literary sense for a change in the rhyme pattern to accompany a change in the subject matter, and conversely for a sentence of (say) three couplets to have a rhyme pattern to itself, this flexibility eventually clinched the decision to present the English as continuous text without stanza divisions. It also means that each translation is exactly as long as the original, with the line-numbers corresponding, so that the English version can help readers follow the details of the Spanish original.

The only disadvantage of this decision has been that the translations have occasionally been in danger of sounding like Ogden Nash. Much as I admire Ogden Nash, I have tried to avoid such an impression, and only gone in for virtuoso rhymes when the ballad is in any event a light-hearted one. The translation has occasionally taken liberties by varying the consonants in the rhyme, or by including an extra final consonant – e.g. in Mariana, no.7, *steel, uncongealed, heel* –. These variations are in practice unnoticeable in speech or a sung performance.

LENGTH OF LINE

The Spanish lines are usually of eight syllables, although an extra unstressed syllable often creeps in at the start of a line in actual performance. English ballad lines are sometimes longer, and it seemed at first that a longer line might be needed for the English translations. On the other hand, English words, though they tend to look longer on the page than their Spanish counterparts, also tend to have fewer syllables. In the event some of the English versions have nine syllables to a line (with the last stress on the eighth syllable), but the majority have been prepared with six-syllabled lines (with the last stress on the fifth syllable). These shorter lines occasionally have to omit minor details of the Spanish, but everything important is included, and the corresponding lightness and lilt probably makes them more successful in general than the longer lines, which may seem needlessly wordy in comparison.

RHYTHM

Rhythm, in both Spanish and English, depends on the pattern created, within each line of verse, by the stressed and the unstressed syllables. In Spanish, as in English, in all words of more than one syllable, one of the syllables is pronounced louder than the others (that is, with a greater force of air being breathed out). This is the stressed syllable. Many Spanish monosyllables are always unstressed; in English we can often choose in practice whether to stress monosyllables or not. The Spanish ballad lines have no fixed rhythm other than the requirement always to have the seventh syllable of each line stressed, and even if they did, Spanish stress patterns tend to get a bit lost in song, since in Spanish it is possible for the stresses of the music to override the stresses of the words without anyone feeling awkward about it (Spanish has no schwa vowels, like the *-er* in English *paper*, and Spanish unstressed vowels are the same phonetically as stressed ones, only less loud). In English, however, regular rhythm is essential in all songs and in almost all poetry, and the pattern of stressed and unstressed vowels has to fit the beats of the music. If a composer cannot do this, the result sounds unnatural, or forced, or as if the singer is merely singing the first thing that comes into his head. Sounding natural does not come naturally. English schwa prevents *paper* from sounding at all natural if the *-er* is on a musically-stressed note. So if the English is to be as performable as the Spanish, it is essential for the translations to be given a constant rhythm, and the basic pattern chosen is one that is quite common in English, and also known in Spanish (the old *arte mayor*), in which (using "." for unstressed vowels and "/" for stressed vowels) the basic rhythmic unit is "./." (as in *How we brought the good news from Ghent to Aix*). So in these English translations the standard rhythm of each couplet is:

[./.]./../.
[./.]./../(.)

which means that the two lines can run fluently into each other. Often at the start of a couplet an extra unstressed syllable has been added, or deleted, as happens at times in the Spanish. Occasionally an extra final unstressed syllable has been added (e.g. in Fonte Frida, no.8, lines end in *nightingale* and *enemy*). But the central "[/..]/../" of each line is meant to be consistent. This pattern is often based on colloquial rather than formal speech rhythm, particularly when translating direct speech, where, for example, English "going" is usually treated as a monosýllable.

WORDS

The translation has been prepared couplet by couplet, and ideally all the meaning of the Spanish couplet will be there in the English couplet. Sometimes there will be a little bit extra for the sake of clarity, fluency or the rhythm. The meaning is meant to be the same; on the other hand, the syntax has often been changed. Sticking closely to the original syntax is one of the grosser and most unappealing symptoms of translationese. It is the task of all translators (at any level) to translate the meaning rather than the words; that is, in this case, to attempt to produce what the original texts might have written were they expressing themselves in Modern English rather than sixteenth-century Spanish. This cannot always be achieved, but it is the right aim, and it is what these translations have been aiming for. Other things being equal, of course, the closer the translation is to the original the better.

This, then, is what the translations have been aiming for. English readers and performers will be the ones to decide if they succeed.

THE SPANISH TEXTS

The 71 ballads included here were all initially chosen from Marcelino Menéndez y Pelayo's *Antología de poetas líricos castellanos*, Vols. VIII and IX: *Primavera y flor de romances* (Madrid, Biblioteca Clásica, 1899) and Vol. X: *Romances populares recogidas de la tradición oral* (1900). Vol. VIII and the first half of Vol. IX contained a reprint of F.J. Wolf and C. Hofmann's *Primavera ...* (Berlin, Asher, 1856), and together became Vol. VIII of Menéndez y Pelayo's *Obras Completas* (ed. Enrique Sánchez Reyes, Santander, CSIC, 1945); the second part of Vol. IX and Vol. X together became Vol. IX of the *Obras*. (This is the best place to look for ballads other than those chosen here). Subsequently, where it has been possible to find an earlier source, I have done so, and reprinted that source rather than Menéndez y Pelayo's version. These sources, mostly of the 16th, but a few of the early 17th and some of the late 19th centuries, are often not even internally consistent in editorial criteria, and are collectively inconsistent in many details; modern editors often choose to apply the same modern editorial criteria to all their texts, but I have consciously decided not to. The resulting lack of editorial consistency among the texts here collected is in no way a disadvantage (given the facing translation). Nonetheless, I have consistently added punctuation, capital letters and accents according to modern taste, transcribed the letters "u" and "v" as "u" when representing a vowel and as "v" when representing a consonant, resolved any abbreviations (such as "p̃mos"> "primos" in no.31, line 21), and separated any contracted words which Modern Spanish would prefer to print as two separate words (e.g. "dellos" > "de ellos"). I have left spellings such as "ss", "ç", "y" for modern "i", "b" for modern "v" and vice versa, or an unexpectedly absent or present "h", and left separate words that Modern Spanish would prefer to print as one word (e.g. "Dad me" has not been altered to "Dadme" in no.64, line 1), with the single exception of printing when appropriate "a un" as "aun" (or "aún") to distinguish it from "a un". A very few self-evident misprints in the originals have also been corrected.

SOURCES

After each Spanish text is printed a reference to its source, plus the ballad's number in Menéndez y Pelayo (e.g. M32) and, when applicable, its number (e.g. S17) in Colin Smith, *Spanish Ballads* (Oxford, Pergamon, 1964 and reprints). The page or folio numbers in these source references refer to the following editions:

1550: Cancionero de Romances (Anvers 1550), ed. Antonio Rodríguez Moñino, Madrid, Castalia, 1967. (Originally prepared at Antwerp by Martín Nucio).

Argote: Gonzalo Argote de Molina, Nobleza del Andalucía, Jaén, Instituto de Estudios Giennenses, 1957. (Originally published in 1588).

Encina: Juan del Encina, Obras Completas, Vol. III, ed. Ana María Rambaldo, Madrid, Espasa-Calpe, 1978. (Encina lived 1469-1529).

Escobar: Juan de Escobar, Historia y Romancero del Cid (Lisboa, 1605), ed. Antonio Rodríguez Moñino, Madrid, Castalia, 1973.

Estébanez: Serafín Estébanez Calderón, Escenas Andaluzas, Madrid, Colección Escritores Castellanos, 1883.

General: Hernando del Castillo, Cancionero General, Madrid, La Sociedad de Bibliófilos Españoles, 1882. (Originally published in 1511).

JMP: Juan Menéndez Pidal, Poesía Popular. Colección de los viejos romances que se cantan por los asturianos en la danza prima, esfoyazas y filandones, recogidos y anotados por Juan Menéndez Pidal, Madrid, García, 1885.

Pérez de Hita: Ginés Pérez de Hita, Guerras Civiles de Granada, ed. Paula Blanchard-Demouge, Madrid, Centro de Estudios Históricos, 1913. (Originally published in 1595).

Pliegos: Pliegos góticos de la Biblioteca Nacional, 6 vols, Madrid, Joyas Bibliográficas, 1957-61. (Sixteenth-century broadsheets).

Praga: Pliegos sueltos españoles en la Universidad de Praga, 2 vols, Madrid, 1960. (Sixteenth-century broadsheets).

Ribera / Boehl: J. N. Boehl von Faber, <u>Floresta de rimas</u> <u>antiguas castellanas</u>, Hamburg, Perthes y Besser, 1821. (From multiple sources, including San Juan de Ribera´s <u>Nuevos romances</u> of 1605.)

RMP: Ramón Menéndez Pidal, <u>Poesía popular y poesía</u> <u>tradicional en la literatura española</u>, Oxford, Clarendon Press, 1922.

Rom. Trad.: Ramón Menéndez Pidal et al., eds, <u>Romancero</u> <u>tradicional de las lenguas hispánicas</u>, 12 vols (so far), 1957 - .

Sepúlveda: Lorenzo de Sepúlveda, <u>Romances nuevamente sacados</u> <u>de historias antiguas de la Crónica de España</u>, New York, Hispanic Society of America, 1903. (Originally published at Antwerp, 1551).

Silva: <u>Silva de Romances (Zaragoza, 1550-1551)</u>, ed. Antonio Rodríguez Moñino, Zaragoza, Publicaciones de la Cátedra, 1970.

Silva Barc: <u>Silva de varios romances</u>, Barcelona, 1557. (No modern edition; originally prepared by Jaime Cortey. The only accessible surviving copy seems to be the one at Wolfenbüttel in West Germany).

Sin año: <u>Cancionero de romances impreso en Amberes sin año</u>, ed. Ramón Menéndez Pidal, Madrid, Consejo Superior de Investigaciones Científicas, 1945. (Originally prepared by Martín Nucio, undated but probably in 1548).

Timoneda, RA and RE: Juan Timoneda, <u>Rosas de Romances</u>, Oxford, Dolphin, 1963. (Originally Valencia, 1573). The first part (of four) is the <u>Rosa de Amores</u> (RA) and the second part <u>Rosa Española</u> (RE).

REFERENCES

There is an enormous bibliography of works on the ballads, which is not to be exhaustively recapitulated here. References in the notes to particular authors are to the following:

J. M. Aguirre, "Moraima y el prisionero: ensayo de interpretación", in <u>Studies of the Spanish and Portuguese Ballad</u>, ed. N. D. Shergold, London, Tamesis, 1972, 53-72.

M. Alvar, <u>El Romancero: tradicionalidad y pervivencia</u>, 2nd ed., Barcelona, Planeta, 1974.

C. V. Aubrun, "Le romance ´gentil dona gentil dona´. Une énigme littéraire", <u>Iberoromania</u>, 18, 1983, 1-8.

P. Bénichou, Creación poética en el romancero tradicional, Madrid, Gredos, 1968.

F. Caravaca, "El romance del Conde Arnaldos en textos posteriores al del Cancionero de Romances de Amberes s.a.", Boletín de la Biblioteca Menéndez y Pelayo, 46, 1970, 3-70.

D. Catalán, "El romancero medieval", in El Comentario de textos, 4: La poesía medieval, Madrid, Castalia, 1983, 451-89.

G. Cirot, "Sur les romances ´del maestre de Calatrava´", Bulletin Hispanique, 34, 1932, 1-26.

R. Collins, Early Medieval Spain: Unity in Diversity, 400.- 1000, London, MacMillan, 1983.

M. Díaz Roig, El Romancero Viejo, Madrid, Cátedra, 1976.

W. J. Entwistle, "The adventure of Le Cerf au pied blanc in Spanish and elsewhere", Modern Language Review, 18, 1925, 435-48.

W. J. Entwistle, "The ´Romancero del Rey Don Pedro´ in Ayala and the Cuarta Crónica General", Modern Language Review, 23, 1930, 306-26.

D. W. Foster, The Early Spanish Ballad, New York, Twayne, 1971.

A. M. Howell, "Some notes on early treaties between Muslims and the Visigothic Rulers of Al-Andalús", Actas del I Congreso de Historia de Andalucía: Andalucía Medieval, Tomo I, Córdoba, Monte de Piedad, 1978, 3-14.

M. A. Ladero Quesada, Granada, historia de un país islámico, Madrid, Gredos, 1969.

D. W. Lomax, The Reconquest of Spain, London, Longman, 1978.

A. Mackay, "The ballad and the frontier in Late Medieval Spain", Bulletin of Hispanic Studies, 53, 1976, 15-33.

B. Mariscal de Rhett, ed., La muerte ocultada, Madrid, Gredos, 1984-85 (= Vol. 12 of Menéndez Pidal et al. ´s Romancero ...).

Juan de Mena, Laberinto de Fortuna, ed. J. G. Cummins, Madrid, Cátedra, 1979.

R. Menéndez Pidal et al., eds, Romancero tradicional de las lenguas hispánicas (español - portugués - catalán - sefardí), 12 vols (so far), Madrid, Gredos, 1957 -.

R. Menéndez Pidal, ed., Flor Nueva de Romances Viejos, Madrid,
Espasa-Calpe, 1938 and many reprints.

L. Mirrer-Singer, "Reevaluating the fronterizo ballad: the Romance de
la morilla burlada as a pro-Christian text", La Corónica, 13, 1985,
157-67.

G. Moya, Don Pedro, el Cruel: biología, política y tradición
literaria en la figura de Pedro I de Castilla, Madrid, Júcar, 1974.

A. R. Nykl, "Two Arabic words in the Romancero", Modern Philology, 17,
1919-20, 167-68.

E. R. Rogers, The Perilous Hunt: Symbols in Hispanic and European
Balladry, Lexington, Kentucky University Press, 1980.

C. Smith, Spanish Ballads, Oxford, Pergamon, 1964 and reprints.

L. Spitzer, "The folkloristic pre-stage of the Spanish romance ´Count
Arnaldos´", Hispanic Review, 23, 1955, 173-87.

J. Torres Fontes, "La historicidad del romance Abenámar, Abenámar",
Anuario de Estudios Medievales, 8, 1972-73, 225-56.

For further bibliography, see:

D. Catalán, "Bibliografía", in D. Catalán et al., eds, El Romancero
en la tradición oral moderna, Madrid, Cátedra-Seminario Menéndez
Pidal (=CSMP), 1972, 303-37.

S. G. Armistead, "A critical bibliography of the Hispanic Ballad in
oral tradition (1971-79)", in S. G. Armistead et al., eds, El
Romancero Hoy, 3 vols (=Romancero y Poesía Oral, vols 2-4), Madrid,
CSMP, 1979, Vol. 3, 199-310.

A. Sánchez Romeralo et al., eds, Bibliografía del Romancero Oral, I,
Madrid, CSMP, 1980.

LOVE AND ADVENTURE BALLADS

The ballads in this collection have been divided into three main categories; 'Love and Adventure' ballads, 'Cycle' ballads, and 'Frontier' ballads. Unlike the others, the 'love and adventure' ballads have no connection with any historical events; or rather, if they once did, that connection is no longer visible, nor is it necessary to our understanding of the ballad's plot. The appeal of these ballads is usually to fundamental emotions recognized by the audience and based on such human relationships as faithfulness, unfaithfulness, obsession, frustration, seduction, recognition, etc. Genuinely felt desire is usually presented as its own justification, such that the unfaithful wife and the Princess who takes a lover despite her father's wishes are sympathetic characters, whose essential goodness is often, but not always, symbolized by a happy ending. Women in general are presented as being more warm, human, intelligent and direct than men, a balance of perspective which may be determined by the fact that more often than not it seems to be women who sing and remember the ballads best. Yet it is inappropriate to generalize (as some modern specialists in Folk Literature have tended to do) and see ballads as variants on a few basic themes. Not only are the ballads individual, but different performers can put different nuances into the same tale, and different members of the audience can react in different ways to the same performance. Many ballads are subtle enough for each one to deserve consideration on its own merits, which is why this introduction is much shorter than the notes.

1. BLANCANIÑA

"Blanca soys, señora mía,
más que el rayo del sol –
¿Si la dormiré esta noche
desarmado y sin pavor?
que siete años avía, siete,
que no me desarmo, no;
más negras tengo mis carnes
que un tiznado carbón."
"Dormilda, señor, dormilda
desarmado, sin temor,
que el conde es ydo a la caça
a los montes de León."
"¡Ravia le mate los perros
y águilas el su halcón,
y del monte hasta casa
a él arrastre el morón!"
Ellos en aquesto estando,
su marido que llegó:
"¿Qué hazéys, la Blanca Niña,
hija de padre traidor?"
"Señor, peyno mis cabellos,
peyno los con gran dolor
que me dexéys a mí sola,
y a los montes os vays vos."
"¡Essa palabra, la Niña,
no era sino trayción!
¿Cúyo es aquel cavallo
que allá baxo relinchó?"
"¡Señor, era de mi padre,
y embió os lo para vos!"
"¿Cúyas son aquellas armas
que están en el corredor?"
"¡Señor, eran de mi hermano,
y oy os las embió!"
"¿Cúya es aquella lança?
Desde aquí la veo yo."
"¡Tomalda, conde, tomalda,
matadme con ella vos,
que aquesta muerte, buen conde,
bien os la merezco yo!"

"You´re whiter, my lady,
than the sun at midday;
can I sleep here tonight
unarmed, unafraid?
5 After seven long years
my armour I hold,
and my body is black,
blacker than coal."
"Sleep here, my lover,
10 no armour keep on,
for the Count is out hunting
in the wilds of León."
"May his dogs die of rabies,
his hawk killed by eagles,
15 and may his great horse
drag him home by the heels!"
But her husband returns
a little while later:
"Blancaniña, where are you,
20 like your father, a traitor!"
"I´m combing my hair,
upset that you´ve gone
and left me alone
while you´re in León."
25 "Your answer is faithless,
my lady, I know,
for whose is the horse
that neighed down below?"
"My Lord, it´s my father´s,
30 he´s sent it to you."
"And whose is the armour
I´m now walking through?"
"My Lord, it´s my brother´s,
he´s sent it you too."
35 "And whose is the lance
I can see in my way?"
"Oh, take it and kill me,
with no more delay,
for so I deserve
40 to die here today!"

(1550:317-18; S64, M136)

2. THE UNHAPPY WIFE

"La bella mal maridada
de las lindas que yo vi;
veo te tan triste, enojada -
la verdad dila tú a mí:
si has de tomar amores,
por otro no dexes a mí.
Que a tu marido, senõra,
con otras dueñas lo vi
besando y retoçando,
mucho mal dize de ti
jurava y perjurava
que te avía de herir."
Allí habló la señora,
allí habló y dixo assí:
"¡Saca me tú, el cavallero,
tú, sacasses me de aquí!
Por las tierras donde fueres
bien te sabría yo servir:
yo te haría bien la cama
en que ayamos de dormir,
yo te guisaré la cena
como a cavallero gentil,
de gallinas y de capones
y otras cosas más de mil.
Que a este mi marido
ya no lo puedo sufrir,
que me da muy mala vida
qual vos bien podéys oýr."
Ellos en aquesto estando,
su marido, helo aquí:
"¿Qué hazéys, mala traydora?
¡Oy avedes de morir!"
"Y ¿por qué, Señor, por qué?
Que nunca os lo merecí;
nunca besé a hombre,
mas hombre besó a mí;
¡las penas que él merescía,
Señor, daldas vos a mí!
Con riendas de tu cavallo,
Señor, açotes a mí;
con cordones de oro y sirgo
biva ahorques a mí;

"The unhappy wife,
your beauty I see,
but now you are crying -
explain it to me.
Look no further than me
if you're looking for lovers,
for your husband, my lady,
I've seen him with others,
caressing them, kissing them,
laughing at you,
and swearing aloud
of the harm he would do."
The lady replies,
the knight hears her say:
"Take me, my Lord,
please take me away,
and wherever you go
I'll look after and keep you,
I'll make the bed well
where we're going to be sleeping,
I'll cook you fine meals,
fit for a knight,
chickens and turkeys,
a thousand delights;
for this husband of mine
I can no longer serve,
he treats me so badly,
as I know you have heard."
But while they're together
her husband comes by -
"What are you doing, faithless!
Today you will die!"
"But I do not deserve it -
why, my Lord, why?
I've not kissed another,
though another kissed me;
the punishment he'd have,
give it to me,
with the reins of your horse,
My Lord, now beat me!
With silk and gold strings
hang me alive!

en la huerta de los naranjos
biva entierres tú a mí,
en sepoltura de oro
y labrada de un marfil;
pongas me encima un mote,
Señor, que diga assí:
´Aquí está la flor de las flores,
por amores murió aquí.
Qualquier que muere de amores
mande se enterrar aquí:
que assí hize yo, mezquina,
que por amores me perdí´".

In the orchard of orangetrees,
bury me live!
45 In a fine golden tomb,
with ivory lined,
an inscription on top
that carries this sign:
´The flower of flowers
50 lies dead inside;
who else dies for love
should be lain here beside,
since I suffered for love,
and for love I have died´."

(Sepúlveda:257–59; S65, Ml42)

3. GERINELDOS

"Gerineldos, Gerineldos,
mi camarero pulido,
¡Quién te tuviera esta noche
tres horas a mi servicio!"
"Como soy vuestro criado,
Señora, burláis conmigo."
"No me burlo, Gerineldos,
que de veras te lo digo."
"¿A cuál hora, bella Infanta,
cumpliréis lo prometido?"
"Entre la una y las dos,
cuando el rey´esté dormido."
Levantóse Gerineldos;
abre en secreto el rastrillo,
calza sandalias de seda
para andar sin ser sentido;
tres vueltas le da al palacio,
y otras tantas al castillo.
"Abráisme," dijo, "Señora;
abráisme, cuerpo garrido."

"Gerineldos, my page,
Gerineldos, you´re fine,
and for three hours tonight
I want you to be mine."
5 "But I am your servant,
Princess, you are joking."
"Not so, Gerineldos,
the truth I have spoken."
"What time, then, my Princess,
10 your promise you´ll keep?"
"Between one and two,
when the King is asleep."
Gerineldos has risen
and opened the door,
15 his sandals of silk
make no sound on the floor,
three times round the palace,
round the castle three more.
"Open, my beauty,
20 Open, Princess."

"¿Quién sois vos, el caballero
que llamáis así al postigo?"
"Gerineldos soy, Señora,
vuestro tan querido amigo."
Tomáralo por la mano;
a su lecho lo ha subido,
y besando y abrazando
Gerineldos se ha dormido.
Recordado había el rey
del sueño despavorido;
tres veces lo había llamado,
ninguna le ha respondido.
"Gerineldos, Gerineldos,
mi camarero pulido,
si me andas en traición
trátasme como a enemigo;
o con la Infanta dormías,
o el alcázar me has vendido."
Tomó la espada en la mano,
con gran saña va encendido,
fuérase para la cama,
donde a Gerineldos vido.
Él quisiéralo matar,
mas crióle desde niño.
Sacara luego la espada,
entre entrambos la ha metido,
para que al volver del sueño
catasen que el yerro ha visto.
Recordado hubo la Infanta;
vio la espada y dio un suspiro.
"Recordad, heis, Gerineldos,
que ya érades sentido,
que la espada de mi padre
de nuestro yerro es testigo."
Gerineldos va a su estancia;
le sale el rey de improviso.
"¿Dónde vienes, Gerineldos,
tan mustio, descolorido?"
"Del jardín vengo, Señor,
de coger flores y lirios,
y la rosa más fragante
mis colores ha comido."
"Mientes, mientes, Gerineldos,
que con la Infanta has dormido:
testigo de ello mi espada,
en su filo está el castigo."

"But who is this man
disturbing my rest?"
"It's me, Gerineldos,
the one you love best."
25 She's taken his hand,
into bed they both creep,
they kiss and make love
and then fall asleep.
The King jumps awake
30 from his bed terrified,
he's called Gerineldos,
who hasn't replied.
"Gerineldos, my page,
Gerineldos, you're fine,
35 but are you a traitor,
an enemy of mine?
You're in bed with the Princess,
or else you are spying."
With his sword in his hand
40 he sets out in a rage,
he comes to her bed
and discovers his page.
He wanted to kill him,
but he's raised him as son,
45 so he takes out the sword,
puts it next to each one,
so they'll see when they wake
that he knows what they've done.
The Princess awakes,
50 sees the sword, and she shudders:
"Wake up, Gerineldos,
for you've been discovered;
the sword of my father
knows we are lovers."
55 Gerineldos returns,
but the King comes between.
"You look pale, Gerineldos,
where have you been?"
"I come from the garden,
60 from picking the flowers,
and the sweetest of roses
has weakened my powers."
"You lie, Gerineldos,
with the Princess you stayed;
65 my sword is the witness,
be warned by its blade."

(Estébanez:256-58; S55, M.X,p.161)

4. RICO FRANCO

A caça yvan, a caça,
los caçadores del rey;
ni fallavan ellos caça,
ni fallavan qué traer.
Arrimaran se a un castillo
que se llamava Maynés;
dentro estava una donzella,
muy fermosa y muy cortés.
Siete condes la demandan,
y assí fazían tres reis.
Robárala Rico Franco,
Rico Franco aragonés.
Llorando yva la donzella
de sus ojos tan cortés;
falágala Rico Franco,
Rico Franco aragonés:
"Si lloras tu padre o madre,
nunca más vos los veréis;
si lloras los tus hermanos,
yo los maté todos tres."
"Ni lloro padre ni madre,
ni hermanos todos tres,
mas lloro la mi ventura
que no sé quál ha de ser.
Prestédesme, Rico Franco,
vuestro cuchillo lugués;
cortaré fitas al manto,
que no son para traer."
Rico Franco de cortese
por las cachas lo fue tender;
la donzella, que era artera,
por los pechos se lo fue a meter.
Ansí vengó padre y madre
y aun hermanos todos tres.

(Sin año:191-92; S63, M119)

Out hunting, out hunting
the men of the King,
have not found any prey,
have not caught anything.
5 To Castle Mainés
they come and ride in.
Inside there´s a maiden,
courtly and fair,
seven counts and three Kings
10 have asked for her there,
but she´s with Rico Franco,
(he´s from Aragón);
he´s taken her captive,
she weeps on and on;
15 Rico Franco cajoles her,
(he´s from Aragón):
"If you weep for your parents,
well, they´re dead and gone,
if you mourn your three brothers,
20 I´ve killed every one."
"I don´t weep for my parents
or all their three sons;
but I fear for my future,
I weep for it bitterly –
25 Rico Franco, please lend me
your sharp knife from Italy,
I´ll cut flares for my cloak,
it´ll make me look pretty."
Rico Franco then gives her
30 the handle in pity;
she stabs him to death –
she´s more skilful than others –
and avenges her father
and mother and brothers.

5. THE PRISONER (1)

Por el mes era de mayo,
quando haze la calor,
quando canta la calandria
y responde el ruyseñor,
quando los enamorados
van a servir al amor:
sino yo, triste, cuytado,
que bivo en esta prisión,
que ni sé quándo es de día,
ni quándo las noches son,
sino por una avezilla
que me cantava al albor.
Matome la un vallestero –
¡Déle Dios mal galardón!
Cabellos de mi cabeça
llegan me al corvejón,
los cabellos de mi barba
por manteles tengo yo,
las uñas de las mis manos
por cuchillo tajador.
Si lo hazía el buen rey,
haze lo como señor;
si lo haze el carcelero,
házelo como traydor.
Mas ¡quién agora me diesse
un páxaro hablador,
si quiera fuesse calandria
o tordico o ruyseñor,
criado fuesse entre damas
y abezado a la razón,
que me lleve una embaxada
[a] mi esposa Leonor,
que me embíe una empanada,
no de trucha ni salmón
sino de una lima sorda
y de un pico tajador,
la lima para los hierros
y el pico para la torre!"
Oýdolo avía el rey,
mandóle quitar la prisión.

(1550:300-01; M114a).

"The month is now May,
the summer´s beginning,
the clear nightingale
and the lark are both singing,
5 young people in love
with their loving are busy,
but I am alone
and sad in this prison;
I can´t tell when it´s night,
10 I can´t tell when it´s morning;
a bird used to sing
and announce it was dawning,
but an archer has killed it –
may God harshly reward him!
15 The hairs from my head
reach down to my ankles,
the hairs of my beard,
I use them as blankets,
the nails of my hands;
20 I use them as blades;
if the King has decreed this
his decision he´s made,
but if it´s the jailer
then I´ve been betrayed.
25 I need someone to give me
a bird that can talk,
a nightingale, lark,
a thrush or a hawk,
that´s been trained among women
30 to reason and more;
it could carry the word
to my wife Leonor
to send me a pie,
not of salmon or trout,
35 but containing a pick
and a file to get out,
the pick for the tower
and the file for my chains."
The King heard his cry
40 and has freed him again.

6. THE PRISONER (2)

Que por mayo era, por mayo,	And now it is May,
quando los grandes calores,	the heat is now growing,
quando los enamorados	all the young lovers
van servir a sus amores;	to love are now going,
sino yo, triste, mezquino,	5 but here I am, sad,
que yago en estas prisiones,	alone in this prison,
que ni sé quándo es de día	I can´t tell if it´s night,
ni menos quándo es de noche,	or if the sun´s risen;
sino por una avezilla	there once was a bird
que me cantava al alvor;	10 who sang me the dawn,
matómela un ballestero;	but an archer has shot him -
¡déle Dios mal galardón!	Curse the day he was born!

(General:550 [no.461]; Ml14)

---

7. MARIANA

"Vengo brindado, Mariana,
para una boda el domingo."
"Esa boda, Don Alonso,
debiera ser conmigo."
"No es conmigo, Mariana,   5
es con un hermano mío."
"Siéntate aquí, Don Alonso,
en este escaño florido,
que me lo dejó mi padre
para el que case conmigo."   10
Se sentara Don Alonso;
presto se quedó dormido.
Mariana, como discreta,
se fue a su jardín florido.
Tres onzas de solimán   15
cuatro de acero molido,
la sangre de tres culebras,
la piel de un lagarto vivo,
y la espinilla de un sapo,
todo se lo echó en el vino.   20

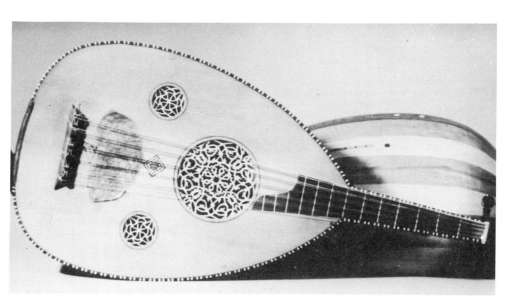

"I´m going to a wedding, Mariana,
the wedding on Sunday will be."
"But I tell you that wedding, Alonso,
that wedding, it should be with me."
"Oh it isn´t my wedding, Mariana,   5
I´m going to my brother´s, you see."
"Well, come and sit down here, Alonso,
come, sit on this flowery chair,
for my father bequeathed it, Alonso,
to the one who would marry me here."   10
Alonso sat down as invited
and sleep then invaded his mind;
Mariana went out to her garden
to find what she needed to find:
three ounces of fearsome corrosive,   15
four ounces of slivers of steel,
the skin from a still-living lizard,
the blood of three snakes uncongealed,
and she poured it all into the bottle
with a wart a toad grew on its heel.   20

"Bebe vino, Don Alonso,
Don Alonso, bebe vino."
"Bebe primero, Mariana,
que así está puesto en estilo."
Mariana, como discreta,   25
por el pecho lo ha vertido.
Don Alonso, como joven,
todo el vino se ha bebido;
con la fuerza del veneno
los dientes se le han caído.   30
"¿Qué es esto, Mariana?
¿Qué es esto que tiene el vino?"
"Tres onzas de solimán,
cuatro de acero molido,
la sangre de tres culebras,   35
la piel de un lagarto vivo
y la espinilla del sapo,
para robarte el sentido."
"!Sáname, buena Mariana,
que me casaré contigo!"   40
"No puede ser, Don Alonso,
que el corazón te ha partido."
"!Adiós, esposa del alma!
Presto quedas sin marido;
¡Adiós, padres de mi vida!   45
Presto quedaron sin hijo.
Cuando salí de mi casa
salí en un caballo pío;
y ahora voy para la iglesia
en una caja de pino."   50

(JMP:164-65; S68, M.X,p.98)

8. FONTE FRIDA

Fonte frida, Fonte frida,
Fonte frida y con amor,
do todas las avezicas
van tomar consolación;
si no es la tortolica,   5
que está viuda y con dolor.
Por aý fuera a passar
el traydor del ruyseñor;
las palabras que dezía
llenas son de trayción: 10
"Si tú quisiesses, Señora,

"Would you like to drink wine now, Alonso,
Don Alonso, would you like some wine?"
"But it´s only polite, Mariana,
for you to drink yours before mine."
She´s used all her skill, Mariana,   25
to pour her wine back as before,
while the young unsuspecting Alonso
has drained it till there´s nothing more,
and the poison is sharp and so rapid
his teeth fall right out on the floor -   30
"But what is all this, Mariana,
and what´s the wine doing this for?"
"Three ounces of fearsome corrosive,
four ounces of slivers of steel,
the skin from a still-living lizard,   35
the blood from three snakes uncongealed,
in the wine, with a little toad´s pimple,
mean this pain is the last that you´ll feel."
"Cure me, my sweet Mariana,
I promise that I´ll marry you."   40
"No, that cannot happen, Alonso,
your heart is now cracking in two."
"Farewell to the love I´d have married,
whose time without me has begun!
Farewell to my father and mother,   45
who´ll have to live on with no son!
When I left from our gateway this morning
I rode on this white horse of mine;
but now I´ll go on to the churchyard
encased in a coffin of pine."   50

There´s a crystal-cool spring, Fonte Frida,
Fonte Frida, a haven for lovers,
where all the young birds come together
enjoying themselves with the others;
except for the lonely young turtle-dove,   5
a widow who silently suffers.
That sweet-singing traitor, the nightingale,
came to the water one night,
and his treacherous words to the widow
held a dangerous edge of delight: 10
"Would you like me to come round and serve you?

yo sería tu servidor."
"¡Vete de aý, enemigo,
malo, falso, engañador!
Que ni poso en ramo verde,   15
ni en prado que tenga flor,
que si hallo el agua clara
turbia la bevía yo;
que no quiero haver marido,
porque hijos no haya, no.   20
No quiero plazer con ellos,
ni menos consolación.
¡Déxame, triste enemigo,
malo, falso, mal traydor,
que no quiero ser tu amiga,   25
ni casar contigo, no!"

(Silva:213; S61, M116)

---

9. CONDE CLAROS (1)

Media noche era por filo,	Twelve o´clock, midnight,
los gallos querían cantar.	the cocks sing their best;
Conde Claros con amores	Count Claros, in love,
no podía reposar.	is unable to rest;
Dando muy grandes sospiros 5	his emotion has led him
que el amor le hazía dar,	to sigh and to weep,
por amor de Clara Niña,	his love for the Princess
no le dexa sossegar.	will not let him sleep.
Quando vino la mañana	And now the night´s over,
que quería alborear, 10	the dawn comes instead,
salto diera de la cama,	as sharp as a falcon
que parece un gavilán.	he leaps from his bed,
Bozes da por el palacio,	and calls in his palace
y empeçara de llamar:	with no time to lose
"Levanta, mi camarero, 15	"Bring me, my page,
dame vestir y calçar."	my clothes and my shoes."
Presto estava el camarero	The pageboy has brought him
para avérselo de dar;	his clothes all together;
diérale calças de grana,	his trousers of scarlet,
borzeguíes de cordován, 20	his boots of fine leather,
diérale jubón de seda	his jacket of silk
aforrado en zarzahán,	with a striped silk lining,
diérale un manto rico	his richly-made cape,
que no se puede apreciar,	there isn´t one finer,
trezientas piedras preciosas 25	attached to the collar

     Would you like me to act as your knight?"
     "You´re wicked, you´re false, you´re an enemy,
     leave me alone, leave me here,
     for I´m not going to sit on green branches   15
     or in fields where bright flowers appear,
     and I´ll only drink water when muddied
     even if I´ve discovered it clear -
     for I don´t want to marry another,
     I don´t want to have children again,   20
     I don´t want any family pleasures,
     nor a husband to keep me from pain;
     so leave me alone, you´re a traitor,
     a wicked false enemy too,
     for I certainly won´t be your lover,   25
     and neither will I marry you."

---

al derredor del collar.		are three hundred diamonds;
Tráele un rico cavallo,		he brings him his horse -
que en la corte no ay su par,		in the court there´s no rival -
que la silla con el freno		worth more than a city
bien valía una ciudad,	30	are its reins and its bridle;
con trezientos cascaveles		three hundred bells
al rededor del petral.		on its breaststrap are lying,
Los ciento eran de oro,		a hundred of gold,
y los ciento de metal,		a hundred of iron,
y los ciento son de plata	35	a hundred of silver,
por los sones concordar;		in tune they all ring
y vase para el palacio,		as he rides to the palace,
para el palacio real,		the home of the King,
a la Infanta Clara Niña,		to find Claraniña
allí la fuera a hallar.	40	the royal Princess,
Trezientas damas con ella		who has three hundred maids,
que la van a acompañar,		not a single one less,
tan linda va Clara Niña		and that she´s the most beautiful
que a todos haze penar.		all sadly confess.
Conde Claros que la vido,	45	Claros dismounts
luego va descavalgar,		as soon as he´s seen her
las rodillas por el suelo		and kneels on the ground
le començo de hablar:		before Claraniña;
"¡Mantenga Dios a Tu Alteza!"		"God bless you, Your Highness"
"¡Conde Claros, bien vengáys!"	50	"Count Claros, you´re blest",

Las palabras que prosigue
eran para enamorar.
"Conde Claros, Conde Claros,
El Señor de Montalván,
¡cómo avéys hermoso cuerpo,
para con moros lidiar!"
Respondiera el Conde Claros,
tal respuesta le fue a dar:
"Mi cuerpo tengo, Señora,
para con damas holgar.
Si yo os tuviesse esta noche,
Señora, a mi mandar,
otro día en la mañana
con cient moros pelear;
si a todos no los venciesse,
que me mandasse matar."
"Calledes, conde, calledes,
y no os queráys alabar -
el que quiere servir damas
assí lo suele hablar,
y al entrar en las batallas
bien se saben escusar."
"Si no lo creéys, Señora,
por las obras se verá.
Siete años son passados
que os empecé de amar,
que de noche yo no duermo,
ni de día puedo holgar."
"Siempre os preciastes, Conde,
de las damas os burlar.
Mas déxame yr a los baños,
a los baños a bañar,
quando yo sea bañada
estoy a vuestro mandar."
Respondiérale el buen conde,
tal respuesta le fue a dar:
"Bien sabedes vos, Señora,
que soy caçador real;
caça que tengo en la mano
nunca la puedo dexar."
Tomárala por la mano,
para un vergel se van.
A la sombra de un ciprés,
debaxo de un rosal,
de la cintura arriba
tan dulces besos se dan;
de la cintura abaxo
como hombre y muger se han.

and she plays on his passion
with what she says next:
"You have, my Count Claros,
My Lord Montalbán,
55 a fine body for fighting
with Moors, a fine man."
Claros replies,
these words he's said:
"My body is best
60 with women in bed;
and if I can have you
tonight at my will,
fight a hundred fierce Moslems
next morning I will,
65 if I don't beat them all,
then let me be killed."
"Don't say that, Count Claros;
there's no need to boast;
when flattering women
70 men do that most,
and then in the battle
they run from the host."
"If you don't believe me,
you'll see that it's true;
75 for the last seven years
I've been longing for you,
I'm restless at night
and all the day too."
"My Count, you have always
80 made fun of the women,
so let me go bathing
(I'm on my way swimming)
and when I return
I'll be here at your bidding."
85 But this is the answer
she's heard the Count say:
"I am a huntsman
in the King's pay,
and a bird in the hand
90 can't be let slip away."
He leads her away
to a garden nearby,
in the shade of a pine
by a rosebush they lie;
95 from the waist up
kissing sweet as they can,
from the waist down
join woman and man.

Mas la fortuna adversa,
que a plazeres da pesar;
por aý passó un caçador
que no deviera passar,
en busca de una podenca
que ravia devía matar.
Vido estar al Conde Claros
con la Infanta al bel holgar.
El conde, quando le vido,
empeçóle de llamar:
"Ven acá tú, el caçador;
assí Dios te guarde de mal,
de todo lo que has visto
tú nos tengas poridad.
Darte yo mil marcos de oro,
y si más quisieres, más;
casarte con una donzella
que era mi prima carnal;
darte he en arras y en dote
la villa de Montalván.
De otra parte la Infanta
mucho más te puede dar."
El caçador sin ventura
no les quiso escuchar,
vase para los palacios
a do el buen rey está.
"Manténgate Dios, el rey,
y a tu corona real;
una nueva yo te trayo
dolorosa y de pesar,
que no os cumple traer corona
ni en cavallo cavalgar;
la corona de la cabeça
bien la podéys vos quitar,
si tal desonrra como ésta
la oviesseys de comportar.
Que he hallado la Infanta
con Claros de Montalván,
besándola y abraçando
en vuestro huerto real:
de la cintura abaxo
como hombre y muger se han."
El rey con muy grande enojo
al caçador mandó matar,
porque había sido osado
de tales nuevas le dar.
Mandó llamar sus alguaziles
a priessa y no de vagar;

100 But Fortune is harsh
and turns joy to despair;
there comes in a huntsman,
who shouldn´t be there,
trying to find
105 a lost rabid hound;
he sees Claraniña
making love with the Count.
When the Count sees the huntsman
he summons him down:
"Come here, my good huntsman,
110 God keep you from harm;
don´t say that you´ve seen us,
don´t raise an alarm.
A thousand gold coins
I can give you or more,
115 I can give you my cousin
to marry, I´m sure,
you can have as a dowry
rich Montalbán,
and the Princess will too
120 give as much as she can."
A curse on the huntsman,
he didn´t agree,
he rode to the palace
her father to see:
125 "God bless you, My King,
and your royal crown,
I bring you sad news
that will bow your head down,
for you cannot ride proudly
130 or hold your head high,
you´ll lose all your kingdom
your hopes all awry
if you let this dishonour
unpunished go by;
135 I´ve just seen the Princess
and Count Montalbán
in your royal garden
kissing close as they can,
from the waist downward
140 joined woman with man."
The King is so angry
he orders the death
of the huntsman who dared
accuse the Princess.
145 Then he summons his guards
without a delay,

mandó armar quinientos hombres
que los hayan de acompañar
para que prendan al conde
y le hayan de tomar,
y mandó cerrar las puertas,
las puertas de la ciudad.
A las puertas del palacio,
allá le fueron a hallar.
Preso llevan al buen conde
con mucha seguridad,
unos grillos a los pies
que bien pesan un quintal,
las esposas a las manos
que era dolor de mirar,
una cadena a su cuello
que de hierro era el collar.
Caválganle en una mula
por más desonrra le dar,
metiéronle en una torre
de muy gran escuridad.
Las llaves de la prisión
el rey las quiso llevar
porque sin licencia suya
nadie le pueda hablar.
Por él rogavan los grandes
quantos en la corte están,
por él rogava Oliveros,
por él rogava Roldán,
y ruegan los doze pares
de Francia la natural,
y las monjas de Santa Ana
con las de la Trinidad
llevavan un crucifixo
para al buen rey rogar.
Con ellas va un arçobispo
y un perlado y cardenal
mas el rey con grande enojo
a nadie quiso escuchar;
antes, de muy enojado,
sus grandes mandó llamar.
Quando ya los tuvo juntos
empeçoles de hablar.
"Amigos e hijos míos,
a lo que los hize llamar,
ya sabéys que el Conde Claros,
el Señor de Montalván,
de cómo le he criado
hasta ponello en edad,

150 and brings five hundred knights
with him on the way
to seek out the Count
wherever he goes;
he orders the gates
of the city to close,
but in front of the palace
155 and capture the Count
so he can't get away,
the heaviest irons
they put on his feet,
the cuffs on his hands
160 are painful to see,
with a chain round his neck
like a necklace of steel,
he's set on a mule
more dishonoured to feel,
165 he's locked in a tower
as dark as can be,
and the King takes the keys
of the dungeon off with him
so noone can see him
170 without his permission.
All of the nobles
at court want to help,
Oliver goes,
Roland as well,
175 the twelve noble knights
of France want him freed,
the Nuns of the Trinity
and St Anne's nuns proceed
to the King with their crosses,
180 they all intercede;
the archbishop, the cardinal,
and prelate all pray,
but the King is so angry
he sends them away –
185 or rather in fury
he summons his court,
and when they're together
he says what he's thought:
"My friends and relations,
190 you all understand
that noble Count Claros,
the Lord Montalbán,
was brought up by me
till he grew to a man;

y le he guardado su tierra
que su padre le fue a dar –
el que morir no deviera,
Reinaldos de Montalván –.
Por hazelle yo más grande
de lo mío le quise dar;
hízele governador
de mi reyno natural.
Él, por darme galardón,
mirad en qué fue a tocar;
que ¡quiso forçar la Infanta,
hija mía natural!
Hombre que lo tal comete,
¿qué sentencia le han de dar?"
Todos dizen a una voz
que lo hayan de degollar,
y assí la sentencia dada
el buen rey la fue a firmar.
El arçobispo que esto viera
al buen rey fuera a hablar,
pidiéndole por merced
licencia le quiera dar
para yr a ver al conde
y su muerte le denunciar.
"Plázeme" dixo el buen rey,
"Plázeme de voluntad,
mas con esta condición,
que sólo havéys de andar
con aqueste pagezico
de quien puedo bien fiar."
Ya se parte el arçobispo
y a las cárceles se va.
Las guardas desque lo vieron
luego le dexan entrar.
Con él yva el pagezico
que le va a acompañar.
Quando vido estar al conde
en su prisión y pesar,
las palabras que le dize
dolor eran de escuchar.
"Pésame de vos, el conde,
quanto me puede pesar,
que los yerros por amores
dignos son de perdonar.   [...]
Por vos he rogado al rey;
nunca me quiso escuchar.
Antes ha dado sentencia
que os hayan de degollar.

195 from the death of his father
I guarded his lands
(he should never have died,
Reynard Montalbán),
even more of my kingdom
200 to give him I planned,
I made him a governor
of part of my lands;
now see the reward
he has placed in my hand!
205 Raping the Princess,
my daughter and heiress,
for a man who does that,
what sentence is fairest?"
They have to agree,
210 execution in shame,
the sentence is given,
the King signs his name.
The Archbishop sees it
and asks for permission
215 to do a sad duty
and go to the prison
to explain to the Count
the fatal decision;
"Yes", says the King,
220 "but on this condition,
I´ll let you go in
if you go there alone
with only this page
whose loyalty´s known."
225 To the dungeon descends
the loyal archbishop
and when the guards see him
they open the prison
to him and the page
230 who is going there with him;
he sees the sad Count
in captive submission,
it´s painful to speak
but still harder to listen:
235 "I´m greatly upset,
My Count, by this mission,
for mistakes made by lovers
should be forgiven;   [...]
I´ve prayed to the King,
240 but he wouldn´t listen;
he´s decreed execution,
the sentence is given.

Yo vos lo dixe, sobrino,
que os dexássedes de amar,
que el que las mugeres ama
a tal galardón le dan
que haya de morir por ellas
y en las cárceles penar."
Respondiera el buen conde
con esfuerço singular:
"¡Calledes, por Dios, mi tío,
no me queráys enojar!
Quien no ama a las mugeres
no se puede hombre llamar.
Mas la vida que yo tengo
por ellas quiero gastar."
Respondió el pajezico,
tal respuesta le fue a dar:
"Conde, bien aventurado
siempre os deven de llamar,
porque muerte tan honrrada
por vos havía de passar.
Más embidia he de vos, Conde,
que manzilla ni pesar;
más querría ser vos, Conde,
que el rey que os manda matar,
porque muerte tan honrrada
por mí hoviesse de passar.
Llaman yerro a la fortuna
quien no la sabe gozar.
La priessa del cadahalso
vos, Conde, la devéys dar,
si no es dada la sentencia
vos la devéys de firmar."
El conde que esto oyera
tal respuesta le fue a dar:
"Por Dios, te ruego, el page,
y en amor de caridad,
que vayas a la Princesa
de mi parte a le rogar
que suplico a su alteza
que ella me salga a mirar,
que en la hora de mi muerte
yo la pueda contemplar.
Que si mis ojos la veen
mi alma no penará."
Ya se parte el pagezico,
ya se parte, ya se va,
llorando de los sus ojos
que quería rebentar.

My nephew, I told you
to stop chasing women,
245 for incautious lovers
often reach this position
of dying for them,
or of lying in prison."
Count Claros replies
250 with fighting words then:
"My uncle, please stop,
I´ll be angry again:
those who do not love women
cannot be called men
255 and I´m happy to give
my life up for them."
The bishop´s young page
replies to him then:
"My Count, they should call you
260 most favoured of men,
when your life has so come
to an honourable end!
For you I feel envy,
not sorrow, my friend,
265 I would rather be you
than the powerful King,
for to die in such honour
is a wonderful thing!
Those who cannot enjoy love
270 call loving a sin;
so run to the block,
be proud to climb in,
yourself sign the sentence
instead of the King."
275 The Count hears the page
and makes a request;
"I beg you do this
at a lover´s behest,
that you go on now for me
280 and tell the Princess
that I´m begging Her Highness
to come to my death
so I can see her
at my very last breath,
285 for if I see her
my soul will find rest."
The page sets off running,
he rushes off first,
he´s crying so hard
290 his eyes want to burst,

Spanish	Line	English
Topara con la Princesa;		he finds the Princess
bien oyréys lo que dirá:		and tells her the worst:
"Agora es tiempo, Señora,		"And there´s time, my Princess,
que hayáys de remediar,		for you to recover,
que a vuestro querido, el conde,	295	as they take to his death
lo llevan a degollar."		Count Claros, your lover."
La Infanta que esto oyera		The Princess collapses
en tierra muerta se cae.		and faints on the ground,
Damas, dueñas y donzellas		and none of the maids there
no la pueden recordar,	300	can bring her around
hasta que llegó su aya,		till the nurse who once held her
la que la fue a criar:		hurries on down;
"¿Qué es aquesto, la Infanta?		"My Princess, what is this;
aquesto, ¿qué puede estar?"		what can this be?"
"¡Ay, triste de mí, mezquina!	305	"I don´t know what to do,
que no sé qué puede estar;		take pity on me;
que si al conde me matan		if my Claros is killed
yo me havré desesperar."		then desperate I´ll be!"
"Saliéssedes vos, mi hija,		"So go, my Princess,
saliéssedes lo a quitar."	310	you must set him free."
Ya se parte la Infanta,		Claraniña is running
ya se parte, ya se va,		as fast as she can
fuese para el mercado		down to the square
donde lo han de sacar.		where they´re taking her man;
Vido estar el cadahalso	315	the platform´s prepared
en que lo han de degollar,		according to plan;
damas, dueñas y donzellas		the old and young women
que lo salen a mirar,		are gathering there.
vio venir la gente de armas		She sees the armed guards
que lo traen a matar,	320	take him into the square,
los pregoneros delante		and before them the criers
por su yerro publicar.		his crime now declare.
Con el poder de la gente		There are so many people
ella no podía passar:		she cannot get through -
"¡Apartad vos, gente de armas!	325	"Let me through, all you guards
Todos me hazed lugar!		let me come in too,
Si no, ¡por vida del rey,		if not - then the King
a todos mande matar!"		will kill all of you!"
La gente, que la conosce,		The guards recognize her
luego le hazen lugar	330	and let her go through.
hasta que llegó al conde		She reaches the Count
? le empeçara de hablar:		and shouts to him too:
"¡Esforçá, esforçá, el buen conde!		"Don´t give up, my Count Claros,
No queráys desmayar!		be brave, there´s still time,
que aun que yo pierda la vida	335	for I´m going to save your life
la vuestra se ha de salvar."		even if I lose mine."
El alguazil que esto oyera		The constable hears her
començo de caminar,		and goes straightaway

vase para los palacios,
a donde el buen rey está:
"Cavalgue, La Vuestra Alteza,
a priessa, no de vagar,
que salida es la Infanta
para el conde nos quitar;
los unos manda que maten,
y los otros enforcar –
si Tu Alteza no socorre
yo no puedo remediar."
El buen rey de que esto oyera
començo de caminar
y fuese para el mercado
a do el conde fue a hallar.
"¿Qué es esto, Infanta?
Aquesto,¿qué puede estar?
La sentencia que yo he dado,
vos la queréys revocar?
Yo juro por mi corona,
por mi corona real,
que si heredero tuviesse
que me hoviesse de heredar,
que a vos y al Conde Claros
vivos os haría quemar."
"Que vos me matéys, mi padre,
muy bien me podéys matar,
mas suplico a Vuestra Alteza
que se quiera él acordar
de los servicios passados
de Reynaldos de Montalván,
que murió en las batallas
por tu corona ensalçar;
por los servicios del padre
al hijo deves galardonar;
por mal querer de traydores
vos no le devéys matar,
que su muerte será causa
que me hayáys de disfamar.
Mas suplico a Vuestra Alteza
que se quiera consejar,
que los reyes con furor
no deven de sentenciar,
porque el conde es de linage
del reyno más principal,
porque él era de los doze
que a tu mesa comen pan.
Sus amigos y parientes
todos te querrían mal,

340 to the King at the Palace
and there has to say:
"Come quickly, Your Highness,
come now, don´t delay,
the Princess has come
to take him away;
345 she wants some of us killed,
she wants some of us hung,
and I cannot resolve this
until you have come."
The King when he hears this
350 sets off then and there
and goes to the Count
in the old market-square:
"What is this, my Princess?
What can have arisen?
355 Do you think you can alter
a sentence I´ve given?
I swear by my crown
that if I ever learn
that you´ve got an heir
360 who´ll inherit in turn,
then, you and the Count,
I´ll have you both burned!"
"Then kill me, my father,
you easily could;
365 but I beg of Your Highness,
recall, if you would,
the services done you
by Reynard, the Good;
defending your crown
370 he died at the sword,
and his son, the Count Claros
deserves the reward;
his enemies hate him,
but don´t kill him, you´ll learn
375 at once, if you kill him,
my shame is confirmed.
I beg of Your Highness,
consider again;
Kings shouldn´t pass sentence
380 in anger and pain;
and the Count is a noble,
the best in the land,
for he´s one of the twelve
who eat at your hand;
385 his friends and relations
will all be annoyed

rebolver te hían guerra,
tus reynos se perderán."
El buen rey que esto oyera
començara a demandar:
"Consejo os pido, los míos,
que me queráys consejar."
Luego todos se apartaron
por su consejo tomar;
el consejo que le dieron,
que le haya de perdonar,
por quitar males y bregas,
y por la Princesa afamar.
Todos firman el perdón;
el buen rey fue a firmar.
También le aconsejaron,
consejo le fueron dar,
pues la Infanta quería al conde,
con él aya de casar.
Ya deshierran al buen conde,
ya lo mandan desferrar.
Descavalga de una mula
el arçobispo a desposar;
él tomóles de las manos,
assí los huvo de jurar;
los enojos y pesares
en plazer hovieron de tornar.

and attack your own kingdom,
it could be destroyed."
The King, when he´s heard her,
390 says to his court:
"I need your advice,
come tell me your thoughts."
So they go to one side
to decide what is best;
395 the advice that they give
is to pardon him next,
to avoid any war,
and restore the Princess.
They all sign the pardon,
400 the King signs it too,
they give him advice
about what he should do;
the Princess loves the Count,
so let marriage ensue.
405 They take off the chains
and the irons from the Count,
the Archbishop, to marry them,
has to dismount,
he holds both their hands
410 and joins them together;
so sorrow and pain
have turned into pleasure.

(Silva:390-96; S54, M190)

10. CONDE CLAROS (2)

"Pésame de vos, el conde,
porque vos mandan matar,
pues el yerro que tú hezistes
no fue mucho de culpar,
que los yerros por amores
dinos son de perdonar.
Yo rrogué por vos al rrey
que vos mandase soltar,
mas el rrey, con gran enojo,
no me lo quiso escuchar.
Díxome que no rrogase,
que no se puede escusar,
la sentençia ya es dada,
no se puede rrevocar,
que dormistes con la infanta

"My Count, I´m distressed
that they´ve sent you to die,
for there´s really no blame
to be felt in your crime.
5 Crimes caused by love
should be forgiven,
so I begged of the King
that your freedom be given,
but the King was so angry
10 he´d not even listen.
He made me be quiet,
said it can´t be arranged,
he´s given the sentence,
it cannot be changed,
15 for you slept with the Princess

que avíades de guardar.
El cadahalso está hecho
donde os an de degollar.
Más os valiera, sobrino,
de las damas no curar,
que quien más las damas sirve
tal merçed deve esperar,
que de muerto o perdido
ninguno puede escapar."
"Tales palabras, mi tío,
no las puedo soportar;
más quiero morir por ellas
que bevir sin las mirar.
Quien a mí bien me quisiere,
no me cure de llorar,
que no muero por traidor
ni por los dados jugar:
muero yo por mi señora,
que no me puede penar,
pues el yerro que yo fize,
no fue mucho de culpar."

(Encina:305-06; M.Ap55)

when you were her guard;
so you´ll be beheaded
out there in the yard.
Not to sleep with the girls,
20   my nephew, is best,
and those who love most
this reward should expect _
none can escape
ruin or death."
25   "Your words, my good uncle,
I cannot agree with them,
I´d much rather die
if I cannot now be with them.
If you´re wishing me well
30   keep as calm as you´re able,
I don´t die as a traitor,
or for gambling at table,
I won´t even suffer,
for my lady I die,
35   and there´s really no blame
to be felt in my crime."

11. DEATH CONCEALED

A cazar va el rey don Pedro,
a cazar como solía;
le diera el mal de la muerte,
para casa se volvía.
A la entrada de la puerta
vio un pastor que le decía:
"Albricias, Señor Don Pedro,
que dármelas bien podía;
que Doña Alda ya parió,
y un hijo varón tenía."
"Pues, si parió Doña Alda,
¡hijo sin padre sería!"
Con estas palabras y otras,
el rey subió para arriba.
"Haga la cama, mi madre;
haga la cama de oliva;
aprisa, aprisa con ella,
que presto me moriría.
No diga nada a Doña Alda,
a Doña Alda de mi vida,

King Pedro, out hunting
as often he goes,
falls mortally ill
and has to come home.
5   There at his doorway
a shepherd he sees:
"Greetings, King Pedro,
give greetings to me,
for she´s just had a boy,
10   Doña Alda, your Queen!"
"If Alda has borne him,
he´ll fatherless be!"
He goes with these words
to the very top room -
15   "Make my bed, mother,
the best you can do,
quickly, but quickly,
I´m bound to die soon -
but say nothing to Alda,
20   the Queen of my heart,

que no sepa de mi muerte
hasta los cuarenta días."
Don Pedro que se murió,
Doña Alda nada sabía.
Viniera Pascua de Flores,
Doña Alda no ha oído misa.
"Diga, diga, la mi suegra,
¿qué vestido llevaría?"
"Como eres alta y delgada,
lo negro bien te estaría."
"Yo non quiero llevar luto,
que voy de linda parida."
A la entrada de la iglesia
toda la gente la mira.
"Diga, diga, Don Melchor,
consejero de mi vida,
¿por qué me mira la gente?
¿Por qué la gente me mira?"
"Diréte una cosa, Alda,
que de saberse tenía:
aquí se entierran los reyes
cuantos lo son de Castilla,
y aquí se enterró Don Pedro,
la prenda que más querías."
"¡Oh, mal haya la mi suegra,
que engañada me traía!
¡Que en vez de venir de luto,
vengo de linda parida!"

(JMP:181-82; M.X,p.110)

don't tell her I've died
until forty days pass."
Don Pedro has died,
but Alda knows nothing;
she has not been to Mass
and now Easter is coming -
"Tell me, Queen Mother,
what dress should I wear?"
"You're tall and you're thin,
so black suits you there."
"I'm a happy new mother,
I shouldn't wear black!"
The people at church
all stare at her back -
"Tell me, Melchor,
adviser and friend,
why are all of them staring
again and again?"
"Alda, I'll tell you,
it must be revealed,
here there lie buried
all the Kings of Castille,
and here lies King Pedro
your husband concealed."
"A curse on his mother
who kept the news back!
I've come as a mother
but I should be in black!"

(line numbers: 25, 30, 35, 40, 45)

12. THE LADY AND THE SHEPHERD

Estáse la gentil dama
paseando en su vergel;
los pies tenía descalços
que era maravilla ver.
Hablávame desde lexos,
no le quise responder.
Respondíle con gran saña:
"¿Qué mandáis, gentil mujer?"
Con una boz amorosa
començó de responder:
"Ven acá tú, el pastorcico,
si quieres tomar plazer;
siesta es de medio día,

The noble young lady
walks in her garden,
no shoes on her feet,
she looks like a marvel;
she calls from afar,
I don't want to respond,
but I say to her angrily
"What is it you want?"
With love in her voice
she answers to me:
"Come here, my shepherd,
if pleasure you seek;
it's time at midday

(line numbers: 5, 10)

y ya es hora de comer;
si querrás tomar posada,
todo es a tu plazer."
"No era tiempo, Señora,
que me aya de detener;
que tengo muger y hijos
y casa de mantener;
y mi ganado en la sierra
que se me yva a perder,
y aquellos que lo guardan
no tenían qué comer."
"Vete con Dios, pastorcillo,
no te sabes entender.
Hermosuras de mi cuerpo
yo te las hiziera ver;
delgadita en la cintura,
blanca soy como el papel,
la color tengo mezclada
como rosa en el rosel,
las teticas agudicas
que el brial quieren hender,
el cuello tengo de garça,
los ojos de esparver,
pues lo que tengo encubierto
maravilla es de lo ver."
"Ni aunque más tengáys, Señora,
no me puedo detener."

for food and for leisure
15 and if you come here
it is all for your pleasure."
"I haven´t got time
to stop or to eat,
I´ve a wife and my children
20 and household to keep;
I must go to the mountains
and round up my sheep,
the shepherds who guard them
have nothing to eat."
25 "God be with you, good shepherd,
but you don´t know what´s best,
my body´s a beauty,
I´d show you the rest,
I´m slim at the waist,
30 my skin, it is fair,
it´s white and it´s pink
as a rose can compare,
my nipples push out
through the gown, they´re so tight,
35 my neck, it is slender,
my eyes, they are bright;
for all that´s now covered
is fine to see too."
"Whatever you have,
40 I have no time for you."

(Rom. Trad. X (Pliego suelto):39-40; S66, M145)

13. THE WHITE-FOOTED DEER

Tres hijuelos avía el rey,
tres hijuelos, que no más;
por enojo que uvo de ellos
todos maldito los ha.
El uno se tornó ciervo,
el otro se tornó can,
el otro se tornó moro,
passó las aguas del mar.

The King had three sons,
just three and no more,
but he is so angry
he´s put spells on them all;
5 the first is a stag,
the second a hound,
the third is a Moor
who sails the world round.

Andávase Lançarote
entre las damas holgando;
grandes bozes dio la una:
"Cavallero, ¡estad parado!
si fuesse la mi ventura
cumplido fuesse mi hado
que yo casasse con vos
y vos comigo de grado,
y me diéssedes en arras
aquel ciervo del pie blanco."
"Daros lo he yo, mi Señora,
de coraçón y de grado,
y supiesse yo las tierras
donde el ciervo era criado."
Ya cavalga Lançarote,
ya cavalga y va su vía;
delante de sí llevava
los sabuesos por la traýlla.
Llegado avía a una hermita
donde un hermitaño avía.
"¡Dios te salve, el hombre bueno!"
"Buena sea tu venida;
caçador me parescéys
en los sabuessos que traýa."
"Digas me tú, el hermitaño,
tú que hazes santa vida:
esse ciervo del pie blanco,
¿dónde haze su manida?"
"Quedáys os aquí, mi hijo,
hasta que sea de día;
contaros he lo que vi
y todo lo que sabía.
Por aquí passó esta noche,
dos horas antes del día,
siete leones con él
y una leona parida;
siete condes dexa muertos
y mucha cavallería.
Siempre Dios te guarde, hijo,
por do quier que fuer tu yda,
que quien acá te embió
no te quería dar la vida."
¡Ay, dueña de Quintañones!
De mal fuego seas ardida;
que tanto buen cavallero
por ti ha perdido la vida.

Lancelot's spending
10 much time with the girls,
and one of them cries
"Good knight, please come here;
I'd be delighted,
my future assured,
15 if you would be mine
and I would be yours,
and you gave me as dowry
that white-footed deer."
"I'll give it you, Lady,
20 without sorrow or fear,
if you tell me the land
where the deer has appeared."
Lancelot rides
away on his steed,
25 and with him his hounds,
all on the lead;
he comes to a cave
where a hermit he sees:
"God bless you, good hermit."
30 "I welcome you too;
you seem like a hunter
from the hounds here with you."
"Tell me, good hermit,
you live your life there,
35 that white-footed stag,
just where is its lair?"
"Stay here, my son,
until it is day,
and all that I've seen
40 and I know, I will say;
there came with him this night,
two hours before dawn,
seven lions and a lioness,
with cubs newly-born.
45 He has killed seven Counts,
and knights, many more.
Take care, my good son,
wherever you ride,
for whoever has sent you
50 doesn't want you alive."
Oh Maid Quintañones,
you deserve to be burned,
for so many knights
have never returned!

(1550:282-83; S58, M147)

14. ROSA FRESCA

"Rosa fresca, Rosa fresca,
tan garrida y con amor,
quando yo os tuve en mis braços
no vos supe servir, non;
y agora que os serviría
no vos puedo haver, non."
"Vuestra fue la culpa, amigo,
vuestra fue, que mía no,
embiástesme una carta
con un vuestro servidor,
y en lugar de recaudar
él dixera otra razón:
que érades casado, amigo,
allá en tierras de León,
que tenéys muger hermosa
e hijos como una flor."
"Quien os lo dixo, Señora,
no vos dixo verdad, no,
que yo nunca entré en Castilla,
ni allá en tierras de León,
sino cuando era pequeño,
que no sabía de amor."

"My pretty young Rose,
of beauty and charm,
I knew nothing of love
when you came to my arms,
5 and now that I know
I find you´re alarmed."
"That´s your fault, my friend,
the blame isn´t mine.
You sent me a letter;
10 your servant declined
to read me the letter,
and told me instead
that you lived in Lcón
with the wife that you wed,
15 that she is a beauty,
and so are your sons."
"If he told you that
he was lying at once,
I´ve not been to Castille
20 nor beyond to León
since before I knew love
because I was too young."

(Silva:212; S62, M115)

15. THE PRINCESS AND GALVÁN

Bien se pensava la reyna
que buena hija tenía,
que del conde Don Galván
tres vezes parido havía;
que no lo sabía ninguno
de los que en la corte havía
sino fuesse una donzella
que en su cámara dormía,
y por enojo que huviera
a la reyna lo dezía.
La reyna se la llamava,
y a su cambra la metía,
y estando en este cuydado
de palabras la castiga:
"Ay, hija, si virgo estáys
reyna seréys de Castilla;
hija, si virgo no estáys,

The Princess was a virgin,
or so thought the Queen,
but three times to Galván
pregnant she´d been.
5 Noone at Court
knew of the three
except for her maid,
who slept at her feet.
But one day she was angry
10 and went to the Queen,
so the Queen called her daughter
to come and be seen.
The Princess arrived
and this warning received:
15 "If you´re still a virgin
then you will be Queen,
but if you are not,

¡de mal fuego seáys ardida!"
"Tan virgo estoy, la mi madre,
como el día que fuy nascida –
Por Dios, os ruego, mi madre,
que no me dedes marido;
doliente soy del mi cuerpo
que no soy para servillo."

(Silva:210-11; M159)

burnt alive may you be!"
"I´m as virgin today
20 as always I´ve been,
but I beg you, my mother,
find no husband for me,
for my body´s so painful,
no wife could I be."

16. DOÑA ALDA

En París está Doña Alda,
la esposa de Don Roldán;
trezientas damas con ella
para la acompañar.
Todas visten un vestido,
todas calçan un calçar,
todas comen a una mesa,
todas comían de un pan,
sino era Doña Alda
que era la mayoral.
Las ciento hilavan oro,
las ciento texen cendal,
las ciento tañen instrumentos
para Doña Alda holgar.
Al son de los instrumentos
Doña Alda adormido se ha;
ensoñado avía un sueño,
un sueño de gran pesar.
Recordó despavorida
y con un pavor muy grande,
los gritos dava tan grandes
que se oýan en la ciudad.
Allí hablaron sus donzellas,
bien oyréys lo que dirán:
"¿Qué es aquesto, mi Señora?
¿Quién es el que os hizo mal?"
"Un sueño soñé, donzellas,
que me ha dado gran pesar:
que me veýa en un monte,
en un desierto lugar;
de so los montes muy altos
un açor vide volar.
Tras de él viene una aguililla
que lo ahinca muy mal.

Alda´s in Paris,
Roland´s betrothed;
her three hundred maids
all wear the same clothes;
5 all wear the same dresses,
all wear the same shoes;
and at the one table
all eat the same food,
but Alda, their mistress,
10 to eat has refused.
A hundred spin gold,
a hundred weave satin,
a hundred play music
to keep Alda happy.
15 At the sound of the music
she´s fallen asleep,
and dreams a bad dream
that is painful and deep.
She jumps awake startled
20 by terror and pity,
the shouts that she gives
can be heard in the city –
her maids hurry round,
you´ll hear what they say,
25 "What is this, my lady?
Who´s hurt you this way?"
"I´ve just had a dream,
and it caused me great pain:
I´m alone in a wilderness
30 on a wide plain,
from the top of the mountains
a hawk comes out flying
with an eagle pursuing
closely behind,

El açor con grande cuyta
metió se so mi brial;
el aguililla con grande yra
de allí lo yva a sacar,
con las uñas lo despluma,
con el pico lo deshaze."
Allí habló su camarera,
bien oyréys lo que dirá:
"Aquesse sueño, Señora,
bien os lo entiendo soltar.
El açor es vuestro esposo
que viene de allén la mar,
el águila sodes vos
con la qual ha de casar,
y aquel monte es la yglesia
donde os han de velar."
"Si assí es, mi camarera,
bien te lo entiendo pagar."
Otro día de mañana
cartas de fuera le traen,
tintas venían de dentro,
de fuera escritas con sangre:
que su Roldán era muerto
en la caça de Ronces Valles.

(1550:182; S44, M184)

35 the hawk in its panic
flies under my dress,
but the eagle has snatched it,
by fury possessed,
with its claws tears its feathers,
40 with its beak tears the rest."
Straightway replied
her trusted old maid,
"My lady, your dream
can be quickly explained;
45 the hawk is your husband
back from the sea,
and you are the eagle,
and married you'll be,
and the plain is the church,
50 who will look after you."
"I'll gladly repay you
if these words are true."
But the very next morning
came letters that said –
55 written outside in blood,
inside running red –
that at Roncesvalles
her Roland lay dead.

17. ROSA FLORIDA

En Castilla está un castillo
que se llama Rochafrida,
al castillo llaman Rocha
y a la fonte llaman Frida.
El pie tenía de oro
y almenas de plata fina;
entre almena y almena
está una piedra çafira.
Tanto relumbra de noche
como el sol a medio día.
Dentro estava una donzella
que llaman Rosa Florida;
siete condes la demandan,
tres duques de Lombardía,
a todos les desdeñava,
tanta es su loçanía.
Enamoró se de Montesinos,

In Castille there's a castle
called Rocafrida;
the Castle is strong,
cold is the river;
5 the base is of gold,
the turrets of silver;
between two of the turrets
there shines a sapphire,
as brilliant at night
10 as the sun's noonday fire;
and inside the castle
is Rosa Florida.
Three nobles from Italy,
seven counts ask to see her,
15 but so great is her pride
that she won't let them be there.
She loves Montesinos,

de oýdas, que no de vista.
Una noche estando assí
gritos da Rosa Florida;
oyera la un camarero
que en su cámara dormía:
"¿Qué es aquesto, mi Señora,
¿qué es esto, Rosa Florida?
O tenedes mal de amores,
o estáys loca sandía."
"Ni yo tengo mal de amores,
ni estoy loca sandía,
mas llevasses me estas cartas
a Francia la bien guarnida,
diesses las a Montesinos,
la cosa que yo más quería;
dile que me venga a ver
para la Pascua Florida;
darle he yo este mi cuerpo,
el más lindo que hay en Castilla,
si no es el de mi hermana,
que de fuego sea ardida;
y si de mí más quisiere
yo mucho más le daría,
darle he siete castillos,
los mejores que ay en Castilla."

20 she´s heard all about him,
so great´s her obsession
one night she starts shouting –
A page in her room
has heard from his bed:
"My Rosa Florida,
what is it you´ve said?
25 You must be in love,
or you´re losing your head."
"No, I´m not ill with love,
and I´ve still kept my head,
but carry these letters
30 to France now instead,
to the one I love most,
Count Montesinos,
and say that next Easter
he must come and see us;
35 I´ll give him my body,
the best in Castille
(apart from my sister´s –
cursed may she be!);
And if he wants more
40 I´ve more to command,
he can have seven castles,
the best in the land!"

(1550:253; S48, M179)

18. MELISENDA

Todas las gentes dormían
en las que Dios tiene parte;
no duerme la Melisenda,
la hija del emperante,
de amores del Conde Ayruelo;
no la dexan reposar.
Salto diera de la cama
como la parió su madre;
vistiérase un alcandora,
no hallando su brial.
Va se para los palacios
donde sus damas están;
dando palmadas en ellas
las empeçó de llamar:
"Si dormides, mis donzellas,
si dormides, ¡recordad!

All of the Christians
are taking their rest,
but not Melisenda,
the Royal Princess;
5 she´s in love with Ayruelo,
and awake in distress.
As naked as naked
she leaps from her bed,
she can´t find her dress,
10 puts a gown on instead,
and goes to the rooms
where her ladies are resting,
beats on their backs
and starts to address them:
15 "Wake up, my ladies,
if you´re sleeping, awake,

Las que sabedes de amores,
consejo me queráys dar;
las que de amores no sabedes
tengades me poridad.
Amores del Conde Ayruelo
no me dexan reposar."
Allí hablara una vieja,
vieja es de antigua edad:
"Agora es tiempo, Señora,
de los plazeres tomar,
que si esperáys a la vejez
no vos querrá un rapaz."
Desque esto oyó Melisenda,
no quiso más esperar,
y va se a buscar al Conde
en los palacios do está.
topara con Fernandillo,
un alguazil de su padre.
"¿Qué es aquesto, Melisenda?
Esto, ¿qué podría estar?
o vos tenéys mal de amores,
o vos queréys loca tornar."
"Que ni tengo mal de amores,
ni tengo por quien penar;
mas quando fuy pequeña
tuve una enfermedad;
prometí tener novenas
allá en San Juan de Letrán;
las dueñas yvan de día,
donzellas agora van."
Desque esto oyera Hernando,
puso fin a su hablar.
La infanta, mal enojada,
queriendo se de él vengar,
"Prestasses me" dixo a Hernando,
"prestasses me tu puñal,
que miedo me tengo, miedo,
de los perros de la calle."
Tomó el puñal por la punta,
los cabos le fue a dar;
diera le tal puñalada
que en el suelo muerto cae,
y va se para el palacio
a do el Conde Ayruelo está.
Las puertas halló cerradas,
no sabe por do entrar;
con arte de encantamento
las abrió de par en par.

if you know about love
your counsel I´ll take,
if you don´t know of love
then my secret please keep -
it´s my love for Ayruelo
that won´t let me sleep."
There spoke an old woman,
as old as could be,
"It´s time now, Princess,
your pleasures to seize;
if you wait till you´re old
then no man you´ll please."
Melisenda hears this
and runs off straightaway
to the rooms where the Count
has chosen to stay,
but she meets Fernandillo,
one of the guards -
"What´s up, Melisenda?
Do you know where you are?
Are you suffering from love,
are you going insane?"
"I´m not suffering from love,
noone´s giving me pain;
when young I was ill,
and after that plight
I promised in Rome
that we´d pray I´m all right,
the women by day,
the maidens by night."
Hernando hears this
and makes her be still,
but the Princess is angry,
so strong is her will:
"Lend me, Hernando,
lend me your knife,
there are dogs in the street
and I fear for my life."
He gives her the handle,
the blade in his hand,
she stabs him so much
he can no longer stand,
and she goes to the room
of Ayruelo, her man.
She finds the doors locked,
with no way inside,
but she whispers a spell
and the doors open wide.

Al estruendo el Conde Ayruelo
empeçara de llamar:
"¡Socorred, mis cavalleros!
¡Socorred sin más tardar!
Creo son mis enemigos
que me vienen a matar."
La Melisenda, discreta,
le empeçara de hablar:
"No te congoxes, Señor,
no quieras pavor tomar,
que yo soy una morica
venida de allende el mar."
Desque esto oyera el Conde
luego conoscido la ha.
Fue se el Conde para ella,
las manos le fue a tomar
a la sombra de un laurel
de Venus es su jugar.

65 Ayruelo has heard this,
aloud he has cried
"Help me, my knights,
without any delay,
my enemies come
70 to kill me today."
Melisenda is clever,
this answer she´s made:
"Don´t worry, My Lord,
don´t be afraid,
75 I´m just a young Moslem,
from home I have strayed."
Ayruelo has now
recognized Melisenda,
he´s taken her hand
80 to hold and befriend her,
in the shade of a laurel
their loving is tender.

(Praga, I:273-74; S49, Ml98)

19. THE PRINCESS IN THE TREE

A caçar va el cavallero,
a caçar como solía;
los perros lleva cansados,
el falcón perdido avía.
Arrimara se a un roble,
alto es a maravilla;
en una rama más alta
viera estar una infantina;
cabellos de su cabeça
todo el roble cobrían.
"No te espantes, cavallero,
ni tengas tamaña grima;
fija soy yo del buen rey
y de la reyna de Castilla.
Siete fadas me fadaron
en braços de una ama mía,
que andasse los siete años
sola en esta montiña.
Oy se cumplían los siete años,
o mañana en aquel día.
Por Dios te ruego, cavallero,
lleves me en tu compañía,
si quisieres por muger,

·The knight is out hunting,
an ordinary day,
his hounds are all tired,
his hawk´s flown away;
5 he stops by an oak tree,
the highest and best,
and there at the top
he sees a Princess;
the hair from her head
10 spreads right over the tree –
"Don´t be startled good knight,
or worried by me,
I´m the child of the King
and the Queen of Castille;
15 in the arms of my nurse
seven fairies decreed
that I´d spend seven years
on this mountain in sorrow;
the seven years end
20 today or tomorrow –
I beg you, good knight,
take me off to your home,
if you wish as your wife,

si no, sea por amiga."
"Esperéys me vos, Señora,
fasta mañana, aquel día -
yré yo tomar consejo
de una madre que tenía."
La niña le respondiera
y estas palabras dezía:
"¡O mal aya el cavallero
que sola dexa la niña!"
Él se va a tomar consejo
y ella queda en la montiña.
Aconsejó le su madre
que la tomasse por amiga.
Quando volvió el cavallero,
no hallara la montiña;
vido la que la llevavan
con muy gran cavallería.
El cavallero desque la vido
en el suelo se caýa.
Desque en sí uvo tornado
estas palabras dezía:
"Cavallero que tal pierde
muy gran pena merescía.
Yo mesmo seré el alcalde,
yo me seré la justicia,
que le corten pies y manos
y lo arrastren por la villa."

or as lover alone."
25 "Please wait, my Princess,
just one other day,
I´ll go to my mother
to see what she´ll say."
The Princess replies
30 in an angrier tone:
"A curse on the knight
who leaves me alone!"
She stays in the tree
and he goes to his mother;
35 his mother suggests
he should take her as lover;
but when he returns
she isn´t in sight -
then he sees she´s been taken
40 by a large group of knights;
and when he has seen her
he falls to the ground,
and these words he says
when at last he comes round:
45 "If you don´t take your chance
you deserve to fall down;
I´ll pass my own sentence
in my own lawyers´ gown,
that I lose hands and feet
50 and be dragged round the town!"

(1550:254-55; S67, M151)

20. ARNALDOS

¡Quien hubiese tal ventura
sobre aguas de la mar
como hubo el infante Arnaldos
la mañana de San Juan!
Andando a buscar la caza
para su halcón cebar
vio venir una galera
que venía en alta mar.
Las áncoras tiene de oro
y las velas de un cendal;
marinero que la guía
va diciendo este cantar:
"Galera, la mi galera,
Dios te me guarde de mal,

Upon the high seas
to have such good fortune
as Infante Arnaldos
on St John´s day morning!
5 To feed to his hawk
for new prey he was searching
when from over the sea
a galley came near him -
golden the anchors,
10 silken the sails,
and the sailor who steered it
sang in this way:
"My galley, my galley,
God keep you from harm,

de los peligros del mundo,   15   from the world and its dangers
de fortunas de la mar,   from the sea and its storms,
de los golfos de León   from the rocks of León,
y estrecho de Gibraltar,   and the Strait of Gibraltar,
de las fustas de los moros   from attacks by the Moslems
que andaban a saltear."   20   who come to assault you!"
Allí habló el infante Arnaldos,   Arnaldos called out,
bien oiréis lo que dirá: these words he was saying:
"Por tu vida, el marinero,   "I beg you, come back,
vuelve y repite el cantar."   and sing that again!"
"Quien mi cantar quiere oír   25   "To hear what I sing
en mi galera ha de entrar."   come aboard, come this way."
Tiró la barca el navío   The ship sent its boat,
y el infante fue a embarcar;   he went out and stayed;
alzan velas, caen remos,   they left all their oars,
comienzan a navegar;   30   they began to set sail.
con el ruido del agua   The water was soothing,
el sueño le venció ya.   he fell in a dream,
Pónenle los marineros   and they put their irons on him,
los hierros de cautivar;   their prisoner to keep,
a los golpes del martillo   35   but the blows of the hammer
el infante fue a acordar.   awakened the Prince –
"Por tu vida, el buen marino,   "I beg you, good sailor,
no me quieras hacer mal: don´t harm me like this:
hijo soy del rey de Francia,   I´m the French King´s son, grandson
nieto del de Portugal.   40   of the King Portuguese,
Siete años había, siete,   and for seven long years
que fui perdido en la mar."   I was lost on the sea!"
Allí le habló el marinero: The sailor replied
"Si tú me dices verdad,   "If that is the truth,
tú eres nuestro infante Arnaldos, 45   you´re our own Prince Arnaldos,
y a ti andamos a buscar."   we´re looking for you!"
Alzó velas el navío   The ship kept on sailing,
y se van a su ciudad.   they came to their town;
Torneos y más torneos,   great celebrations,
que el conde pareció ya.   50   their Prince had been found.

(RMP)

21. ESPINELO

Muy malo estava Espinelo,   Espinelo is ill
en una cama jazía,   and lying in bed;
los bancos eran de oro,   its boards are of silver,
las tablas de plata fina,   of gold is its head,
los colchones en que duerme   5   the mattress he lies on

eran de olanda muy rica,
las sávanas que le cubren
en el agua no se vían:
la colcha que encima tiene
sembrada de perlería.
A su cabecera assiste
Mataleona, su amiga,
con las plumas de un pavón
la su cara le resfría.
Estando en este solaz
tal demanda le hazía:
"Espinelo, Espinelo,
¡cómo nasciste en buen día!
El día que tú nasciste
la luna estava crescida
que ni punto le faltava,
ni punto le fallescía.
Contasses me tú, Espinelo,
contasses me la tu vida."
"Yo te la diré, Señora,
con amor y cortesía.
Mi padre era de Francia,
mi madre de Lombardía.
Mi padre con su poder
a toda Francia regía.
Mi madre como señora
una ley introduzía
que muger que dos pariesse
de un parto y en un día
que la den por alevosa
y la quemen por justicia
o la echen en la mar
porque adulterado havía.
Quiso Dios y mi ventura
que ella dos hijos paría
de un parto y en un hora,
que por deshonra tenía.
Fuera se a tomar consejo
con tan loca fantasía,
a una captiva mora
sabia en nigromancía.
"¿Qué me aconsejas tú, mora,
por salvar la honra mía?"
Respondiera le: "Señora,
yo de parescer sería
que tomasses a tu hijo,
el que se te antojaría,
y lo eches en la mar

has a soft linen sheen
and the sheets are so fine
they can hardly be seen,
the blanket that's on him
10 is covered with pearls;
and Mataleona
is with him, his girl.
With the plumes of a peacock
she's cooling his head,
15 and as they are resting
his lover has said:
"My love, Espinelo,
born at a good time,
the moon shone as full
20 as it could in its prime
on the day you were born,
when you came to this earth –
Please tell, Espinelo,
of your life and your birth."
25 "I'll be glad, my good lady,
now I've got the chance;
my mother's Italian,
my father's from France;
my father, the King
30 of all France has once been.
A law was proposed
by my mother, the Queen,
that a woman with twins,
both born the same day,
35 should be held as a traitor
and burnt straightaway,
or thrown in the sea
as an adulterous lover;
but God and my fortune
40 decreed that my mother
gave birth to two twins;
her dishonour discovered,
she ran in despair
to the Court's prison bars,
45 where she found a girl Moslem
who knew of the Stars:
"Advise me, good Moor.
how can I be saved?"
The Moorish girl answered,
50 this answer she gave,
"Take one of your sons,
the one you think best,
put him into the sea

en una arca de valía,
bien embetumada toda
con mucho oro y joyería,
porque quien al niño hallasse
de criarlo holgaría."
Cayera la suerte en mí,
y en la gran mar me ponía,
la qual estando muy brava
arrebatado me havía
y puso me en tierra firme
con el furor que trahía
a la sombra de una mata
que por nombre "Espino" havía,
que por esso me pusieron
de Espinelo nombradía.
Marineros navegando
hallaron me en aquel día,
llevaron me ha presentar
al gran Soldán de Suría.
El Soldán no tenía hijos,
por su hijo me tenía;
el Soldán agora es muerto –
yo por el Soldán regía."

55 in a thick and strong chest,
all covered in pitch,
with gold and with jewels,
so whoever then finds him
is glad and not cruel".
60 My mother chose me,
put me on the wide sea,
and the sea was as rough
as rough as could be,
it brought me to shore
65 and left me there free,
beneath an "espino",
a shady thorn-tree,
so the name "Espinelo"
was given to me.
70 The sailors who found me
that day on the beach
the Sultan of Syria
eventually reached;
the Sultan was childless,
75 adopted me there,
and so now that he's died
I reign as his heir."

(Timoneda, RA:32r-33v; Ml52)

22. THE HUSBAND'S RETURN (1)

"Caballero de lejas tierras,
llegaos acá y paréis,
hinquedes la lanza en tierra,
vuestro caballo arrendéis;
preguntaros he por nuevas;
¿si mi marido conocéis?"
"Vuestro marido, Señora,
decid de qué señas es."
"Mi marido es mozo y blanco,
gentilhombre y bien cortés,
muy gran jugador de tablas
y también del ajedrez.
En el pomo de su espada
armas trae de un marqués,
y un ropón de brocado
y de carmesí el envés.
Cabe el fierro de la lanza
trae un pendón portugués,

"Knight from afar,
come here and get down,
pull up your horse,
rest your lance on the ground,
5 and give me some news
if my husband you've found."
"Your husband, my lady,
please say what he's like."
"He's fair and he's noble,
10 he's young and polite,
he plays well at the tablas,
and also at chess,
and the crest on his sword-hilt
is of a Marqués,
15 his robe's of brocade
and crimson his vest;
there's a Portuguese banner
by the end of his lance,

que ganó en unas justas
a un valiente francés."   20   which he won in a joust
"Por esas señas, Señora,   off a noble from France."
tu marido muerto es.   "Your husband is dead,
En Valencia le mataron   if his signs they are these,
en casa de un ginovés,   he was killed in Valencia,
sobre el juego de las tablas   25   by a wild Milanese;
lo matara un milanés;   where there´d set up some <u>tablas</u>
muchas damas lo lloraban,   a rich Genoese,
caballeros con arnés,   many women and knights
sobre todos lo lloraba   wept at the slaughter,
la hija del ginovés.   30   and there wept most of all
Todos dicen a una voz   the Genoese daughter;
que su enamorada es.   all of them say
Si habéis de tomar amores,   that she was his lover -
por otro a mí no dejéis."   and if <u>you</u> want some love,
"No me lo mandéis, Señor,   35   take me and no other."
Señor, no me lo mandéis,   "Don´t ask me, Good Sir,
que antes que eso hiciese,   I´ll not love anyone,
Señor, monja me veréis."   rather than that
"No os metáis monja, Señora,   I´ll end up a nun."
pues que hacello no podéis,   40   "No, don´t be a nun,
¡que vuestro marido amado   that wouldn´t be wise,
delante de vos lo tenéis!"   for your own loving husband´s
                                                  in front of your eyes!"

(Ribera / Boehl:245; M156)

23. THE HUSBAND'S RETURN (2)

Estando yo ante mi puerta   Embroidering silk
labrando la fina seda,   I sat by the door
vi venir un caballero   when a knight from the Sierra
por alta Sierra Morena.   Morena rode forth;
Con las armas en el caballo   5   he looked like my husband,
a mi marido semeja.   his armour and horse,
Atrevíme a preguntarle   so I dared to enquire
si venía de la guerra.   if he came from the wars -
"De la guerra, no, Señora,   "No, I´m not from the wars,
pero vengo cerca de ella.   10   but I come from nearby;
¿Por qué lo entruga, Señora?   Why do you ask me?
¿Por qué lo entruga, doncella?"   My lady, say why."
"Porque tengo a mi marido   "My husband has been
ha siete años en la guerra.   seven years at the war,
De los siete años que estuvo,   15   and for seven long years
nunca me envió una letra."   I´ve heard nothing at all."
"Diga, diga, La Señora,   "Tell me, what is he like,

diga de qué señas era."
"Era alto como un pino,
y galán como una estrella.
Llevaba un caballo blanco
todo cubierto de seda."
"Por las señas que me dabais
en la guerra muerto queda;
su cuerpo revuelto en sangre,
su boca llena de arena."
"¡Ay, triste de mí, cuitada!
¡Ay, de mi suerte tan negra!
Siempre truje toca blanca,
¡ahora vestiréla prieta!
Tres hijos que me quedaron
los criaré en mi tristeza,
y en cuanto manejen armas
mandarélos a la guerra
para vengar a su padre
que le mataron en ella."
"Non se aflija, La Señora,
no se acordoje, mi dueña,
nin vista los negros paños,
¡que yo su marido era!"

(JMP:152; M.X,p.83)

so I can be sure."
"Like a star he shines out,
20 like a pinetree he´s tall,
and his horse, it is white,
with silk on it all."
"From what you have told me
he´s lying there dead,
25 blood over his body,
sand over his head."
"A curse on my fate!
Alas and alack!
I´ve always worn white,
30 but now I´ll wear black!
Three sons I have left,
and when they are older
they´ll go to the war
like their father, as soldiers,
35 and then their poor father,
avenged he will be ..."
"Don´t weep, my good lady,
no sorrow you´ll see;
and don´t dress in black -
40 your husband is me!"

24. VIRGIL AND THE VIRGIN

Mandó el rey prender Virgilios
y a buen recaudo poner
por una trayción que hizo
en los palacios del rey,
porque forçó una donzella
llamada Doña Ysabel.
Siete años lo tuvo preso
sin que se acordasse de él,
y un domingo, estando en missa,
mientes se le vino de él.
"Mis cavalleros, Virgilios,
¿qué se avía hecho de él?"
Allí habló un cavallero
que a Virgilios quiere bien:
"Preso lo tiene tu alteza
y en tus cárceles lo tien."
"Via, comer, mis cavalleros,
cavalleros, via, comer.

The King ordered Virgil
to prison confined,
for committing at court
a treacherous crime;
5 he´d assaulted a virgin
by name Isabel;
the King then forgot him,
seven years he was held,
till one Sunday at Mass
10 the thought came to the King -
"My knights, about Virgil,
what´s happened to him?"
A knight and companion
of Virgil replied
15 "My Lord, he´s in prison,
you locked him inside."
"Come eat up, my knights,
come eat up with me,

Después que ayamos comido
a Virgilios vamos ver."
Allí hablara la reyna:
"Yo no comeré sin él."
A las cárceles se van
a donde Virgilios es.
"¿Qué hazéys aquí, Virgilios?
Virgilios, ¿aquí qué hazéys?"
"Señor, peyno mis cabellos
y las mis barvas también;
aquí me fueron nacidas,
aquí me han encanecer,
que oy se cumplen siete años
que me mandaste prender."
"Calles, calles tú, Virgilios,
que tres faltan para diez."
"Señor, si manda Tu Alteza
toda mi vida estaré."
"Virgilios, por tu paciencia,
comigo yrás a comer."
"Rotos tengo mis vestidos,
no estoy para parecer."
"Que yo te los daré, Virgilios,
yo dar te los mandaré."
Plugo a los cavalleros,
y a las donzellas también;
mucho más plugo a una dueña
llamada Doña Ysabel.
Ya llaman un arçobispo,
ya la desposan con él;
tomara la por la mano
y lleva se la a un vergel.

20 then when we have eaten
Virgil we´ll see."
But the Queen said "Without him
I won´t have my meal."
They went to the prison
where he was confined,
25 "What have you been doing
for all of this time?"
"I´ve been combing my hair,
and my beard the same way,
in here it has grown,
30 and in here will go grey,
since you had me arrested,
seven years to the day."
"But Virgil, don´t say that,
it´s three more for ten."
35 "My Lord, if you wish it,
my life will here end."
"I´m pleased with your patience,
so come eat with me."
"My clothes are in rags,
40 unfit I will be."
"Then I´ll give you some, Virgil,
now that you´re free."
The knights were delighted,
the ladies as well,
45 and more happy than all
was Doña Isabel –
They called the Archbishop
to marry the pair,
then they went hand in hand
50 to the rose garden there.

(1550:252-53; M111)

25. THE SPECTRE

"¿Dónde va usted, caballero?
"¿Dónde va usted por ahí?"
"Voy en busca de mi esposa,
que hace años que la vi."
"Su esposa de usted se ha muerto
y yo la vide enterrar;
las señales que llevaba
yo se las puedo explicar.
La cara era de cera

"Where are you going,
Sir, where do you go?"
"To look for my wife
I last saw years ago."
5 "Your wife´s dead and buried,
I saw, so I know,
I can tell you the way
that she looked, it was so:
waxen her face,

y los dientes de marfil,
y el pañuelo que llevaba
era rico carmesí;
la llevaban cuatro duques,
caballeros más de mí."
"Haya muerto o no haya muerto,
a su casa me he de ir."
Al subir las escaleras
una sombra vide allí;
mientras más me retiraba
más se acercaba hacia mí.
"Siéntese usted, caballero,
no te asustes tú de mí,
que soy tu querida esposa
que hace un año que morí.
Los brazos que te abrazaban
a la tierra se los di;
la boca que te besaba
los gusanos dieron fin -
Cásate, buen caballero,
cásate, y no andes así;
la primer hija que tengas,
ponle Rosa como a mí,
pa cuando a llamarla fueras
que te acuerdes tú de mí."

10 ivory teeth,
the richest of crimsons
was her handkerchief,
and four noble dukes
bore her beneath."
15 "Dead or alive,
I must come back home here."
As I went up the stairs
a spectre appeared,
the more I retreated
20 the more it came near:
"Sit down, my good knight,
there is nothing to fear,
for I am your wife,
I´ve been dead for a year.
25 The arms that embraced you
I´ve left in the ground,
the mouth that once kissed you
the worms roam around -
Good husband, get married,
30 and happy you´ll be;
call the first of your daughters
Rosa, like me,
so whenever you call her
my memory you´ll see."

(M.X,p.192)

26. GALLARDA

Estábase la Gallarda
en su ventana florida;
vio venir un caballero,
venir por la calle arriba.
"Sube arriba, caballero,
Sube, sube, por tu vida."
"De subir tengo, Señora,
aunque me cueste la vida."
Al abrir la primer puerta
le entrara gran pavorida:
viera cien cabezas de hombre
colgadas en una viga.
También vio la de su padre,
que muy bien la conocía.
"¿Qué es aquello, la Gallarda,
que tienes n´aquella viga?"

Gallarda is sitting
at her window-seat
when she sees a fine knight
come along up the street -
5 "Come up here, I beg you,
come up here, good knight."
"Yes, I will come up,
though it cost me my life."
As he opens the door
10 he takes a great fright,
for a hundred men´s heads
hang from the rafters,
and among them the knight
has discovered his father´s -
15 "What are these things hanging
from here, my Gallarda?"

"Son cabezas de lechones
criados en mi montisa."
"¡Voto al diantre la montiña
que tales lechones cría!"
"Habla bien, mozo, si sabes,
habla bien con cortesía,
que antes de la media noche
la tuya allí se pondría."
Gallarda pone la mesa,
caballero no comía;
Gallarda escanciaba vino,
caballero no bebía.
Allá para media noche
Gallarda se revolvía.
"¿Qué es lo que buscas, Gallarda,
que tanto te revolvías?"
"Busco mi puñal dorado
que a mi lado lo tenía."
"Tu puñal de oro, Gallarda
la vida te costaría."
Metióselo en el costado
y al corazón le salía.
"Abre las puertas, portera,
ábrelas, portera mía."
"No abriré, no, caballero,
no abriré yo, por mi vida;
que si lo sabe Gallarda
Gallarda me mataría."
"No tengas miedo a Gallarda,
que ya muerta la tenías."
"¡Oh, bien haya el caballero,
la madre que lo paría!
¡Cuántos de los caballeros
entraban y no salían!
Tengo de dirme con él,
servirle toda mi vida."

(JMP:196-97; M.X,p.124)

"The heads of some owls
that lived in my garden."
"A curse on the land
20 that owls like these harbours!"
"Take care, if you know,
be calm, be polite,
or your head will be with them
later tonight."
25 Gallarda brings food,
the knight doesn't eat it,
Gallarda brings wine,
the knight doesn't need it.
Midnight is coming,
30 Gallarda looks round;
"What is it, Gallarda?
What haven't you found?"
"My gold-handled knife,
I had it just here."
35 "Your gold-handled knife
will be costing you dear",
and he pushes it in
through her ribs to the heart.
"Porter, the doors,
40 pull them apart."
"No Sir, I can't open,
although I am willing,
for if she finds out
Gallarda will kill me."
45 "There's no need to fear,
for I've just killed Gallarda."
"Oh, blessings on you
and your mother and father!
There've gone in but not out
50 oh, so many knights!
But I must come with you,
your servant for life."

CYCLE BALLADS

Ballads 1-26 recounted isolated episodes. Even if they were originally part of a longer tale, those ballads are self-contained units. But many of the ballads came in what are known as "cycles"; that is, a series of ballads on the same story, recounting separate parts of the tale. The ballads do not necessarily follow each other neatly, and ballads from the same cycle can be inconsistent with each other in quite important details. Nor should we envisage performers singing the "cycle" ballads one after the other in order to tell a whole tale; although the ballads from the same story are often printed together in the *Romanceros*, it is not normal to find them in proximity on the "pliegos sueltos". Indeed, for understandable reasons such as a desire for variety and not to bore the public, the performable "pliegos" tended to include a mixture of ballad types, often with just one ballad from a cycle. This seems to imply that the stories were, at least at one time, well enough known for an episode to be intelligible in itself. Some of the ballads printed so far may have been similarly accompanied in prerecorded times also, and the present division into separate types is for administrative convenience rather than because they are impermeable compartments. The ballads of the cycles have largely died out now in the modern ballad tradition, for they are mostly concerned with outstanding events of Medieval Spanish history now long forgotten. Yet they are very well known to literary historians and deserve to be remembered if only by specialists. It is often thought that these ballads are the "fragments" of earlier, unattested and now lost, long epics. This theory is unnecessary, since the evidence supposedly in its support equally well supports the rival theory that the ballad cycles themselves may often be very old. The fact that these ballads have a loose connection with historical fact does not make them greatly different from the others; many of the same clichés, phrases and plot-mechanisms will recur here.

I have chosen not to include samples of all the "cycles". There are no ballads here on the Infantes de Lara or Fernán González. They are printed here in chronological order of subject (not necessarily of text). Since El Cid is the best known Spanish hero, there are many of his ballads here (37-52); the others are a selection of those on King Rodrigo (27-30), Roncesvalles (31-32), Bernardo del Carpio (33-36) and King Pedro "El Cruel" (54-58).

RODRIGO, THE LAST VISIGOTHIC KING

The Iberian Peninsula was invaded by Moslems, mostly Berber troops ("moros") under Arab commanders, in the year 711. The Visigothic Kingdom, which had been the culturally outstanding area of Western Europe in the seventh century, failed dismally to repel them, and by 718 all of the peninsula except the North-West was under Moslem military control. Moslem Spain came in the tenth century to be another outstanding cultural centre. The Christians succeeded in taking over about half the peninsula by 1085, and then nearly all of it in the thirteenth century, leaving only the (also culturally brilliant) Kingdom of Granada, which survived till 1492. The Christians had great difficulty in understanding why the Moslems had been able to sweep in, and the popular imagination decided that it was divine punishment for the sins of the last Visigothic King. Balladeers adapted this plot to the clichés of the genre, with the result that the tale came to be that the last Visigothic King, Rodrigo, had raped the daughter of the Visigothic noble, Count Julián, who lived at Ceuta on the Moroccan coast, and that Julián then enlisted Moslem troops to take revenge. Julián certainly existed, but the tale of lust and revenge is fiction. (So is some modern historians' idea that Visigothic Spain was "in decline". It was not; for the history of Spain to 1000, Collins' book is indispensable).

27. KING RODRIGO AND LA CAVA

Amores trata Rodrigo;	Rodrigo's in love
descubierto a su cuydado	and his passion reveals,
a La Cava lo dezía,	he's telling La Cava
de quien era enamorado.	of the love that he feels,
Mirava su lindo rostro,	5 he looks at her eyes,
mirava su rostro alindado,	at her beautiful face,
sus lindas y blancas manos	her shining white hands,
él se las está loando:	and he praises her grace –
"Querría que me entendieses	"Please understand
por la vía que te hablo;	10 when I talk in this way,
darte ía mi coraçón	that I'd give you my heart
y estaría al tu mandado."	and I'd do as you say."
La Cava, como es discreta,	La Cava is cautious
a burlas lo havía echado.	and assumes that he's joking,
El rey le haze juramento	15 but then the King swears
que de veras se lo a hablado.	it's the truth that he's spoken.
Toda vía lo disimula	She still won't agree,
y burlando se a escusado.	and runs off with a smile.
El rey va a tener la siesta	The King goes to his rooms
y en un retrecte se a entrado;	20 to rest for a while,

con un paje de los suyos
por La Cava a embiado.
La Cava, muy descuidada,
cumplió luego su mandado.
El rey, luego que la vido,   25
a le de rezio apretado,
haziendo le mil offertas
si ella hazía su rogado.
Ella nunca hazer lo quiso,
por quanto él la a mandado;   30
y assí el rey lo hizo por fuerça
con ella y contra su grado.
La Cava se fue enojada
y en su cámara se a entrado;
no sabe si lo dezir   35
o si lo tener callado.
Cada día gime y llora,
su hermosura va gastando.
Una donzella su amiga
mucho en ello havía mirado   40
y hablóle de esta manera,
de esta suerte le a hablado:
"Agora siento, La Cava,
un coraçón engañado,
en no me dezir lo que sientes   45
de tu tristeza y tu llanto."
La Cava no se lo dize,
mas al fin se lo a otorgado;
dize cómo el rey, Rodrigo,
la a por fuerça desonrado,   50
y porque más bien lo crea
a se lo luego mostrado.
La donzella, que lo vido,
tal consejo le ha dado:
"Escríveselo a tu padre   55
tu desonra demostrando."
La Cava lo hizo luego
como se lo a aconsejado,
y da la carta a un donzel
que de La Cava es criado.   60
Enbarcárase en Tarifa
y en Ceuta la huvo levado,
donde era su padre, el conde,
y en sus manos la huvo dado.
Su madre como lo supo   65
grande llanto a començado;
el conde la consolava
con que la haría bien vengado

then he sends a page asking
La Cava to come,
and she unsuspecting
his bidding has done;
the King, when she's there,
pulls her close to his chest
and offers rewards
if she grants his request,
but she's never agreed,
whatever he's said,
so Rodrigo has forced her
unwilling in bed;
La Cava, distraught,
to her bedroom has fled
should she keep it a secret,
or tell it instead?
She's losing her beauty
from crying each day;
her friend at the court
sees her wasting away,
and can't understand,
so's decided to say:
"La Cava, I'm worried,
please tell me your fears,
don't hide the real reason
for all of your tears."
La Cava is quiet,
but at last her friend hears
she was roughly deflowered
by Rodrigo the King,
and she shows her the scars
that prove everything.
Her friend then suggests,
when she's seen the scars on her,
to write to her father,
recount the dishonour;
She writes straightaway,
she agrees that she ought,
entrusting the letter,
to her servant at court;
in a boat from Tarifa
for Ceuta he's bound,
then the letter he gives
to her father the Count.
When her mother is told
she collapses in tears;
he curses the King
and consoles his wife's fears,

de la desonra tan grande
que el rey les havía causado.

70 he´ll avenge the dishonour
that very same year.

(Silva Barc:44-46; M3)

28. JULIÁN IN CEUTA

En Ceupta está Iulián,
en Ceupta la bien nombrada.
Para las partes de aliende
quiere embiar su embaxada.
Moro viejo la escrevía
y el conde se la notava;
después de averla escripto
al moro luego matara.
Embaxada es de dolor,
dolor para toda España.
Las cartas van al rey moro,
en las quales le jurava
que si le dava aparejo
le dará por suya España.
¡Madre España, ay de ti!
En el mundo tan nombrada,
de las partidas la mejor,
la mejor y más ufana,
donde nasce el fino oro
y la plata no faltada,
dotada de hermosura
y en proezas estremada,
por un perverso traydor
toda eres abrasada;
todas tus ricas ciudades
con su gente tan galana
las domeñan hoy los moros
por nuestra culpa malvada,
si no fueran las Asturias
por ser la tierra tan brava.
El triste rey Don Rodrigo,
el que entonces te mandava,
viendo sus reynos perdidos
sale a la campal batalla.
El qual en grave dolor
enseña su fuerça brava,
mas tantos eran los moros
que han vencido la batalla.
No paresce el rey, Rodrigo,

Julián is in Ceuta,
the fortress renowned;
from there over Africa
his message goes round.
5 An old Moslem prepared it;
he checked what it said,
and then once it was written
he struck him down dead.
For Spain it´s a message
10 of sorrow and war:
to the King of the Moslems
in the letter he swore
that if he gave him help
he´d win Spain for the Moors.
15 Oh Spain, our poor country,
renowned through the world,
the best and the proudest,
a jewel, a pearl,
where gold can be found,
20 and silver as well,
whose beauty´s renowned,
whose virtues excel;
you´re all being burned
by a renegade traitor,
25 your rich cities and people
are noble by nature
but ruled now by Moslems -
and we are to blame;
except the Asturians,
30 still proud without shame.
Poor King Rodrigo,
once ruler of Spain,
though his lands are all lost
he fights once again,
35 and shows that he´s brave
though in sorrow and pain;
but the Moors are so many
they win and remain.
Rodrigo has vanished,

ni nadie sabe do estava.
iO maldito de ti, Don Orpas,
obispo de mala andança!
En esta negra conseja
uno a otro se ayudava.
iO dolor sobre manera!
iO cosa nunca cuydada!
Que por sola una donzella
la qual Cava se llamava
causen estos dos traydores
que España sea domeñada
y perdido el rey señor
sin nunca de él saber nada.

(1550:198-99; S1, M4)

40 noone knows where he´s staying.
A curse on the bishop
Don Orpas, ill-fated,
who the fearsome revenge
of the Count has thus aided!
45 Grief without measure,
never yet contemplated!
For the sake of a girl
known as La Cava
these two betrayed Spain,
50 which has still not recovered;
Rodrigo was lost
and never discovered.

29. RODRIGO'S RETREAT

Las huestes de Don Rodrigo
desmayavan y huýan
quando en la octava batalla
sus enemigos vencían.
Rodrigo dexa sus tiendas
y del real se salía;
sólo va el desventurado,
que no lleva compañía.
El cavallo de cansado
ya mudar no se podía,
camina por donde quiere,
que no le estorva la vía.
El rey va tan desmayado
que sentido no tenía;
muerto va de sed y hambre
que de velle era manzilla,
yva tan tinto de sangre
que una brasa parescía,
las armas lleva bolladas
que eran de gran pedrería,
la espada lleva hecha sierra
de los golpes que tenía,
el almete abollado
en la cabeça se le hundía,
la cara lleva hinchada
del trabajo que sufría.
Subióse encima de un cerro,
el más alto que veýa;

Rodrigo´s proud army
is running away,
for after eight battles
they´re losing the day.
5 Rodrigo is leaving
his camp on his own,
the unfortunate King
is escaping alone.
His horse is exhausted,
10 just able to roam
and wander at will
and stumble round free,
for the King´s in a daze,
scarcely able to see;
15 a sad figure whose thirst
and hunger are growing,
so reddened by blood
that he seems to be glowing,
his armour all dented
20 that used to be jewelled;
his sword´s like a saw,
the blows were so cruel;
his helmet is battered
and sunk on his head,
25 his face is all swollen
from tears that he´s shed.
He climbs the high hill
that he saw straight ahead

dende allí mira su gente
cómo yva de vencida.
De allí mira sus vanderas
y estandartes que tenía,
cómo están todos pisados,
que la tierra los cubría.
Mira por los capitanes
que ninguno parescía,
mira el campo tinto en sangre
la qual arroyos corría.
El triste de ver aquesto
gran manzilla en sí tenía,
llorando de los sus ojos
de esta manera dezía:
"Ayer era rey de España,
hoy no lo soy de una villa,
ayer villas y castillos,
hoy ninguno posseýa,
ayer tenía criados,
hoy ninguno me servía,
hoy no tengo una almena
que pueda dezir que es mía.
¡Desdichada fue la hora,
desdichado fue aquel día
en que nascí y heredé
la tan grande señoría!
Pues lo havía de perder
todo junto y en un día.
¡O muerte! ¿Por qué no vienes
y llevas esta alma mía
de aqueste cuerpo mezquino?
Pues ¡se te agradescería!

30 and looks down at his army
who´ve scattered and fled,
he looks at the standards
all covered in dirt,
he looks at the banners
all trampled in earth;
35 he looks for his captains,
but none can be seen,
for instead on the ground
their red blood flows in streams;
and when he sees this
40 he is shaken in horror,
tears well from his eyes
and he cries out in sorrow:
"Once I ruled Spain,
now not a town;
45 once I had castles,
now fallen down;
once I had servants,
none serve me now;
Now I haven´t a turret
50 that I can call mine.
Ill-fated the day,
Ill-fated the time
I was born as the heir
of the Kingdom of Spain,
55 for now I have lost it
all in a day!
So Death, hurry down
and free my poor soul
from this miserable body,
60 it´s happy to go!"

(Silva:133; S3, M5)

30. RODRIGO'S PENANCE

Después que el rey Don Rodrigo
a España perdido havía,
yva se desesperado
por donde más le plazía;
mete se por las montañas,
las más espessas que havía,
porque no le hallen los moros
que en su seguimiento yvan.
Topado ha con un pastor

King Don Rodrigo,
when he´d lost Spain,
in great desperation
ran away cross the plain,
5 and into the mountains,
the worst he could find,
to escape from the Moslems
who followed behind.
He met there a shepherd

que su ganado traýa;
díxole, "Dime, buen hombre,
lo que preguntar quería,
si hay por aquí poblado
o alguna casería
donde pueda descansar,
que gran fatiga traýa."
El pastor respondió luego
que en balde la buscaría,
porque en todo aquel desierto
sola una hermita havía,
donde estava un hermitaño
que hazía muy santa vida.
El rey fue alegre de esto,
por allí acabar su vida.
Pidió al hombre que le diesse
de comer, si algo tenía.
el pastor sacó un çurrón,
que siempre en él pan traýa;
dio le de él y de un tasajo
que a caso allí echado havía.
El pan era muy moreno,
al rey muy mal le sabía;
las lágrimas se le salen,
detener no las podía,
acordándose en su tiempo
los manjares que comía.
Después que hovo descansado
por la hermita le pedía;
el pastor le enseñó luego
por donde no erraría.
El rey le dio una cadena
y un anillo que traýa –
joyas son de gran valer
que el rey en mucho tenía –.
Començando a caminar
ya cerca el sol se ponía.
Llegado es a la hermita
que el pastor dicho le havía;
él, dando gracias a Dios,
luego a rezar se metía.
Después que hovo rezado
para el hermitaño se yva;
hombre es de auctoridad
que bien se le parescía.
Preguntóle el hermitaño
cómo allí fue su venida.
El rey, los ojos llorosos,

10 tending his sheep
and asked him "Good shepherd,
please answer to me,
is there near here
a village or town?
15 For I am exhausted,
I need to lie down."
But in vain, for this answer
the shepherd then gave,
that in all that wild country
20 was only a cave
with a saintly old hermit,
sure to be saved;
but the King was delighted,
he'd make it his grave.
25 He said he was hungry
and begged to be fed,
so the shepherd took out
his bag with his bread,
and also some meat
30 that he'd happened to bring;
but the bread was so coarse
it could not please the King,
and his tears started flowing,
they couldn't keep in,
35 as he thought of the fine food
and banquets there'd been.
He rested, then asked
for the way to the cave,
and the shepherd then showed him
40 so he'd not lose the way.
The King gave the shepherd
a chain and a ring,
valuable jewels,
fit for a King.
45 Then he started to walk
with the sun going down
till the cave that the shepherd
had shown him he found.
He gave thanks to Lord God
50 and started to pray,
and then after his prayer
he went into the cave;
the hermit looked saintly
and ancient and wise,
55 and asked Don Rodrigo
why he'd arrived;
The King was in tears,

aquesto le respondía:
"El desdichado Rodrigo
yo soy, que rey ser solía;
vengo a hazer penitencia
contigo en tu compañía.
No recibas pesadumbre,
por Dios y Santa María."
El hermitaño se espanta;
por consolallo dezía:
"Vos cierto havéys elegido
camino qual convenía
para vuestra salvación
que Dios os perdonaría."
El hermitaño ruega a Dios
por si le revelaría
la penitencia que diesse
al rey que le convenía;
fuele luego revelado
de parte de Dios un día
que le meta en una tumba
con una culebra viva,
y esto tome en penitencia
por el mal que hecho havía.
El hermitaño al rey
muy alegre se bolvía,
contóselo todo al rey
cómo passado lo havía.
El rey de esto muy gozoso
luego en obra lo ponía;
métese como Dios manda
para allí acabar su vida.
El hermitaño muy santo
mírale el tercero día.
Dize, "¿Cómo os va, buen rey?
¿Va os bien con la compañía?"
"Hasta ahora no me ha tocado,
porque Dios no lo quería.
Ruega por mí, el hermitaño,
porque acabe bien mi vida."
El hermitaño llorava,
gran compassión le tenía,
començóle a consolar
y esforçar quanto podía.
Después buelve el hermitaño
a ver ya si muerto havía.
Halla que estava rezando
y que gemía y plañía;
preguntóle cómo estava.

and thus he replied:
"I´m poor Rodrigo,
60 I used to be King,
I´ve come to do penance
with you for my sin,
for God and Saint Mary,
please do let me in".
65 The hermit was startled,
but comforted him -
"I´m sure that you´ve chosen
the suitable place
to come and be saved,
70 so may God give you grace."
The hermit then prayed
for God to reveal
the appropriate pain
for Rodrigo to feel;
75 the Lord came and told him
the action to take,
"Put the King in a tomb
with a poisonous snake,
and let this be his penance,
80 the amends he must make."
The hermit returned
very pleased with these words
and explained to the King
the guidance he´d heard;
85 the King was delighted,
without a delay
he went as God ordered
to die in this way.
The hermit looked in
90 upon the third day,
and cried to the King:
"How are you and your friend?"
"He´s not bitten me yet,
so I´ve not made amends -
95 pray to God, my good hermit,
let me have this good end!"
The hermit in sorrow
and pity and tears
encouraged the King
100 and quietened his fears;
and returned a while later
to see if he´d died,
but found he was praying;
the King wept and cried
105 and replied to the hermit

"Dios es en la ayuda mía,"
respondió el buen rey Rodrigo,
"la culebra me comía.
Come me ya por la parte
que todo lo merescía
por donde fue el principio
de la mi muy gran desdicha."
El hermitaño lo esfuerça;
el buen rey allí moría.
Aquí acabó el Rey Rodrigo,
al cielo derecho se yva.

(Silva:135-36; M7)

     "God has had pity",
and then the King shouted
"The snake has now bitten,
it´s biting the part
110 that deserves the most blame,
the part that has caused
my misfortune and shame!"
The hermit then blessed him,
the King died that day,
115 and so good Rodrigo
went to heaven straightway.

THE BATTLE OF RONCESVALLES

     This ballad and the following one are based on the French legends concerning the battle of Roncesvalles. In 778 an army of Charlemagne's, the Frankish ruler, went to Moslem Zaragoza under the apprehension that some of the inhabitants would open the city gates for them. This turned out not to be true, and they retreated to France across the high pass at the Western end of the Pyrenees, known as Roncesvalles. There the rearguard was attacked and defeated by Basques, perhaps with some Moslem help. (For a fuller account, as usual, see Collins; the Basques destroyed another Frankish army there in 824 also). This insignificant defeat grew in the French imagination into a glorious victory over the Moslems, until by the eleventh century most Frenchmen actually believed they had helped drive the Moslems out of much of Spain. (Some French historians may still believe this). The *Chanson de Roland* elaborated this episode into a superb work of literature; it may have been translated into Spanish (one fragment survives, although there is no way we can tell the length of the whole), and it inspired Spanish imitations and expansions of particular episodes (including the Alda ballad, no.16).

31. THE FLIGHT OF MARSIN

Ya comiençan los franceses
con los moros pelear,
y los moros eran tantos,
no los dexan ressollar.
Allí habló Baldovinos,   5
bien oyréys lo que dirá:
"Ay, compadre Don Beltrán,
mal nos va en esta batalla;
más de sed que no de hambre
a Dios quiero yo dar el alma.   10
Cansado traygo el cavallo;
más, el braço del espada.
Roguemos a Don Roldán
que una vez el cuerno taña;
oýr lo ha el emperador,   15
que está en los Puertos de España,
que más vale su socorro
que toda nuestra sonada."
Oýdo lo ha Don Roldán,
en las batallas do estava: 20
"No me lo roguéys, mis primos,
que ya rogado me estava.
mas rogaldo a Don Renaldos,
que a mí no me lo retrayga,
ni me lo retrayga en villa,   25
ni me lo retrayga en Francia,
ni en cortes del Emperador
estando comiendo a la tabla;
que más querría ser muerto
que sufrir tal sobarvada."   30
Oýdo lo ha Don Renaldo
que en las batallas andava.
Començara a dezir,
estas palabras hablava:
"O mal oviessen franceses   35
de Francia la natural,
que a tan pocos moros como éstos
el cuerno mandan tocar,
que si me toman los corajes
que me solían tomar   40
por estos y otros tantos
no me daré sólo un pan."
Ya le toman los corajes
que le solían tomar;
assí se entra por los moros   45
como segador por pan,

The French are attacking the Moslems,
the French are beginning to fight,
but the ranks of the Moors are so many
the French cannot have a respite;
and Baldwin has made a suggestion, 5
let us hear all the words of this knight:
"My friend and companion, Sir Bertrand,
this battle is one of our worst,
I feel like surrendering my soul up
to God from my desperate thirst, 10
and my horse is exhausted beneath me
but I fear that my sword-arm fails first;
we´d better beseech our Lord Roland
to take up the horn by his side
and blow a loud note to our comrades 15
who through the high passes now ride,
we have to attempt to get help now,
forgetting our military pride."
But Roland has heard this entreaty
for he´s in there fighting ahead; 20
"My cousins, don´t ask me to do this,
you say what´s already been said,
for I don´t want the world to reproach me,
so go and ask Reynard instead;
I don´t want them to think me a coward 25
in every French city and square,
in all of the courts of the Emperor,
nor whenever a banquet´s prepared;
if I´m to have that reputation
I´d rather die fighting in there." 30
But Reynard has heard what he answered
while battling his share of the fight,
and has started to call to the Frenchmen,
let us hear all the words of this knight:
"I cannot believe you are Frenchmen, 35
disgracing the land you were born,
in the face of so very few Moslems
you want to call help on the horn,
when if I can just call on my courage,
the courage I usually call, 40
by two times the number of Moslems
I wouldn´t be worried at all."
And now he has called on his courage,
the courage he usually feels,
and takes out his sword to the Moslems 45
like a scythe to the summer wheatfields,

assí derriba cabeças
como peras de un peral.
Por Ronces Valles arriba
los moros huyendo van.   50
Allí salió un perro moro
(que en mala ora lo parió su madre):
"¡Alcaria, moros, alcaria,
sí mala ravia vos mate!
que soys ciento para uno,   55
ýs les fuyendo delante.
¡O mal aya el rey Marsín,
que soldada os manda dare,
mal aya la reyna mora
que vos lo manda pagare,   60
mal ayáys vosotros, moros,
que la venís a ganare!"
De que esto oyeron los moros,
aun ellos bolvido han,
y bueltas y rebueltas,   65
los franceses fuyendo van.
A tan bien se los esfuerça
esse arçobispo Turpín:
"¡Buelta, buelta, los franceses,
con coraçón a la lid!   70
¡Más vale morir con honrra
que con desonrra bivir!"
Ya bolvían los franceses
con coraçón a la lid;
tantos matan de los moros   75
que no se puede dezir.
Por Ronces Valles arriba
fuyendo va el Rey Marsín,
cavallero en una zebra,
no por mengua de rocín;   80
la sangre que de él salía
las yervas haze teñir,
las bozes que él yva dando
al cielo quieren subir:
"¡Reniego de ti, Mahoma!   85
Y'aun de quanto hize en ti.
Hize te el cuerpo de plata,
pies y manos de marfil,
y por más te honrar, Mahoma,
la cabeça de oro te hiz.   90
Sessenta mil cavalleros
ofrecílos yo a ti,
mi muger Abrayma, mora,
ofreció te treynta mil,

he scatters the heads of the enemy
like slicing ripe pears off a tree;
so ahead up the pass, Roncesvalles,
the Moslems are starting to flee.   50
But a Moslem cries out to reproach them
(cursed was the day of his birth):
"You´re shameful to Allah, you Moslems,
disgracing the face of the Earth!
There´s a hundred of you for each Christian   55
and yet you are running away,
a bad day for your King and your ruler
Marsín, when you´re here in his pay,
and his Queen who has bid him protect you,
for her this is too a bad day,   60
and a bad day for all Moslem soldiers -
Fight to take victory away!"
As soon as the Moslems have heard this
they come straight back into the fight,
the Frenchmen are halted and routed   65
and now they are taking to flight;
but Archbishop Turpin revives them,
let us hear all the words of this knight:
"Come back, oh come back, you French soldiers,
come back and start fighting again,   70
much better to perish with honour
than carry on living in shame!"
The French have come back to the battle,
the French begin fighting again,
and so many Moslems are slaughtered   75
that very few Moslems remain.
Now on up the pass, Roncesvalles,
rides Marsín, the great King of the Moors,
he´s fleeing away on his zebra,
that he´d chosen instead of his horse;   80
the blood that is flowing out from him
is spreading out red on the ground,
the cries that he makes to the heavens
are echoing up and around:
"I disown what I gave you, Mahomet,   85
I disown you as well, I repeat,
I´ve made you an image of silver
with ivory fingers and feet,
Mahomet, the head is all golden,
your honour from this is complete.   90
And also to you I have offered
sixty thousand of all our best men,
my wife, a good Moslem, Abrayma,
offered thirty more thousand up then,

mi hija Mata Leona   95
ofrecióte quinze mil;
de todos éstos, Mahoma,
tan sólo me veo aquí,
y aun mi braço derecho,
Mahoma, no lo trayo aquí.   100
Cortómelo el encantado,
esse Roldán, paladín,
que si encantado no fuera
no se me fuera él assí.
Mas yo me vo para Roma,   105
que cristiano quiero morir;
ésse será mi padrino,
esse Roldán, paladín,
ésse me baptizará,
esse arçobispo Turpín -   110
mas perdona me, Mahoma,
que con cuyta te lo dixe,
que yr no quiero a Roma,
curar quiero yo de mí."

(Pliegos, I:131-32; S41, M.Ap. 50)

---

32. THE DEAD KNIGHT'S FATHER

Por la matança va el viejo,	Over the battlefield
por la matança adelante;	goes the old man,
los braços lleva cansados	from searching the bodies
de los muertos rodear.	tired are his hands;
Vido a todos los franceses,	5 he´s found all the Frenchmen
y no vido a Don Beltrán.	except for Beltrán.
Siete vezes echan suertes,	Seven times they drew lots,
quién lo bolverá a buscar;	who would go from their band,
echan las tres con malicia,	the first three they cheated
las quatro con gran maldad.	10 and the same the next four,
Todas siete le cupieron	and in all of the seven
al buen viejo de su padre.	his father was drawn.
Buelve riendas al cavallo	He saddled his horse
y él se lo buelve a buscar,	and went looking once more,
de noche por el camino,	15 by day, on the paths,
de día por el xaral.	by night, anywhere.
A la entrada de un prado,	At the edge of a meadow,
saliendo de un arenal,	by some sand there was there,
vido estar en esto un moro	was a Moslem, a sentry,
que velava en el adarve.	20 guarding the fort;

my daughter, young Mataleona,   95
offered fifteen more thousand again,
but of all these brave soldiers, Mahomet,
I´m the only one left here, alone,
and Mahomet, I´ve had to abandon
the right arm that once was my own;   100
their valiant champion, Roland,
succeeded in taking my arm –
he must have had heaven´s assistance
preserving him safely from harm;
and so I shall travel to Rome now,   105
for Christian I´m wanting to die,
their valiant champion, Roland,
will be godfather there in reply,
and the Christian Archbishop, yes, Turpin,
is the one I´ll be there baptized by ...   110
But no, no, Mahomet, I´m sorry,
the pain made me say what I said,
for of course I´m not travelling to Rome now,
I´ll recover without them instead."

Hablóle en algaravía,
como aquel que bien la sabe:
"Digas me tú, el morico,
lo que quiero preguntar:
cavallero de armas blancas   25
¿si lo viste acá passar?
Si lo tienes preso, Moro,
de oro te lo pesarán,
y si tú lo tienes muerto
des me lo para enterrar,   30
porque el cuerpo sin el alma
muy pocos dineros vale."
"Esse cavallero, amigo,
dime tú qué señas ha."
"Armas blancas son las suyas,   35
y el cavallo es alazán,
y en el carrillo derecho
él tenía una señal,
que siendo niño pequeño
se la hizo un gavilán "   40

he asked him in Arabic –
as he´d been taught –
"Tell me, good Moslem,
what I ask you to say,
has a knight in white armour
come by this way?
If he´s your prisoner,
his weight´s yours in gold;
if he lies dead there
his body I´ll hold,
for a body is worthless
that hasn´t a soul."
"My friend, tell me how
I´ll know which is your knight?"
"His horse coloured chestnut,
his armour is white,
he carries a scar
on his cheek, on the right,
where a sparrowhawk gave him,
when little, a fright."

"Esse cavallero, amigo,   "My friend, in the meadow
muerto está en aquel pradal;   dead lies your knight,
dentro en el agua los pies,   his feet in the water,
y el cuerpo en un arenal.   he´s stretched on the sand,
Siete lançadas tenía,   45 seven times pierced by lances
passan le de parte a parte."   from his heels to his hands."

(Silva:182-83; M185)

BERNARDO EL CARPIO

The French Roncesvalles legends inspired not only imitation (31-32) but resentment, which crystallised in the legend of Bernardo el Carpio, who was supposed to be a victorious Spanish commander against the French, and is the subject of the next four ballads here (there are several others). Whether the legend of Bernardo existed before the eleventh century is unclear, but it is certainly fictional in all important details. Yet the nationalism that probably inspired the concoction of the story falls out of the general memory, for the part of the tale that survives in ballads concerns his birth, and inheritance.

33. BERNARDO'S BIRTH

En los reynos de León   Alfonso "The Chaste"
el casto Alfonso reynava.   in León, where he reigned,
Hermosa hermana tenía,   had a beautiful sister,
Doña Ximena se llama.   Ximena by name.
Enamorárase de ella   5 The Count of Saldaña
esse Conde de Saldaña,   her lover became,
mas no bivía engañado   and she loved in return,
porque la infanta lo amava.   so it wasn´t in vain.
Muchas vezes fueron juntos,   They were often together,
que nadie lo sospechava;   10 seen by noone,
de las vezes que se vieron   but so close were the two
la infanta quedó preñada.   she conceived a young son;
La infanta parió a Bernaldo   once Bernardo was born,
y luego monja se entrava.   she retired as a nun;
Mandó el rey prender al conde   15 the King locked up the Count
y ponerle muy gran guarda.   for what he had done.

(1550:205; S4, M8)

34. BERNARDO AT COURT

En corte del casto Alfonso	At the court of Alfonso
Bernaldo a plazer vivía	Bernardo is living,
sin saber de la prisión	not knowing his father
en que su padre yazía.	is lying in prison;
A muchos pesava de ella	noone will tell him,
mas nadie gelo dezía,	and sadly they´ve hidden it,
ca no osava ninguno,	for decrees of the King
que el rey gelo defendía.	have expressly forbidden it;
Y sobre todos pesava	especially sad
a dos deudos que tenía;	are two of his kinsmen,
uno era Vasco Meléndez	Vasco Meléndez
a quien la prisión dolía,	dislikes that decision,
y el otro Suero Velázquez	and Suero Velázquez
que en el alma lo sentía.	resents the imprisonment.
Para descubrir el caso	They want him to know;
en su poridad metían	So they use their ability
a dos dueñas hijas dalgo	to send for two girls
que eran de muy gran valía.	of the highest nobility,
Una era Urraca Sánchez,	Urraca de Sánchez´s
la otra dizen María;	the first that they beckon,
Meléndez era el renombre,	María Meléndez´s
que sobre nombre tenía.	the name of the second,
Con estas dueñas fablaron	they ask them in secret
en gran poridad un día,	so noone will know:
diziendo: "Nos vos rogamos,	"Please do us this favour,
Señoras, por cortesía,	my ladies, please go
que le digáys a Bernaldo	and say to Bernardo,
por qualquier manera o vía,	the best way you know,
cómo yaze preso el Conde,	that his father Count Sancho
su padre, Don Sancho Díaz;	is lying in prison,
que trabaje de sacarlo,	he must try to release him,
si pudiere, en qualquier guisa,	it´s his duty and mission,
que nos al rey le juramos	and if you tell Bernardo
que de nos no lo sabría."	we can swear that we didn´t."
Las dueñas quando lo oyeron	When the girls hear this,
a Bernaldo lo dezían.	without a delay
Quando Bernaldo lo supo,	they explain to Bernardo,
pesó le a gran demasía,	who´s struck with dismay,
tanto que dentro en el cuerpo	and he feels that his blood
la sangre se le bolvía.	is all draining away;
Yendo para su posada	he goes back to his room,
muy grande llanto hazía;	he cries out in pain,
vistióse paños de duelo	then in black he comes back
y delante el rey se yva.	to the palace again.
El rey, quando assí lo vido,	The King when he sees him
de esta suerte le dezía:	misunderstands:

Line numbers in centre: 5, 10, 15, 20, 25, 30, 35, 40, 45

"Bernaldo, ¿por aventura
codicias la muerte mía?"
Bernaldo dixo: "Señor,
vuestra muerte no quería,   50
mas duele me que está preso
mi padre gran tiempo havía;
Señor, pido os por merced,
y yo vos lo merescía,
que me lo mandedes dar."   55
Empero el rey, con gran yra,
le dixo: "Partíos de mí,
y no tengáys osadía
de más esto me dezir,
ca sabed que os pesaría;   60
ca yo vos juro y prometo
que en quantos días yo viva
de la prisión no veades
fuera a vuestro padre un día."

"Are you coming against me?
Will I die at your hands?"
"No, no" says Bernardo,
"That´s not what I planned;
but I´m grieved that my father´s
been captive for years,
and I beg you a favour,
it´s one I deserve,
that you give him to me ..."
The King´s anger appears
and he sends him away,
saying "Never you dare
to ask me again
or you´ll pay then and there,
for I promise you now
for as long as can be
that you´ll not see your father
coming out free."

---

35. BERNARDO'S CHALLENGE

Por las riberas de Arlança
Bernaldo el Carpio cavalga
con un cavallo morzillo
enjahezado de grana,
gruessa lança en la su mano,   5
armado de todas armas.
Toda la gente de Burgos
le mira como espantada,
porque no se suele armar
si no a cosa señalada.   10
También lo mirava el rey,
que fuera vuela una garça;
diziendo estava a los suyos:
"Ésta es una buena lança;
si no es Bernaldo del Carpio,   15
éste es Muça, el de Granada."
Ellos estando en aquesto
Bernaldo que allí llegava.
Ya sossegado el cavallo
no quiso dexar la lança,   20
mas puesta encima del ombro
al rey de esta suerte hablava:
"Bastardo me llaman, Rey,
siendo hijo de tu hermana,

Bernaldo con gran tristeza
aquesto al rey respondía:
"Señor, rey soys y faredes
a vuestro querer y guisa;
empero yo ruego a Dios,
también a Santa María,
que vos meta en coraçón
que lo soltedes ayna,
ca yo nunca dexaré
de vos servir toda vía."
Mas el rey, con todo esto,
amávale en demasía,
y ansí se pagava de él
tanto quanto más le vía;
por lo qual siempre Bernardo
ser hijo del rey creýa.

(Silva:140-42; M9)

65 Bernardo's in tears
but he sadly agrees,
"My Lord, you are King,
you can do as you please,
but I pray to the Virgin,
70 and God, on my knees,
that they soften your heart
and you let him go free,
for Bernardo your servant
forever will be."
75 Alfonso still loves him
too much to complain,
treats him as son
over again,
so always Bernardo's
80 in favour remained.

Alongside the river Arlanza
Bernardo del Carpio appears;
his horse is dark red and its harness
shines scarlet and bright as he nears;
Bernardo wears all of his armour,   5
he carries his lance in his hand;
and all the Castilians of Burgos
in pride and astonishment stand,
for he wouldn't put on all his armour
unless something special were planned.   10
The King sees him coming towards him -
the King is out hunting once more -
and he says to the men that are with him
"That soldier's a fine one for sure -
he must be Bernardo del Carpio,   15
unless he is Muza the Moor."
While they've been talking about him
Bernardo has quickly arrived;
he pulls up his horse to attention
but won't put his lance to one side;   20
he holds it up over his shoulder
and speaks to Alfonso with pride;
"They say I'm a bastard, Alfonso,
of Jimena, your sister, the son,

y del noble Sancho Días,   25
esse Conde de Saldaña.
Dizen que ha sido traydor,
y mala muger tu hermana;
tú y los tuyos la avéys dicho,
que otro ninguno no osara,   30
mas quienquiera que lo ha dicho
¡miente por medio la barba!
Mi padre no fue traydor,
ni mi madre muger mala,
por que quando fui engendrado   35
ya mi madre era casada.
Pusiste a mi padre en yerros
y a mi madre en orden sancta;
y porque no herede yo
quieres dar tu reyno a Francia.   40
Morirán los castellanos
antes de ver tal jornada,
montañeses y leoneses,
y essa gente esturiana;
y esse rey de Çaragoça   45
me prestará su compaña
para salir contra Francia
y darle cruda batalla.
Y si buena me saliere
será el bien de toda España;   50
si mala, por la república
moriré yo en tal demanda.
¡Mi padre mando que sueltes,
pues me diste la palabra!
Si no, en campo, como quiera,   55
te será bien demandada."

(Timoneda, RE:10-11; S5, M12)

36. BERNARDO'S INHERITANCE

Con cartas y mensajeros
el rey al Carpio embió.
Bernaldo, como es discreto,
de trayción se receló,
las cartas echó en el suelo   5
y al mensajero habló:
"Mensajero eres, amigo,
no mereces culpa, no,
mas a el rey que acá te embía
diga le tú esta razón: 10

that my father is noble Don Sancho,   25
the Count of Saldãna´s the one;
but they say that my father´s a traitor,
your sister great evil has done;
You and your men have proclaimed this,
though nobody else has dared try;   30
but whoever they are who have said so,
they lie in their teeth, yes they lie!
My father was never a traitor,
my mother no evil has done,
for when they together conceived me   35
they were already married as one;
but you threw the good Count in a dungeon,
and made my poor mother a nun;
now you want to give Frenchmen your kingdom
to prevent me succeeding, their son.   40
Castilians would all rather perish
than see that the kingdom has gone,
and so would the men of Asturias,
La Montaña, the men of León,
and the ruler of proud Zaragoza,   45
though Moslem, would lend me his lance
and his soldiers to help us give battle
and drive back the Frenchmen to France;
and if we succeed in our battle,
the victory belongs to all Spain!   50
And if we should fail, then our dying
will not be entirely in vain.
Now I tell you, release me my father,
you gave me your word that you would;
for if not, as you choose, in a duel   55
revenge will be taken for good."

A messenger carrying letters
from the King to El Carpio was sent,
Bernardo was naturally wary,
suspicious of treacherous intent,
and he threw to the floor the King´s letter   5
and said to the man what that meant:
"I know that you´re only the messenger,
one of my trustworthy friends,
but take this reply to the Court now,
to the King who his messenger sends;   10

que no lo estimo yo a él
ni aun quantos con él son,
mas por ver lo que me quiere
toda vía allá yré yo."
Y mandó juntar los suyos,   15
de esta suerte les habló:
"Quatro cientos soys, los míos,
los que comedes mi pan;
los ciento yrán al Carpio
para el Carpio guardar;   20
los ciento por los caminos
que a nadie dexen passar;
dozientos yréys comigo
para con el rey hablar.
Si mala me la dixere,   25
peor se la he de tornar."
Por sus jornadas contadas
a la corte fue a llegar.
"Mantenga vos Dios, buen rey,
y a quantos con vos están."   30
"Mal vengades vos, Bernaldo,
traydor hijo de mal padre;
di te yo el Carpio en tenencia,
tú tomas lo de heredad."
"Mentides, el rey, mentides,   35
que no dizes la verdad,
que si yo fuesse traydor
a vos os cabría en parte;
acordarse vos devía
de aquella del Enzinal,   40
quando gentes estrangeras
allí os trataron tan mal
que os mataron el cavallo
y aun a vos querían matar.
Bernaldo, como traydor,   45
de entre ellos os fue a sacar.
Allí me distes el Carpio
de juro y de heredad;
prometistes me a mi padre,
no me guardastes verdad."   50
"¡Prendeldo, mis cavalleros,
que ygualado se me ha!"
"Aquí, aquí, los mis dozientos,
los que comedes mi pan,
que oy era venido el día   55
que honrra avemos de ganar."
El rey, de que aquesto viera,
de esta suerte fue a hablar:

just tell him he doesn´t impress me
and neither do those of his court,
but even so I will return there
to see what it is that he´s sought."
He gathered his knights all together, 15
and these are the words that he said;
"In all you are four hundred knights here,
four hundred who eat of my bread;
one hundred will stay at El Carpio
to look after the fort in my stead; 20
a hundred will go to the roadways
to prevent further troops coming in;
two hundred will come along with me
as I enter to talk with the King,
and if he should dare to rebuke me, 25
well, so much the worse then for him."
They took a few days on the journey
but eventually came to the Court –
"May the Good Lord preserve you, Alfonso,
and all you have here in support." 30
"You are here as a rebel, Bernardo,
your father was traitorous too;
I´ve allowed you to live at El Carpio,
but you say it belongs now to you."
"My King, you are lying, you´re lying, 35
and what you have said isn´t true,
and besides, if you think I´m a traitor
then part of the blame lies with you.
I think you had better remember
when foreigners entered your lands; 40
to El Encinal came some soldiers,
and you suffered so much at their hands;
those soldiers were wanting to kill you,
they´d already slaughtered your horse,
when Bernardo, who now you call traitor, 45
rescued you bravely by force;
you gave me El Carpio in payment,
it´s mine and I hold it by right;
you promised you´d give me my father,
a promise you´re breaking tonight." 50
"My noblemen, seize and arrest him!
The rebel refuses to bow!"
"Hurry here, hurry here my two hundred,
your service to me you have vowed,
if we want to stand up for our honour, 55
the time to defend it is now!"
But when the king saw his reaction
these were the words that he spoke:

"¿Qué ha sido aquesto, Bernaldo,
que assí enojado te has?   60
¿Lo que hombre dize de burla
de veras vas a tomar?
Yo te do el Carpio, Bernaldo,
de juro y de heredad."
"Aquestas burlas, el rey,   65
no son burlas de burlar.
Llamastes me de traydor,
traydor hijo de mal padre;
El Carpio, yo no lo quiero,
bien lo podéys vos guardar,   70
que quando yo lo quisiere
muy bien lo sabré ganar."

(1550:206-07; S6, M13A)

THE CID

Rodrigo (Ruy) Díaz (c.1043-99), later known as "El Cid", is the national hero of Castille. He was born into the lower nobility of the village of Vivar, near Burgos, and before he was 30 he seems to have already been commander of the Castilian army. He was twice exiled from Castille by Alfonso VI (probably in 1081, returning after 1086, and then again in 1088), and ended his life as ruler of Valencia, a rich kingdom he captured for himself from the Moslems in 1094. There are a large number of tales about him, mostly fictional, including three quite separate groups of ballads. Nos 37 and 38 here concern his youth; nos 39 to 48 form most of an extended cycle concerning the siege of Zamora in 1072; nos 50 to 52 come from the same tradition as the epic *Poema de Mío Cid*, of which a new translation is available in the *Hispanic Classics* series.

37. XIMENA'S COMPLAINT

En Burgos está el buen rey
assentado a su jantare,
quando la Ximena Gómez
se le vino a querellare;
cubierta paños de luto   5
tocas de negro cendale,
las rodillas por el suelo
començara de fablare:

The King is in Burgos
eating his meal
when the noble Ximena
makes her appeal,
dressed all in black,
with a veil of dark gauze,
she kneels on the ground
and argues her cause.

"Bernardo, now don´t get so angry,
recover the calm that you broke,   60
are you going to feel sorely offended
by something I said as a joke?"
I grant you the right to El Carpio,
a promise I cannot revoke."
"You say it´s a joke, King Alfonso,   65
but it´s no laughing matter at all;
you said that you think I´m a traitor,
my father a traitor you call;
So I´ll let you return to El Carpio,
and guard it with some of your men;   70
if I should have need of it later
I´m sure I can take it again."

"Con manzilla vivo, rey,
con ella murió mi madre.
Cada día que amanesce
veo el que mató a mi padre,
cavallero en un cavallo,
y en su mano un gavilane;
por fazerme más despecho
cévalo en mi palomare,
mátame mis palomillas
criadas y por criare,
la sangre que sale de ellas
teñido me ha mi briale.
Embiéselo a dezire,
embióme a amenazare.
Rey que non faze justicia
non deviera de reynare
ni cavalgar en cavallo
ni con la reyna folgare,
ni comer pan a manteles,
ni menos armas se armare."
El rey quando aquesto oyera
començare de pensar:
"Si yo prendo o mato al Cid
mis cortes rebolverseane;
pues si lo dexo de hazere

"I live in dishonour,
10 my mother has died,
and my father´s assassin
each day I see ride
proud on his horse
with a hawk at his side;
15 it feeds in my dovecot,
to increase my distress,
it´s killing my doves,
the young and the rest
and the blood that runs from them
20 leaves stains on my dress;
I´ve sent to complain,
he sends threats in reply -
No King without justice
on his throne should be seen,
25 nor ride on his horse,
nor play with his Queen,
nor eat off fine linen,
nor lead armies between."
The King hears her words
30 and he´s worried as well:
"If I punish the Cid
then the Court will rebel,
but if I do nothing

Dios me lo ha de demandare.
Mandarle quiero una carta,
mandarle quiero llamare."
Las palabras no son dichas,
la carta camino vae;
mensagero que la lleva
dado la avía a su padre.
Quando el Cid aquesto supo
ansí començó a fablare:
"Malas mañas avéys, Conde,
non vos las puedo quitare,
que carta que el rey vos manda
non me la queréys mostrare."
"Non era nada, mi fijo,
sinon que vades alláe;
fincad vos acá, mi fijo,
que yo yré en vuesso lugare."
"¡Nunca Dios lo tal quisiesse,
ni Sancta María su madre!
Sino que a donde vos fuerdes
tengo yo de yr delante."

in heaven I´ll pay –
35   I´ll send him a letter,
and bring him this way."
The letter is gone
as soon as commanded,
and to the Cid´s father
40   the messenger hands it,
and when the Cid knows
he cannot understand it.
"My father, you´re mean,
and you ought to know better,
45   for I see you don´t want
to show me the King´s letter."
"All the King wants
is for you to go there –
but stay here, my son,
50   and instead I´ll prepare."
"May God and may Mary
forbid that you do,
and grant that where you go
I should go too".

(Escobar:131; S25, M30A)

38. RODRIGO AND FERNANDO

Cavalga Diego Laýnez
al buen rey besar la mano;
consigo se los llevava
los trezientos hijos dalgo.
Entre ellos yva Rodrigo,
el sobervio castellano.
Todos cavalgan a mula,
sólo Rodrigo a cavallo;
todos visten oro y seda,
Rodrigo va bien armado;
todos espadas ceñidas,
Rodrigo estoque dorado;
todos con sendas varicas,
Rodrigo lança en la mano;
todos guantes olorosos,
Rodrigo guante mallado;
todos sombreros muy ricos,
Rodrigo caxco afinado,
y encima del caxco lleva
un bonete colorado.

Diego Laínez
rides to the Court,
and three hundred knights
with him has brought,
5   among them Rodrigo
rides proudly indeed;
all the rest are on mules
but he´s on his steed,
all the rest ride in silk,
10   he´s in breastplate and greaves,
all the rest carry swords,
he´s a dagger of gold,
all the rest have their staffs,
he a fighting lance holds,
15   all the rest have cloth gloves,
he has gloves of chain mail,
all the rest have fine hats,
but Rodrigo´s availed
of his bright-shining helmet,
20   with a red cap impaled.

Andando por su camino,
unos con otros hablando,
allegados son a Burgos;
con el rey se han encontrado.
Los que vienen con el rey
entre sí van razonando,
unos lo dizen de quedo,
otros lo van preguntando:
"¿Aquí viene entre esta gente
quien mató al Conde Laçano?"
Como lo oyera Rodrigo
en hito los ha mirado;
con alta y sobervia voz
de esta manera a hablado:
"Si hay alguno entre vosotros,
su pariente o adeudado,
que le pese de su muerte,
¡salga luego a demandallo!
Yo se lo defenderé
quier a pie, quier a cavallo."
Todos responden a una:
"Demande lo su pecado."
Todos se apearon juntos
para el rey besar la mano;
Rodrigo se queda solo
encima de su cavallo.
Entonces habló su padre,
bien oyréys lo que ha hablado:
"Apeaos vos, hijo mío,
besaréys al rey la mano,
porque él es vuestro Señor,
vos, hijo, soys su vassallo."
Desque Rodrigo esto oyó
sintióse más agraviado,
las palabras que responde
son de hombre muy enojado:
"Si otro me lo dixera
ya me lo hoviera pagado;
mas por mandarlo vos, padre,
yo lo haré de buen grado."
Ya se apeava Rodrigo
para el rey besar la mano,
al hincar de la rodilla
el estoque se ha arrancado.
Espantóse de esto el rey
y dixo como turbado:
"¡Quítate, Rodrigo, allá,
quítate me allá, diablo,

As they ride on the road
the discussions begin;
and now they're in Burgos,
meeting the King.
25 The knights of the King
are wondering now –
some say it soft,
some shout it aloud –
"Is Lozano's assassin
30 there in that crowd?"
Rodrigo has heard them,
he looks bold and proud,
he challenges them,
with his voice strong and loud,
35 "If any of you,
relation or friend,
are upset by his death,
come forth and defend;
and on foot or on horse
40 I'll stand firm to the end!"
They answer together
"His sins will attend."
To kiss the King's hand
all the others dismount;
45 Rodrigo alone
remains on his mount,
but these are the words
of his father the Count –
"Rodrigo, get down,
50 and kiss the King's hand,
for he is your Lord
and you're his to command."
When he hears this
he becomes more annoyed
55 as everyone sees
from the words he employs:
"If anyone else
had said that, he'd pay,
but since you're my father
60 I'll do as you say."
He dismounted and knelt
to the King there beneath,
but the dagger he carries
slips out of its sheath,
65 and the King is so shaken
he cries out in fright:
"Get away now, Rodrigo,
you devilish knight!

que tienes el gesto de hombre
y los hechos de león bravo!"
Como Rodrigo lo oyó
a priessa pide el cavallo;
con una voz alterada
contra el rey assí ha hablado:
"Por besar mano de rey
no me tengo por honrrado;
porque la besó mi padre
me tengo por afrentado."
En diziendo estas palabras
salido se ha del palacio;
consigo se los tornava
los trecientos hijos dalgo;
si bien vinieron vestidos,
bolvieron mejor armados,
y si vinieron en mulas,
todos buelven en cavallos.

Though you look like a man,
70 like a lion you fight!"
Rodrigo gets back
on his horse straightaway,
and these words of anger
he´s chosen to say:
75 "I´ve kissed a King´s hand
but that brings me no honour;
since my father has kissed it
I instead feel dishonoured";
and saying these words
80 he goes out of the Court
with all the three hundred
knights they have brought:
they´ve put on their arms
for their fine silks and jewels,
85 they ride back on horses
instead of their mules.

(Silva:156-57; S26, M29)

39. FERNANDO AND THE ARCHBISHOP

Doliente estava, doliente,
esse buen rey, Don Fernando;
los pies tiene cara a oriente,
y la candela en la mano.
A la cabecera tiene
los sus hijos todos quatro;
los tres eran de la reyna,
y el uno era bastardo.
Esse que bastardo era
quedava mejor librado;
arçobispo de Toledo,
de las Españas primado.
"Si yo no muriera, hijo,
vos fuérades Padre Santo,
mas con la renta que os queda
bien podéys, hijo, alcançallo."

In pain was the King,
Good King Fernando,
facing the East,
candle in hand.
5 at the head of the bed
all four of his sons;
three were the Queen´s,
a bastard was one.
He was the richest,
10 and so would remain,
Toledo´s Archbishop
and Primate of Spain.
"If I wasn´t dying,
my son, you´d be Pope,
15 but with all of this money
you still have the hope."

(Silva:158; S14, M35)

40. FERNANDO AND URRACA

"Morir vos queredes, padre;
 San Miguel vos aya el alma!
Mandastes las vuestras tierras
a quien se vos antojara;
a Don Sancho a Castilla,
Castilla la bien nombrada,
a Don Alonso a León
y a Don García a Vizcaya.
A mí, porque soy muger,
dexáys me deserodada.
Yrme e yo por essas tierras
como una muger errada,
y este mi cuerpo daría
a quien se me antojara,
a los moros por dineros
y a los christianos de gracia.
De lo que ganar pudiere,
haré bien por la vuestra alma."
"¡Calledes, hija, calledes!
No digades tal palabra,
que muger que tal dezía
merescía ser quemada.
Allá en Castilla la Vieja
un rincón se me olvidava:
Çamora avía por nombre,
Çamora la bien cercada.
De una parte la cerca el Duero,
de otra, peña tajada;
del otro la morería,
una cosa muy preciada.
Quien vos la tomare, hija,
¡la mi maldición le caiga!"
Todos dizen "Amén, amén",
sino Don Sancho, que calla.

"My father, you´re dying,
may your soul find its rest!
You´ve given your kingdom
as you thought best,
5 you´ve offered to Sancho
proud ancient Castilla,
León to Alonso,
Biscay to García,
but I am a woman,
10 and left with no home,
I´ll wander the kingdom
a woman alone
and offer my body
to all men I see,
15 to Moslems for money
to Christians for free,
and the money I make
for your soul it shall be."
"Silence, my daughter,
20 those words should be spurned,
a woman who says them
deserves to be burned!
There´s a place in Castilla
that now I recall,
25 the town of Zamora
with fortified walls,
the Duero runs by it,
it´s on a steep hill,
and the old Moslem quarter
30 is beautiful still;
who captures it from you,
my curse is on them!"
And except for Don Sancho
they all say "Amen!"

(Sin año:158; S15, M36).

41. URRACA AND RODRIGO

"¡A fuera, a fuera, Rodrigo,
el sobervio castellano!
Acordarse te devría
de aquel tiempo ya passado
quando fuiste cavallero
en el altar de Santiago,

"Get away, proud Rodrigo,
Castilian son!
You ought to remember
the times that have gone;
5 the King was your guardian
when to court you first came,

quando el rey fue tu padrino,
tú, Rodrigo, el ahijado,
mi padre te dio las armas,
mi madre te dio el cavallo,
yo te calcé las espuelas
porque fuesses más honrrado;
que pensé casar contigo,
mas no lo quiso mi pecado,
cassaste con Ximena Gómez,
hija del Conde Loçano;
con ella uviste dineros,
comigo uvieras estado.
Bien casaste tú, Rodrigo;
muy mejor fueras casado;
dexaste hija de rey
por tomar de su vassallo."
"Si os parece, mi Señora,
bien podemos desligallo."
"Mi ánima penaría
si yo fuesse en discrepallo."
"A fuera, a fuera los míos,
los de a pie y de a cavallo,
pues de aquella torre mocha
¡una vira me han tirado!
No traýa el asta hierro,
el coraçón me ha passado.
¡Ya ningún remedio siento
sino bivir más penado!"

and you were his favourite
knight of St James,
with arms from my father
and a horse from my mother
and spurs from myself,
your honourable lover,
and I thought we would marry,
but that couldn´t be,
for you married Ximena,
of the rich family
of the noble Lozano
when you should be with me –
a good marriage, Rodrigo,
but it wasn´t the best,
you married a vassal
and spurned a Princess."
"If you wish it, Urraca,
I´ll abandon my wife."
"No, no, then I´ll suffer
in the eternal life!"
"Come away, come away,
my soldiers and knights!
from Zamora an arrow
has pierced me tonight,
the shaft isn´t metal
but it´s wounded my heart,
and for all of my life
I´ll be hurt by the dart."

(1550:214; S16, M37)

42. VELLIDO DOLFOS (1)

."¡Rey Don Sancho, Rey Don Sancho!
No digas que no te aviso,
que de dentro de Çamora
un alevoso ha salido;
llámase Vellido Dolfos
hijo de Dolfos Vellido –
quatro trayciones ha hecho,
y con ésta serán cinco.
Si gran traydor fue el padre,
mayor traydor es el hijo."
Gritos dan en el real:
"¡A Don Sancho han mal herido!
¡Muerto le ha Vellido Dolfos,

"King Sancho, King Sancho,
let this be a warning!
From Zamora a traitor
has gone out this morning,
Vellido, of Dolfos
Vellido the son,
four crimes he´s committed,
and this the fifth one,
the father´s a traitor,
but worse is the son!"
There´s a cry in the camp:
"King Sancho has died!
Vellido has stabbed him,

gran trayción ha cometido!"
Desque le tuviera muerto
metióse por un postigo,
por las calles de Çamora
va dando vozes y gritos:
"¡Tiempo es, Doña Urraca,
de cumplir lo prometido!"

the traitor and spy!"
15 When he had killed him
he came through the wall,
in the streets of Zamora
he shouted and called:
"Urraca, you promised,
20 now give me it all!"

(Silva:159; S17, M45)

43. VELLIDO DOLFOS (2)

De Çamora sale Dolfos
corriendo y apresurado,
huyendo va de los fijos
del buen viejo Arias Gonçalo.
En la tienda del buen rey
en ella se avía amparado;
"¡Manténgate Dios, el rey!"
"Vellido, seas bien llegado."
"Señor, tu vassallo soy,
tu vassallo, y de tu vando,
y yo por aconsejarle
a aquel viejo Arias Gonçalo
que te entregasse a Çamora,
pues se te avía quitado,
ha me querido matar,
y de él me soy escapado;
a ti me vengo, Señor,
por ser en el tu mandado,
con desseo de servirte
como qualquier fijo dalgo.
Yo te entregaré Çamora,
aunque pese a Arias Gonçalo,
que por un falso postigo
en ella serás entrado."
El buen Arias, de leal,
al rey avía avisado,
desde el muro del adarve
estas palabras fablando:
"A ti lo digo, el buen rey,
y a todos tus castellanos,
que allá ha salido Vellido,
Vellido, un traydor malvado,
que si traycíon te fiziere
a nos no cos imputado."

Out from Zamora
Vellido has run
escaping the wrath
of Gonzalo´s five sons;
5 to the tent of King Sancho
and safety he comes:
"God bless you, my Lord."
"God bless you, Vellido."
"My Lord, I´m your vassal
10 and you are my leader.
I suggested Gonzalo
should open the doors
of Zamora before you
since rightly it´s yours;
15 he wanted to kill me
so I had to flee,
and that´s why I´m here
and your vassal will be;
I´ll be one of your knights
20 and your fine company.
Gonzalo won´t like it
when Zamora is yours –
you can enter the city
through a little side door."
25 But honest Gonzalo
has gone up this morning
on top of the walls
and shouted a warning:
"I tell you, King Sancho,
30 Castilians all,
Vellido the traitor
has left through our walls,
and if he betrays you
then don´t blame us all."

Oýdo lo avía Vellido
que al rey tiene por la mano:
"Non lo creades, Señor,
lo que contra mí ha fablado,
que Don Arias lo publica
porque el lugar no sea entrado,
porque él sabe bien que sé
por dónde será tomado."
Allí le fablara el rey,
de Vellido confiado:
"Yo lo creo bien, Vellido,
el Dolfos, mi buen criado;
por tanto, vámonos luego
a ver el postigo falso."
"Vámonos luego, Señor,
yd solo, no acompañado,
apartad vos del real."
El buen rey se avía apartado;
con voluntad de fazer
lo que a nadie es escusado,
el venablo que llevava
a Vellido se lo ha dado;
el qual, desque ansí lo vido
de espaldas, y descuydado,
enhestóse en los estrivos,
con fuerça se lo ha tirado.
Diérale por las espaldas
y a los pechos ha passado.
Allí cayó luego el rey
muy mortalmente llagado.
Violo caer Don Rodrigo,
que de Bivar es llamado,
y como lo vio ferido
cavalgara en su cavallo;
con la priessa que tenía,
espuelas no se ha calçado.
Huyendo yva el traydor,
tras él yva el castellano;
si apriessa avía salido,
a muy mayor se avía entrado.
Rodrigo que ya llegava
y el Dolfos que estava en salvo,
maldiciones que se echava
el nieto de Laýn Calvo:
"Maldito sea el cavallero
que como yo ha cavalgado,
que si yo espuela traxera
non se fuera el malvado."

35 Vellido has heard this,
he's by the King's hand:
"My Lord, don't believe him,
Gonzalo has planned
to send you this warning
40 to make you hold back,
since he knows that I know
where you can attack."
The King trusts Vellido
and speaks to him thus;
45 "I believe you, Vellido,
you're faithful and just,
now go to the doorway
and show it to us."
"Let's go straightaway,
50 My Lord, come alone."
They've left from the camp
just the two on their own,
to plan the worst treason
that's ever been known.
55 The King gives Vellido
the dagger he wears;
When Vellido can see him
in front, unawares,
he stands up in his stirrups
60 and hurls it so fast
that it strikes the King's back
and straight through it has passed
mortally wounded
the King has to fall.
65 Rodrigo of Vivar
is watching it all;
when he sees the King wounded
he leaps on his horse,
no time to put spurs on,
70 no time to pause;
the Castilian hero
is chasing the assassin
who faster than ever
for safety is dashing,
75 and reaches Zamora
just in front of Rodrigo,
who curses himself
for not catching Vellido:
"Pity who rides
80 as I do today,
for if I had my spurs
he could not get away."

Todos van a ver al rey,
que mortal estava echado,
todos le dizen lisonjas,
nadie verdad le ha fablado,
si no fue el Conde de Cabra,
un buen cavallero anciano:
"Soys mi rey y mi señor,
y yo soy vuesso vassallo:
cumple que miréys por vos
que es verdad lo que vos fablo,
que del ánima curedes,
del cuerpo non fagáys caso;
a Dios vos encomendad,
pues fue este día aziago."
"Buena ventura ayáys, Conde,
que ansí me eys aconsejado."
En diziendo estas palabras
el alma a Dios avía dado;
de esta suerte murió el rey
por averse confiado.

They all rush to the King
who is lying there dying,
85 but none dare to tell him,
they're flattering and lying,
till the Conde de Cabra,
an old and good knight,
90 says "My Lord and my King,
my master, it's right
that you look to your soul
for I tell you the truth,
you should look to your soul
now your body's no use,
95 and surrender to God,
for today is ill-fated."
"God bless you, good Count,
for the truth you have stated."
As he speaks, so his soul
100 ascends to its maker;
and thus dies King Sancho
from trusting a traitor.

(Escobar:156-57; M46)

44. DIEGO ORDÓÑEZ'S CHALLENGE

Ya cavalga Diego Ordóñez,
del real se avía salido,
de dobles pieças armado
y un cavallo morzillo;
va a reptar los çamoranos
por la muerte de su primo,
que mató Vellido Dolfos,
hijo de Dolfos Vellido.
"¡Yo os riepto, los çamoranos,
por traydores fementidos;
riepto a todos los muertos
y con ellos a los bivos;
riepto hombres y mugeres,
los por nascer y nascidos;
riepto a todos los grandes,
a los grandes y a los chicos;
a las carnes y pescados
y las aguas de los ríos!"
Allí habló Arias Gonçalo,
bien oyréys lo que uvo dicho:

Diego Ordóñez
rides out from the force
in all of his armour
and on his best horse
5 to challenge Vellido
and Zamora besides,
for the King was his cousin
and now he has died:
"I challenge Zamora
10 for treachery given,
I challenge Zamora,
the dead and the living,
both present and future,
their sons and their daughters,
15 I challenge their nobles,
their lesser supporters,
their cattle, their fish,
and the Duero's full waters."
Arias Gonzalo
20 replied as you'll hear:

"¿Qué culpa tienen los viejos?   "You can´t blame the old
¿Qué culpa tienen los niños?   or the boys of few years:
¿Qué merecen las mugeres   why challenge our women
y los que no son nascidos?   and those not yet here?
¿Por qué rieptas a los muertos,   25 Why challenge our dead
los ganados y los ríos?   and our river and cattle?
Bien sabéys vos, Diego Ordóñez,   For, Diego Ordóñez,
muy bien lo tenéys sabido,   you know that the battle
que aquel que riepta consejo   five times must be fought
deve de lidiar con cinco."   30 if you claim so to hate us."
Vellido le respondió: Ordóñez replied:
"¡Traydores eys todos sido!"   "You are all of you traitors!"

(1550:216; S18, M47)

45. URRACA AND GONZALO

Tristes van los çamoranos,   The men of Zamora
metidos en gran quebranto,   are angry and shaken,
reptados son de traydores,   with treachery challenged,
de alevosos son llamados;   for traitors mistaken,
más quieren ser todos muertos   5   instead they´d prefer
que no traydores nombrados.   that their lives be forsaken.
Día era de Sant Millán,   It is San Millán´s day,
esse día señalado;   a great day in the making;
todos duermen en Çamora,   the rest are asleep
mas no duerme Arias Gonçalo.   10 but Gonzalo´s awakened;
Acerca de las dos horas   he gets out of bed
del lecho se ha levantado;   about two, before dawning,
castigando está a sus hijos,   to prepare his four sons
a todos quatro está armando;   for their duels in the morning.
las palabras que les dize   15 He gives to his sons
son de manzilla y quebranto: these grim words of warning:
"Ayude hos Dios, hijos míos,   "God bless you, my loved ones,
guarde os Dios, hijos amados,   God protect you, my sons,
pues sabéys quán falsamente   for you know how falsely
havemos sido reptados;   20 this challenge has come.
tomad esfuerço, mis hijos,   Take more courage and effort
si nunca lo havéys tomado,   than ever you´ve done;
acordaos que descendéys   remember you come
de sangre de Laín Calvo,   from Laín Calvo´s line
cuya noble fama y gloria   25 whose fame and whose glory
hasta oy no se ha olvidado.   still shine in our time;
Pues que sabéys que Don Diego   Diego Ordóñez´s
es cavallero preciado,   a good knight and fine,
pero mantiene mentira   but God is displeased

y Dios de ello no es pagado.
El que de verdad se ayuda
de Dios siempre es ayudado.
Uno falta para cinco
por que no soys más de quatro -
yo seré el quinto, y primero
que quiero salir al campo;
morir quiero y no ver muerte
de hijos que tanto amo.
¡Mis hijos, Dios hos bendiga
como hos bendize mi mano!"
Sus armas pide el buen viejo,
sus hijos lo están armando,
las grevas le están poniendo.
Doña Urraca avía entrado;
los braços le echara encima
muy fuertemente llorando.
"¿Dónde vays, mi padre viejo?
O ¿para qué estáys armado?
Dexad las armas pesadas,
que ya soys viejo cansado,
pues que sabéys si os morís
perdido es todo mi estado.
Acordaos que prometistes
a mi padre Don Fernando
de nunca desmampararme,
ni dexar de vuestra mano."
"Plaze me, Señora hija,"
respondió Arias Gonçalo.
Cavalgara Pedro de Arias,
su hijo que era mediano,
que aun que era moço de días
era en obras esforçado;
dixo: "Cavalgad, mi hijo,
que hos esperan en el campo.
Vays en tal hora y tal punto
que nos saquéys de cuydado."
Sin poner pie en el estribo
Arias Pedro ha cavalgado;
por aquel postigo viejo
galopeando ha llegado
donde estavan los juezes
que le estavan esperando;
partido les han el sol,
dexado les han el campo.

(Timoneda, RE:31-32; M49)

30 because this time he's lying,
    and God protects those
    who their hardest are trying.
    You are no more than four,
    we need one more for five,
35 so I'll go out first,
    and if I don't survive
    then I won't see the death
    of the ones I love best.
    My sons, here I bless you;
40 by God you be blessed."
    He asks for his armour,
    his sons help him dress
    and are putting it on
    when Urraca appears,
45 embraces Gonzalo
    and breaks down in tears -
    "What's this for, Gonzalo,
    where are you going to go?
    That armour's too heavy
50 and you are too old,
    and you know that if you die
    then I cannot hold.
    Remember you promised
    you'd never neglect me,
55 you told King Fernando
    you'd always protect me."
    "You're right, good Urraca,"
    Gonzalo's replied,
    and decides that his fifth son,
60 Pedro, will ride,
    for although he's still young
    he's got courage and pride.
    "Ride out my son,
    they're awaiting you there,
65 you're here just in time
    to relieve our despair."
    Pedro rides off
    without using the stirrups
    and through the old gate
70 he arrives at a gallop
    to where all of the judges
    are waiting for him;
    the lines are drawn fairly -
    let battle begin!

46. FERNANDO ARIAS

Por aquel postigo viejo
que nunca fuera cerrado
vi venir pendón vermejo
con trezientos de cavallo.
En medio de los trezientos
viene un monumento armado
y dentro del monumento
viene un cuerpo sepultado.
Fernán de Arias ha por nombre,
hijo de Arias Gonçalo.
Lloravan le cient donzellas,
todas ciento hijas dalgo,
todas eran sus parientas
en tercero y quarto grado.
Las unas le dizen primo,
otras le llaman hermano,
otras le dezían tío,
otras le llaman cuñado;
sobre todas le llorava
aquessa Urraca Hernando;
o ¡quán bien que la consuela
esse viejo Arias Gonçalo!
"Calledes, hija, calledes,
no hagades tan gran llanto,
que si un hijo me han muerto
aún me quedan otros quatro.
No murió por las tavernas,
menos las tablas jugando,
mas murió sobre Çamora,
vuestra honra defensando."

The old city gate
sees a desperate sight:
a red banner is coming
with three hundred knights,
5 and there in the middle
they carry a bier,
on this a man's body
is being brought near.
His name is Fernando,
10 Gonzalo's third son.
A hundred girls mourn him,
noble, each one,
they all are relations,
some closer than others,
15 some mourn for a cousin,
and some for a brother,
some mourn for an uncle
or brother-in-law;
but Princess Urraca,
20 who's weeping much more,
by Arias Gonzalo
is well reassured:
"Don't weep, good Urraca,
be quiet once more,
25 for if I've lost one son
there still remain four;
and he didn't die drinking
or playing wild games,
he died for Zamora,
30 protecting your name."

(Timoneda, RE:32; S19, M50)

47. SANTA GADEA (1)

En Toledo estava Alfonso
que non cuydava reynar,
desterrárale Don Sancho
por su reyno le tomar;
y Doña Urraca Fernando
mensageros fue a embiar.
Las nuevas que le trayán
a él gran plazer le dan;
"Rey Alfonso, Rey Alfonso,

In Toledo, Alfonso,
not expecting to reign,
exiled by Sancho,
who sent him away,
5 is met by a messenger
from Urraca one day,
and the news that he hears
makes him happy again –
"King Alfonso, Alfonso,

que te embían a llamar,
castellanos y leoneses
por rey alçado te han,
por muerte del Rey Don Sancho
que Vellido fue a matar;
sólo quedava Rodrigo
que no lo quiere aceptar;
porque amava mucho al rey,
quiere que ayas de jurar
que en la su muerte, Señor,
non tuviste que culpar."
"Bien vengáys, los mensageros;
secretos queráys estar,
que si el rey moro lo sabe
él aquí nos detendrá."
El Conde Don Peranzules
un consejo le fue a dar,
que cavallos bien errados
al revés avían de errar.
Descuélganse por el muro,
sálense de la ciudad,
fuéronse para Castilla
do esperándolos están.
Al rey le besan la mano;
el Cid non quiere besar;
sus parientes castellanos
todos juntado se han.
"Heredero soys, Alfonso,
nadie os lo quiere negar,
pero si os plaze, Señor,
non vos deve de pesar,
que nos fagáys juramento
qual vos lo querrán tomar,
vos y doze de los vuessos,
quales vos queráys juntar,
que de la muerte del rey
non tenedes que culpar."
"Plázeme, los castellanos,
todo os lo quiero otorgar."
En Sancta Gadea de Burgos,
allí el rey se va a jurar.
Rodrigo toma la jura;
él la quiere razonar.
En un cerrojo sagrado
le comiença a conjurar.
"Don Alfonso, y leoneses,
venís os vos a salvar,
que en muerte del Rey Don Sancho

10   they're sending for you,
     Leonese and Castilians,
     their Kingdom to rule
     now that Sancho has died
     at the hands of Vellido.
15   Only Rodrigo
     doesn't want you as leader,
     for he loved King Sancho
     and wants you to swear
     in the death of your brother
20   you took no part there."
     "You're welcome my friends,
     but be quiet, as you know
     that the King of Toledo
     would not let us go."
25   Count Peranzules
     sends the word down
     they should put on the horseshoes
     the wrong way around.
     Then they slip down the walls
30   and escape through the town.
     They arrive in Castille,
     the Castilians are waiting,
     they kiss the King's hand
     but the Cid's hesitating,
35   with all the King's family
     there congregating:
     "Alfonso, we know
     that you are the heir,
     but I hope that you're happy
40   and fully prepared
     to swear us the oath
     that we want you to swear,
     with twelve of your men,
     any twelve others,
45   that you had no part
     in the death of your brother."
     "Indeed, my Castilians,
     I'll do as you say."
     To Santa Gadea
50   the King goes straightway;
     the Cid makes him swear
     without any delay,
     with his hands on a bolt;
     the Cid starts to say:
55   "Leonese, and Alfonso,
     you are here to proclaim
     for the death of King Sancho

non tuvistes que culpar,
ni tampoco de ella os plugo,
ni a ella distes lugar;
mala muerte ayáys, Alfonso,
si non dixerdes verdad;
villanos sean en ella,
non fidalgos de solar,
que non sean castellanos
por más deshonra vos dar,
sinon de Asturias de Oviedo,
que non tienen piedad."
"Amén, amén", dixo el rey,
"que nunca fuy en tal maldad."
Tres vezes toma la jura,
tantas le va a preguntar;
el rey, viéndose afincado,
contra el Cid le fue ayrar:
"Mucho me fincáys, Rodrigo,
en lo que no ay que dudar;
cras besarme eys la mano
si agora me hazéys jurar."
"Sí, Señor," dixera el Cid,
"si sueldo me avéys de dar,
que en las tierras de otros reyes
a fijos dalgo lo dan;
cuyo vassallo yo fuere
también me lo ha de pagar.
Si vos dármelo quisierdes,
a mí en plazer me verná."
El rey por tales razones
contra el Cid se fue a enojar;
siempre desde allí adelante
gran tiempo le quiso mal.

60

65

70

75

80

85

90

you're no way to blame,
that you didn't suggest it
and it caused you great pain –
May you die a bad death
if, Alfonso, you lie,
at the hands of wild peasants,
not nobles, you'll die,
and to make your death worse
your pitiless murderers
won't be Castilians
but men from Asturias."
"That's enough" said Alfonso,
"I'd no part in the crime."
For a third time they ask him,
he swears a third time;
he knows he's not trusted
and curses the Cid,
"You should not have mistrusted
my oath as you did;
but you'll kiss my hand
tomorrow, my Cid."
"Yes I will" said the Cid
"if you pay me the price,
for all other kings
will pay for good knights,
and whoever's my master,
he must treat me right;
if you pay what I ask
I'll accept with delight."
And that's why Alfonso
mistrusted the Cid
and from that moment on
hated him as he did.

(Escobar:163-64; M51)

48. SANTA GADEA (2)

En Santa Gadea de Burgos,
do juran los hijos dalgo,
allí le toma la jura
El Cid al rey castellano;
las juras eran tan fuertes
que al buen rey ponen espanto,
sobre un cerrojo de hierro
y una ballesta de palo.

5

In Santa Gadea
where loyal knights kneel,
the Cid takes an oath
from the King of Castille;
the oath is so strong
the King shakes where he's stood,
as he swears on a bolt
and a crossbow of wood.

"Villanos te maten, Alonso,
villanos, que no hidalgos,
de las Asturias de Oviedo,
que no sean castellanos;
mátente con aguijadas,
no con lanças ni con dardos,
con cuchillos cachicuernos,
no con puñales dorados,
abarcas traygan calçadas,
que no çapatos con lazo,
capas traygan aguaderas,
no de contray ni frisado,
con camisones de estopa,
no de holanda ni labrados;
cavalleros vengan en burras,
que no en mulas ni en cavallos,
frenos traygan de cordel,
que no cueros fogueados;
mátente por las aradas,
que no en villas ni en poblado,
sáquente el coraçón
por el siniestro costado;
si no dixeres verdad
de lo que eres preguntado:
¿si fuiste ni consentiste
en la muerte de tu hermano?"
Jurado havía el rey
que en tal nunca se ha hallado,
pero allí hablara el rey
malamente y enojado.
"Muy mal me conjuras, Cid;
Cid, muy mal me has conjurado;
mas hoy me tomas la jura,
mañana me besarás la mano."
"Por besar mano de rey
no me tengo por honrrado;
porque la besó mi padre
me tengo por afrentado."
"Vete de mis tierras, Cid,
mal cavallero provado,
y no vengas más a ellas
dende este día en un año."
"Plázeme", dixo el buen Cid,
"Plázeme", dixo, "de grado,
por ser la primera cosa
que mandas en tu reynado.
Tú me destierras por uno,
yo me destierro por quatro."

"May you die, King Alfonso,
at wild peasant hands,
not from noble Castille
but Asturian lands;
may they kill you with goads
that no noble would hold,
and with horn-handled knives,
not with daggers of gold,
and be wearing rough sandals
not neatly-tied shoes,
and waterproof capes
that no noble would use,
and rough peasant smocks
with no linen whatever;
may they ride up on donkeys,
not horses, together,
whose reins are of string,
not of toughly-worked leather;
and kill you on farmlands
where nobles don´t ride,
and take out your heart
from your left hand side:
if you don´t tell the truth
when I ask to discover
if you had a part
in the death of your brother."
The King swore the oath,
that he had no such part;
then replied with great anger
and pain in his heart:
"My Cid, that´s a bad oath,
a bad oath you planned;
today you imposed it,
but you will kiss my hand."
"To kiss the King´s hand
will not be a great honour;
my father kissed one,
and so I feel dishonoured."
"My Cid, you´re a bad knight,
so get out of here,
don´t come back to my kingdom
for over a year!"
"I will" said the Cid,
"I´ll leave you for sure,
for a new King´s first order
cannot be ignored:
you´ve exiled me one year,
I´ll leave you for four."

Ya se parte el buen Cid
sin al rey besar la mano
con trezientos cavalleros,
todos eran hijosdalgo,   60
todos son hombres mancebos,
ninguno no havía cano,
todos llevan lança en puño
y el hierro acicalado,
y llevan sendas adargas   65
con borlas de colorado;
mas no le faltó al buen Cid
adonde assentar su campo.

(Silva:154-55; S20, M52)

Without kissing his hand
he rides off there and then,
and with him ride also
his three hundred men,
all young men and noble,
not one of them old,
the points are all shining
on the lances they hold,
their shields have red tassels
that swing at their ends;
and the Cid, though an exile,
knows still he has friends.

49. THE CID AND THE POPE

A Concilio dentro en Roma
el Padre Sancto ha llamado;
por obedescer al Papa
esse noble Rey Don Sancho
para Roma fue derecho   5
con el Cid acompañado.
Por sus jornadas contadas
dentro en Roma han apeado.
El rey con gran cortesía
al Papa besó la mano,   10
y el Cid y sus cavalleros
cada qual de grado en grado.
En la Yglesia de Sant Pedro
Don Rodrigo se avía entrado,
a do vido siete sillas   15
de siete reyes christianos,
y vio la del rey de Francia
junto a la del Padre Sancto,
y la del rey su señor
un estado más abaxo.   20
Fuese a la del rey de Francia,
con el pie la ha derribado;
la silla era de marfil,
fecho se ha quatro pedaços.
Tomara la de su rey   25
y subióse en lo más alto.
Habló allí un honrado duque
que dizen el saboyano:
"Maldito seas tú, Rodrigo,

The Pope has just called
a Council in Rome,
so the noble King Sancho
sets off from home,
and the Cid travels with him
directly to Rome.
They've arrived at the court
as quickly as planned,
the King has politely
kissed the Pope's hand,
and so has the Cid
and the knights of his band.
Rodrigo goes into
the Church of St Peter
and sees seven chairs
where the Kings will be seated:
next to the Pope's
is the French ruler's chair,
while the chair of King Sancho
is lower down there.
He goes to the French one,
kicks it down to the floor,
and although it's of ivory
it breaks into four;
he picks up his King's chair
and puts it on high.
The honourable Duke
of Savoy passes by,
saying "Damn you, Rodrigo,

del Papa descomulgado,   30   the Pope will disown you,
porque deshonraste un rey,   you´ve insulted a King,
el mejor y más preciado."   the best that is known."
En oýr aquesto el Cid   The Cid answers back
tal respuesta le uvo dado: with threats of his own:
"Dexemos los reyes, Duque,   35   "If you feel insulted
y si os sentís agraviado   forget the King´s thrones,
ayámoslo los dos solos,   and we´ll settle this now
de mí a vos sea demandado."   we two here alone."
Allegóse cabe el duque,   He goes up to the Duke
un gran rempujón le ha dado; 40   and punches his arm,
el duque sin responderle   but the Duke doesn´t answer
se quedó muy sossegado.   and keeps himself calm.
El Papa, quando lo supo,   The Pope has disowned him
al Cid ha descomulgado;   as soon as he knows,
en saberlo luego el Cid   45   so the Cid when he´s told
ante el Papa se ha postrado.   prostrate he goes,
"Absolvedme" dixo, "Papa;   "Pope, you´ll regret it
si no, seráos mal contado."   if you don´t change your mind."
El Papa, de piadoso,   The Pope is forgiving
respondió muy mesurado: 50   and tranquil and kind:
"Yo te absuelvo, Don Rodrigo,   "I gladly forgive you,
yo te absuelvo de buen grado,   Cid, as I ought,
con que seas en mi corte   if you can behave
muy cortés y mesurado."   with restraint at my court."

(Escobar:146-47; M34)

50. THE CID AND BÚCAR

Helo, Helo, por do viene   He´s coming, the Moslem,
el moro por la calçada!   the road over there,
Cavallero a la gineta   standing up in the stirrups
encima una yegua vaya,   upon his bay mare;
borzeguíes maroquines   5   with boots of fine leather,
y espuela de oro calçada,   spurs made of gold,
una adarga ante los pechos   a shield at his chest,
y en su mano una azagaya.   a spear that he holds;
Mirando estava Valencia,   he looks to Valencia,
cómo está tan bien cercada: 10   strong walls and old,
"O Valencia, O Valencia,   and cries out "Valencia!
de mal fuego seas quemada!   You ought to be burned,
Primero fueste de moros   for once you were ours
que de christianos ganada;   but now Christian you´ve turned
si la lança no me miente   15   but I swear by my lance
a moros serás tornada.   you will soon be returned,

Aquel perro de aquel Cid
prenderélo por la barba,
su muger Doña Ximena
será de mí captivada,
su hija, Urraca Hernando,
será mi enamorada.
Después de yo harto de ella
entregarla he a mi compaña."
El buen Cid no está tan lexos,
que todo bien lo escuchava:
"Venid vos acá, mi hija,
mi hija Doña Urraca,
dexad las ropas continas
y vestid ropas de Pascua.
Aquel moro hi de perro
detenédmele en palabras
mientras yo ensillo a Bavieca
y me ciño la mi espada."
La donzella muy hermosa
se paró a una ventana;
el moro desque la vido
de esta suerte le hablara:
"Alá te guarde, Señora,
mi señora Doña Urraca."
"Assí haga a vos, Señor,
buena sea vuestra llegada.
Siete años ha, rey, siete,
que soy vuestra enamorada."
"Otros tantos ha, Señora,
que os tengo dentro en mi alma."
Ellos estando en aquesto
el buen Cid que assomava.
"¡A Dios, a Dios, mi señora,
la mi linda enamorada!
que del cavallo Bavieca
yo bien oygo la patada."
Do la yegua pone el pie
Bavieca pone la pata.
Allí hablara el cavallo,
bien oyréys lo que hablara:
"Rebentar devía la madre
que a su hijo no esperava."
Siete bueltas la rodea
alderredor de una xara;
la yegua, que era ligera,
muy adelante passava,
fasta llegar cabe el río
adonde una barca estava.

and the infidel Cid
I will take by the beard,
his lady Ximena
20 a prisoner in fear,
his daughter Urraca
will soon be my lover –
when I've had enough
she'll be passed to the others."
25 But the Cid is nearby,
he is able to hear –
"So come, my Urraca,
my daughter, come near,
change from these clothes,
30 in your best ones come here,
and keep him here talking,
the infidel Moor,
while I saddle Babieca
and put on my sword."
35 At the window she waits,
she's a beautiful girl;
the Moslem king sees her
and says when he's near
"May Allah preserve you,
40 Urraca, my dear."
"May he bless you, good King,
you're welcome in here,
for seven long years
has my love been sincere."
45 And you've been in my heart
for these same seven years."
Then as they are talking
the Cid now appears –
"Goodbye, my good lady,
50 my beautiful girl,
for those are the hooves
of Babieca, the feared!"
His mare gallops off
with Babieca behind,
55 and Babieca cries out
the thought in his mind –
"A curse on the mother
her son cannot find!"
Seven times chasing her
60 right round a thicket,
but the mare keeps ahead
running lighter and quicker;
they catch sight of a boat
as they come to a river,

El moro desque la vido
con ella bien se holgava,
grandes gritos da al barquero
que le allegasse la barca.
El barquero es diligente,
tiénesela aparejada,
embarcó muy presto en ella
que no se detuvo nada.
Estando el moro embarcado
el buen Cid que llegó al agua,
y por ver al moro en salvo
de tristeza rebentava;
mas con la furia que tiene
una lança le arrojava,
diziendo: "¡Recoged, yerno,
recogedme aquessa lança,
que quiçá tiempo verná
que os será bien demandada!"

65 and the Moslem´s delighted
and feels he´s delivered,
he calls to the boatman
to bring the boat hither;
the boat is all ready,
70 the man´s on his way,
the Moslem jumps in
without any delay;
when the Cid nears the river
the Moor´s safe afloat
75 and the Cid cries in grief
when he sees the Moor´s boat,
and he throws out his lance
and calls over the water -
"Now pick up my lance,
80 you who wanted my daughter,
and there could come a time
when you´ll pay what you ought to!"

(Silva:175-76; S21, M55)

51. THE "AFRENTA DE CORPES"

De concierto están los condes,
hermanos Diego y Fernando;
afrentar quieren al Cid,
muy gran trayción han armado.
Quieren bolverse a sus tierras,
sus mugeres han demandado,
y luego su suegro el Cid
se las huvo entregado.
"Mirad, yernos, que tratedes
como a dueñas hijas dalgo
mis hijas, pues que a vosotros
por mugeres las he dado."
Ellos ambos le prometen
de obedescer su mandado.
Ya cavalgavan los condes
y el buen Cid ya está a cavallo
con todos sus cavalleros
que le van acompañando;
por las huertas y jardines
van riendo y festejando.
Por espacio de una legua
el Cid los ha acompañado;
quando de ellos se despide

The brothers decide -
The Counts of Carrión -
to commit a wild outrage,
do the Cid a great wrong.
5 Their wives have requested
to go to León,
so their father, the Cid,
has let them go on:
"Fernando and Diego,
10 show respect that is due
to my daughters, the wives
I have given to you."
And both of them promise,
that´s what they´ll do.
15 The Cid and the Counts
have now started to ride
and all of his knights
have set out at his side;
through the orchards and gardens
20 all laughter and smiles,
and the Cid goes on with them
three or four miles.
When he finally leaves them

las lágrimas le van saltando
como hombre que ya sospecha
la gran trayción que han armado.
Manda que vaya tras ellos
Alvar Áñez su criado.
Buelve se el Cid y su gente,
y los condes van de largo.
Andando con muy gran priessa
en un monte avían entrado,
muy espesso y muy escuro,
de altos árboles poblado.
Mandan yr toda la gente
adelante muy gran rato.
Quédanse con sus mugeres
tan solos Diego y Fernando.
Apéanse de los cavallos
y las riendas han quitado;
sus mugeres que lo veen
muy gran llanto han levantado.
Apéanlas de las mulas,
cada qual para su lado,
como las parió su madre
ambos las han desnudado,
y luego a sendas enzinas
las han fuertemente atado.
Cada uno açota la suya
con riendas de su cavallo,
la sangre que de ellas corre
el campo tiene bañado;
mas no contentos con esto
allí se las han dexado.
Su primo que las fallara,
como hombre muy enojado,
a buscar los condes yva;
como no los ha fallado
bolviérase para ellas
muy pensativo y turbado.
En casa de un labrador
allí se las ha dexado.
Va se para el Cid su .tío
y todo se lo ha contado;
con muy gran cavallería
por ellas ha embiado.
De aquesta tan grande afrenta
el Cid al rey se ha quexado;
el rey, como aquesto vido,
tres cortes havía armado.

(Silva:160; S22, M57)

25
30
35
40
45
50
55
60
65
70

tears come to his eyes,
he suspects that some traitorous
trick's been devised,
so he sends Álvar Fáñez
to follow instead,
then he returns home
and the Counts ride ahead.
Into a forest
they hurry to ride,
it's thick and it's dark
and the trees are all high;
then the Counts tell the others
to ride on awhile.
Alone with their wives
the Counts have remained,
they get down from their horses
and take off the reins,
and their wives, when they see th[is]
have started to cry
but they pull down the girls
from the mules to their side,
and they strip them as naked
as when they were born
and they tie them to oaktrees
so fierce that they're torn,
and each beats his own wife
with the reins of his horse
and the blood as it flows
stains the ground in its course;
then they leave them to die
from the pain and the force.
Their cousin has found them
and rides in despair
to look for the Counts
but there's nobody there,
so he hurries on back
in angry distress;
he leaves the two girls
with a farmer to rest,
then explains to the Cid
about all that's been done,
and an army of knights
to the rescue has gone.
The Cid has complained
to the King of the crime,
and the King when he hears
holds three Courts at a time.

52. THE CID'S ARRIVAL AT TOLEDO

Tres cortes armara el rey,
todas tres a una sazón;
las unas armara en Burgos,
las otras armó en León,
las otras armó en Toledo
donde los hidalgos son,
para cumplir de justicia
al chico con el mayor.
Treynta días da de plazo,
treynta días, que más no,
y el que a la postre viniesse
que lo diessen por traydor.
Veynte nueve son passados,
los condes llegados son;
treynta días son passados,
y el buen Cid no viene, non.
Allí hablaran los Condes:
"Señor, daldo por traydor."
Respondiera les el rey:
"Esso non faría, non,
que el buen Cid es cavallero
de batallas vencedor,
pues que en todas las mis cortes
no lo avía otro mejor."
Ellos en aquesto estando
el buen Cid que assomó,
con trezientos cavalleros,
todos hijos dalgo son,
todos vestidos de un paño,
de un paño y de una color,
si no fuera el buen Cid
que traya un albornoz.
"¡Mantenga vos Dios, el rey!
Y ¡a vosotros salve os Dios!
Que no hablo yo a los condes
que mis enemigos son."

The King holds three Courts,
all three are now on,
the first is at Burgos,
the next at León,
5   the third at Toledo
where the nobles have gone
to carry out justice
for the weak and the strong.
Thirty days is the limit,
10 thirty days and no later,
any man who comes after
is held to be traitor.
After twenty-nine days
the Counts have appeared;
15 then the thirtieth comes
and the Cid isn't here.
The Counts ask the King
"Declare him a traitor";
the King has replied
20 "No, I'll not contemplate it;
the Cid is a noble
who wins every fight,
and in all of my Courts
there is not such a knight."
25 And as they are talking
the Cid comes in sight
with three hundred horsemen
- each one a good knight -
all wear the same clothes,
30 the same colour and cloth,
except for the Cid
in a fine albornoz -
"God save you my King,
God keep you from harm;
35 I won't speak to the Counts
who my enemies are".

(Sin año:161; S24, M59)

53. KING BÚCAR'S DECREE

Entre muchos reyes sabios
que huvo en la Andaluzía
reynara un moro viejo
que Rey Búcar se dezía.
Siendo ya de muchos años
que amancebado vivía,
por ruegos de su manceba
que amava mucho y quería,
llamó a Cortes a sus gentes
para un señalado día,
porque en ellas se tratasse
lo que a sus reynos cumplía.
De muchas leyes que pone
ésta de nuevo añadía,
que todo hombre namorado
se casasse con su amiga,
y quien no la obedeciesse
la vida le costaría.
A todos paresce bien,
a muchos les convenía,
si no a un sobrino del rey,
el qual ante de él venía;
con palabras muy quexosas
de esta manera dezía:
"La ley que Tu Alteza puso
cierto que me desplazía.
Todos se alegran con ella,
yo sólo me entristecía,
que mal puedo yo casarme,
siendo casada la mía,
casada, y tal mal casada
que gran lástima ponía.
Una cosa hos digo, Rey,
que a nadie no lo diría:
que si yo mucho la quiero
ella muy más me quería."
Allí hablara el Rey Búcar,
esta respuesta le hazía:
"Siendo casada, qual dizes,
la ley no te comprendía."

In Andalucía
were many wise rulers,
and one of the wisest
was ancient King Búcar.
5 For many long years
he'd a mistress and lover,
then at her request,
who he loved more than others,
he summoned his men
10 one day to the Court
where they could agree
to do what they ought.
To his many good laws
he added another,
15 that "All men in love
must marry their lover;
or else they will die,
with no chance to recover."
All thought it right;
20 most found it convenient;
but one of his nephews
disappointed had been in it,
and begged in despair
that the King should be lenient.
25 "Your Majesty's law,
for me it is bad,
the others are happy
but I am left sad;
for I can't marry mine,
30 she's married already,
so unhappily married
it makes my heart heavy –
And one thing I'll tell you
that I've not said before,
35 that though I love her greatly
she loves me much more".
Búcar replied
"I thought just as you did,
if she's married already,
40 then you're not included".

(Timoneda, RA:16-17; M127)

PEDRO THE CRUEL

Ballads nos. 54 to 58 concern King Pedro of Castille (1350-69); they form a "cycle", although in this case it cannot be envisaged that they were ever part of a single longer unit. Most of Pedro's reign was dominated by the civil war between him and his half-brothers. The previous King, Alfonso XI, died of the Black Death while besieging Gibraltar. Pedro was the legitimate heir, but soon after his accession he seems to have ordered the murder of his father's mistress, Leonora de Guzmán; this naturally antagonized his half-brothers, her sons, and - with the help of the Aragonese - they fought him throughout his reign. This was a furious propaganda war also, and both sides seem to have composed or commissioned libellous stories in the ballad metre to sway the population to their view of the conflict. This was intelligent, if ruthless: the medieval equivalent of the modern gutter-press. Pedro eventually lost; in 1369 his half-brother Henrique, Count of Trastámara, killed him personally and became King Henrique II. The anti-Pedro ballads are, accordingly, those that mostly survive, with the result that Pedro is now generally known as "Pedro el Cruel", but there are hints of pro-Pedro ballads as well. Several entered the general repertoire to be still well-known at the time of the printed collections two centuries later. (Entwistle's brief study is still worth looking at for these ballads).

54. PEDRO AND FADRIQUE

Yo me estava allá en Coymbra,
que yo me la ove ganado,
quando me vinieron cartas
del rey Don Pedro, mi hermano,
que fuesse a ver los torneos   5
que en Sevilla se han armado.
Yo, maestre sin ventura,
yo, maestre desdichado,
tomara treze de mula,
veynte y cinco de cavallo,   10
todos con cadenas de oro,
de jubones de brocado;
jornada de quinze días,
en ocho la avía andado.
A la passada de un río,   15
passándole por el vado,
cayó mi mula conmigo,
perdí mi puñal dorado,
ahogara se me un page
de los míos más privado;   20
criado era en mi sala
y de mí muy regalado.
Con todas estas desdichas
a Sevilla ove llegado,
a la Puerta Macarena   25
encontré con un ordenado,
ordenado de evangelio
que missa no avía cantado:
"¡Manténgate Dios, Maestre!
¡Maestre, bien seáys llegado!   30
Oy te ha nascido hijo,
oy cumples veynte y un año.
Si te pluguiesse, Maestre,
bolvamos a baptizallo,
que yo sería el padrino,   35
tú, Maestre, el ahijado."
Allí hablara el maestre,
bien oyréys lo que ha hablado:
"No me lo mandéys, Señor,
Padre, no queráys mandallo,   40
que voy a ver qué me quiere
el rey Don Pedro, mi hermano."
Di de espuelas a mi mula,
en Sevilla me ove entrado,
de que no vi tela puesta   45
ni vi cavallero armado

I was away in Coimbra,
a town I had captured in war,
when Don Pedro, my King and my brother,
sent orders I couldn´t ignore;
he was holding a joust in Sevilla,   5
and that´s what he wanted me for.
I´m the unlucky Fadrique,
unfortunate Knight of St James;
I saddled up twenty-five horses,
with thirteen more mules in the train,   10
and all of them well decorated
with blankets and fine golden chains.
In eight days we finished the journey,
which is usually one of fifteen;
and as we were crossing a river,   15
at the shallowest part of the stream,
my mule collapsed into the water,
and I lost there my dagger of gold,
and one of my pages was drowned there,
a page I´d looked after from old -   20
I´d brought the boy up in my palace
and trained him to follow my will -;
despite all of these disappointments
we finally came to Seville;
we came to the gate of the city,   25
but as we were ready to pass,
a priest of the church came to meet us,
he still hadn´t sung the day´s mass.
"May the Good Lord preserve you, Fadrique,
Fadrique, I welcome you here;   30
today your first son has been born you,
the day of your twenty-first year,
so if you agree, Don Fadrique,
we ought to go back to baptize him,
and I´ll be your first-born´s godfather,   35
to comfort your son and advise him."
I replied straightaway to the father,
this is what I decided to say:
"Don´t tell me to do this, good father,
don´t say we´ve to go on our way,   40
for I´m going to find out why I´m summoned
by my brother King Pedro today."
I rode through the gate of the city
and spurred my mule into the town,
but I saw no knights ready for jousting,   45
no tournament bunting around;

fuyme para los palacios
del rey Don Pedro mi hermano.
En entrando por las puertas
las puertas me avían cerrado;   50
quitaron me la mi espada
la que traýa a mi lado,
quitaron me mi compañía
la que me avía acompañado.
Los míos desque esto vieron   55
de trayción me han avisado,
que me saliesse yo fuera,
que ellos me pondrían en salvo.
Yo, como estava sin culpa,
de nada ove curado,   60
fuyme para el aposento
del rey Don Pedro mi hermano:
"Mantenga os Dios, el rey,
y a todos de cabo a cabo."
"Mal hora vengáys, Maestre,   65
Maestre, mal seáys llegado.
Nunca nos venís a ver
sino una vez en el año,
y esta que venís, Maestre,
es por fuerça o por mandado.   70
Vuestra cabeça, Maestre,
mandàda está en aguinaldo."
"¿Por qué es aquesso, buen rey?
Nunca os hize desaguisado,
ni os dexé yo en la lid   75
ni con moros peleando."
"¡Venid acá, mis porteros!
¡Hágase lo que he mandado!"
Aún no lo ovo bien dicho,
la cabeça le han cortado;   80
a Doña María de Padilla
en un plato la ha embiado.
Assí hablava con ella
como si estuviera sano;
las palabras que le dize   85
de esta suerte está hablando:
"¡Aquí pagaréys, traydor,
lo de antaño y lo de ogaño,
el mal consejo que diste
al rey Don Pedro tu hermano!"   90
Asióla por los cabellos,
echado se la ha a un alano.
El alano es del maestre,
puso la sobre un estrado;

in surprise I rode on to the palace
where my brother the King could be found.
I rode through the gates of the palace,
they slammed the gates shut when I´d passed,   50
they stripped off the sword I was wearing,
the sword that I´d learnt to hold fast;
they took away all of my soldiers
who´d come from Coimbra with me:
My soldiers foresaw there´d be treachery   55
as soon as this welcome they´d seen
and they shouted that they would protect me
if at once from the palace I´d flee:
but since I was guilty of nothing
I wasn´t the least bit afraid   60
and went to my brother, Don Pedro,
to the room where he usually stayed.
"May the Good Lord preserve you, Don Pedro,
and all who are with you this day."
"You are not in my favour, Fadrique,   65
your presence is not welcome here;
for never you bother to see me
except just the once in the year,
and then when you do come, Fadrique,
it´s because you´ve been ordered or led,   70
and the punishment for this, Fadrique,
is that you should leave us your head."
"But what is this for, Good King Pedro?
I never have given you cause,
I´ve always stood by you in battle   75
and when we were fighting the Moors."
"Come straight over here now, my servants,
carry out what I´ve already said."
As soon as he gave them the order
they ran up and struck him down dead;   80
and to Doña María Padilla
they sent on a plate the man´s head.
The Queen started talking right at it,
as if he could hear what she said,
and the words that she said to Fadrique   85
were as wild as the blood that he bled:
"You traitor, you´ve paid in this manner
for your crimes of this year and of others,
for the treacherous words that you spoke
to Don Pedro, your King and your brother."   90
She picked the head up by the hair
and she threw it to eat to a hound,
but the hound was Fadrique´s, and carried
his head to a board on the ground,

a los aullidos que dava   95
atronó todo el palacio.
Allí demandara el rey:
"¿Quién haze mal a esse alano?"
Allí respondieron todos,
a los quales ha pesado: 100
"Con la cabeça lo ha, Señor,
del maestre, vuestro hermano."
Allí hablara una su tía,
que tía era de entrambos:
"¡Quán mal lo mirastes, rey!   105
Rey, ¡qué mal lo avéys mirado!
Por una mala muger
avéys muerto un tal hermano."
Aún no lo avía bien dicho
quando ya le avía pesado,   110
fuése para Doña María,
de esta suerte le ha hablado:
"Prendelda, mis cavalleros,
ponedme la a buen recaudo,
que yo le daré tal castigo   115
que a todos sea sonado."
En cárceles muy escuras
allí la avía aprisionado,
él mismo le da a comer,
él mismo con la su mano;   120
no se fía de ninguno
sino de un paje que ha criado.

(1550:233-34; M65)

55. PEDRO AND THE SHEPHERD

Por los campos de Xerez
a caça va el rey Don Pedro:
en llegando a una laguna
allí quiso ver un buelo,
vido bolar una garça,   5
desparóle un sacre nuevo,
remontara le un neblí;
a sus pies cayera muerto.
A sus pies cayó el neblí;
tuvo lo por mal agüero.   10
Tanto bolava la garça
paresce llegar al cielo.
Por donde la garça sube

and he screamed and he howled out so loud   95
the whole palace was shaking around,
and the King Don Pedro was asking
"Who can be hurting that hound?"
and his servants returned with the answer,
the terrible sight that they´d found: 100
"He´s howling because he´s bewailing
the head of Fadrique your brother!"
Then an aunt of the King cried aloud –
she was his aunt but also the other´s –
"What a bad thing you´ve done, King Don Pedro,   105
the thing you have done here is wicked!
For the love of the evil María
you have killed your fine brother Fadrique!"
As soon as he heard her, Don Pedro
was sickened by what he had done,   110
and went off to Doña María
and told her her fate had begun:
"Put her in prison, my nobles,
lock her securely away,
and the punishment she´s going to suffer   115
should be known to all men from today."
And there in the palace he keeps her,
in the blackest of dungeons there are,
the King himself gives her her food there,
he hands it to her through the bars   120
and except for a page of his houschold
he trusts none of his men to be guards.

King Pedro was going out hunting
in the wilds near the town of Jerez;
When he got to a marsh he decided
to show off his falcon´s prowess –
He noticed a heron above him   5
and sent a young falcon to fly,
but a peregrine followed the falcon
then plummeted down from the sky.
The peregrine fell at his feet,
and a wind of ill omen blew by,   10
while the heron kept climbing so steeply
it seemed to reach heaven on high –
then from there where the heron ascended

vio baxar un bulto negro;
mientras más se acerca el bulto   15
más temor le va poniendo.
Con el abaxarse tanto
paresce llegar al suelo,
delante de su cavallo,
a cinco passos de trecho.   20
De él salió un pastorcico,
sale llorando y gimiendo,
la cabeça desgreñada;
rebuelto trahe el cabello;
con los pies llenos de abrojos   25
y el cuerpo lleno de vello;
en su mano una culebra,
en la otra un puñal sangriento;
en el ombro una mortaja,
una calavera al cuello;   30
a su lado de trahilla
trahía un perro negro,
los ahullidos que dava
a todos ponía gran miedo;
y a grandes vozes dezía: 35
"¡Morirás, el Rey Don Pedro!
Que mataste sin justicia
los mejores de tu reyno.
Mataste tu proprio hermano
el maestre, sin consejo;   40
y desterraste a tu madre –
a Dios darás cuenta de ello.
Tienes presa a Doña Blanca,
enojaste a Dios por ello,
que si tornas a quererla   45
dar te ha Dios un heredero;
y si no, por cierto sepas
te vendrá desmán por ello.
Serán malas las tus hijas,
por tu culpa y mal govierno: 50
y tu hermano Don Henrique
te havrá de heredar el reyno;
morirás a puñaladas,
tu casa será el infierno."
Todo esto recontado   55
desparesció el bulto negro.

(Timoneda, RE:81–82; M66A)

he saw a black shape coming down,
and as this black shape hurried closer   15
a feeling of fear spread around,
it fell further and faster and finally
came to the ground, where it stayed
right in front of the horse of King Pedro,
only five paces away.   20
From the darkness there came out a shepherd,
he emerged with a cry and a wail,
his hair on his head was all tangled
and savage and matted and scaled,
his feet were all tattered and bleeding,   25
his body was covered in hair;
in one hand a bloodcovered dagger
in the other a viper was there,
the shroud from a corpse round his shoulders,
his neck had a skull hanging round;   30
and he held on a lead there beside him
a fearsome and pitch-black hound;
and all of the hunters were scared
by the wailing that echoed around.
He shouted out loud to King Pedro: 35
"King Pedro, I tell you you´ll die,
for you´ve killed all the best of your kingdom
without justice or chance of reply;
you´ve killed your own brother Fadrique
without any trial or reason,   40
you´ve driven your mother to exile,
you´ll answer to God in due season;
you´re holding Queen Blanca in prison,
and God finds that action displeasing;
for if you return to Queen Blanca,   45
the Lord will allow you a son,
but if you do not, then for certain
your punishment will have begun,
your daughters are bound to be wicked,
the fruit of your own evil reign,   50
and your brother the Count Don Henrique
will rule in Castilian Spain,
you will die from the blows of his dagger
and then disappear into hell!"
As he finished his speech the black shepherd   55
vanished, thus breaking the spell.

56. THE DEATH OF BLANCA

"Doña María de Padilla,
no hos mostredes triste, no;
si me descasé dos vezes
hize lo por vuestro amor,
y por hazer menosprecio   5
a Doña Blanca de Borbón.
Embío luego a Cidonia
que me labren un pendón,
será de color de sangre,
de lágrimas su lavor;   10
tal pendón, Doña María,
se haze por vuestro amor."
Fue a llamar a Alonso Ortiz,
que es un honrado varón,
para que fuesse a Medina   15
a dar fin a la lavor.
Respondiera Alonso Ortiz:
"Esso, Señor, no haré yo,
que quien mata a su señora
es aleve a su señor."   20
El rey no le dixo nada;
en su cámara se entró,
embiara dos maceros
los quales él escogió.
Éstos fueron a la reyna,   25
hallaron la en oración;
la reyna como los vido
casi muerta se cayó,
mas después en sí tornada
con esfuerço les habló: 30
"Ya sé a qué venís, amigos,
que mi alma lo sintió,
y, pues, lo que está ordenado
no se puede escusar, no.
Di, Castilla, ¿qué te hize?   35
No, por cierto, trayción.
¡O Francia, mi dulce tierra!,
¡O mi casa de Borbón!
Oy cumplo deziséys años
en los quales muero yo.   40
El rey no me ha conoscido,
con las virgenes me vo.
Doña María de Padilla,
esto te perdono yo;
por quitarte de cuydado   45
lo haze el rey, mi señor."

"My Doña María Padilla,
there's no need for you to look sad,
for if I've deserted my wife,
it was all for the love that we've had.
And now I will show you how little   5
I care for the Bourbon Queen Blanca;
I'll send to Medina Sidonia
to get them to make me a banner,
to be dyed in a blood-red colour,
and of tears the embroidery too,   10
and this banner, my Doña María,
created for my love for you."
He called for Alonso Ortiz,
an honourable man at the court,
to tell him to go to Medina   15
to finish the deed that he sought;
but Alonso Ortiz wouldn't do it,
and said to the King what he thought:
"Whoever, my Lord, kills his Lady
is traitor as well to his Lord."   20
The King went straight into his chamber
without saying a word to Ortiz,
and he sent out a pair of assassins
he'd chosen himself for the deed.
The assassins set off for the Queen   25
and they found her alone and at prayer;
as soon as the Queen saw them coming
she fainted away in despair;
but then she came back to her senses
and bravely she challenged them there: 30
"I know why you've come here, my friends,
and my heart has been dreading you'd come,
but the orders you carry here with you
cannot be excused, by no one -
for I haven't betrayed you, Castilla,   35
no hatred for you have I shown;
I call to the Bourbons, my family!
And to France, the sweet land of my home!
Today is my sixteenth birthday,
at sixteen to my death I will fall,   40
and I swear that I go as a virgin,
for the King hasn't known me at all -
and Doña María Padilla,
I give you my pardon for this,
for my husband the King has decreed it,   45
so you know now that your love is his."

Los maceros le dan priessa,
ella pide confessión;
perdonara los a ellos,
y puesta en contemplación   50
danle golpes con las maças;
assí la triste murió.

(Timoneda, RE:82-83; M68)

57. THE DEATH OF PEDRO

Encima del duro suelo	Lying flat out,
tendido de largo a largo	stretched on the ground,
muerto yaze el rey, Don Pedro,	King Pedro is dead,
que le matara su hermano.	by his brother struck down;
Nadie lo osa alçar del suelo, 5	no-one will bury him,
nadie quiere sepultallo;	no-one will take him,
antes la gente plebeya	people would rather
querían despedaçallo,	destroy and forsake him,
por ser hombre tan cruel	for he was so wicked,
y tan mal complesionado. 10	so cruel and mistaken.
Ninguno llora por él,	Nobody weeps,
nadie haze por él llanto,	nobody cries,
todos lo tienen por bien,	all are delighted
huelgan de velle finado.	that slaughtered he lies,
Bendizen a Don Henrrique, 15	they bless their King Henry
que es el que lo había matado;	who plunged the knife in;
todos dezían a una:	they all say together
"¡O buen Rey Henrique, honrrado,	"Our honourable King,
Dios te dará galardón	God will reward you
por el bien que has causado 20	for the joy you've created
en apartar de este mundo	in ridding the world
a un tan cruel tirano!"	of a tyrant so hated!"

(Silva:466; M.Ap 15)

The assassins came near in a hurry,
she begged for confession right there,
she pardoned the men for the murder,
and fell to her knees in a prayer;   50
they struck her at once with their maces,
and thus the Queen died in despair.

---

58. THE SIEGE OF BAEZA

Cercada tiene a Baeza
ese arráez Audalla Mir,
con ochenta mil peones,
caballeros cinco mil.
Con él va ese traidor,
el traidor de Pero Gil.
El rey moro, Mohamed,
mandó tocar su añafil;
por la puerta de Bedmar
la empieza de combatir.
Ponen escalas al muro,
comiénzanle a conquerir;
ganada tiene una torre,
non la pueden resistir,
cuando de la de Calonge
escuderos vi salir.
Ruy Fernández va delante,
aquese caudillo ardil;
arremete con Audalla,
comiénzale de ferir,
cortado le ha la cabeza,
los demás dan a fuir.

Besieging Baeza
Audalla Mir fights;
eighty thousand on foot
and five thousand knights,
and the traitor, King Pedro,   5
is taking their part;
the King of Granada
signals to start.
They begin their attack
at the gate of Bedmar,   10
climb the walls on their ladders
and start to advance;
they've captured one tower,
we haven't a chance –
then through the Calonge   15
our knights ride to save us,
Rodrigo Fernández
their leader, the bravest,
rides up to Audalla,
attacks straightaway,   20
and cuts off his head –
then the rest run away.

(Argote:478-79; S27, M.Apl8)

FRONTIER BALLADS

Many ballads are set on or near the fiteenth-century frontier between Christian Andalucía and Moslem Granada. The Kingdom of Granada, covering a fairly thin but long slice of the South Coast, was the only part of the peninsula under Moslem rule and Arabic-speaking after the 1250s, but through diplomacy and luck it survived as an independent state until 1492. For most of the intervening period relations between the communities on each side of the frontier were cautious but peaceful; occasionally hostilities would break out, usually as a result of decisions taken far away by the ruler of Castille or of Granada, but in general there was a frontier community in which both sides respected each other. In this area many ballads were composed and performed throughout the fifteenth century, and although they are in Spanish they are often presented from the point of view of Moslem participants, since - like almost all other ballads - the human emotions aroused in stirring events are seen as more interesting than the events themselves. The subject matter of these ballads usually concerns the comparatively brief but emotionally more intense periods of war rather than of peace. In the following century, when the Moslem kingdom was gone, there was a vogue for setting other ballads on the frontier; some of the ballads printed here come from the fifteenth century, some are romanticizations from the sixteenth, and some (59-60) seem to be partly original but also to include later additional material. For the context of the individual ballads, see the study by Mackay; Ladero's is the best history of Granada.

59. REDUÁN

"Reduán, si te acuerda,
que me diste la palabra
que me darías a Jaén
en una noche ganada;
Reduán, si tú lo cumples
daréte paga doblada,
y si tú no lo cumpliesses
desterrar te de Granada
y echar te en una frontera
do no gozes de tu amada."
Reduán le respondía
sin demudarse la cara:
"Si lo dixe, no me acuerdo,
mas cumpliré mi palabra."
Reduán pide mil hombres,
y el rey cinco mil le dava.
Por essa Puerta de Elvira
se sale gran cavalgada;

"Reduán, you remember
the promise you gave
to capture Jaén
in a night and a day -
5   Reduán, if you do this
I´ll double your pay,
but if you do not
you´ll be exiled from here:
your love in Granada,
10 you on the frontier."
Reduán is not shaken
by what he has heard -
"I´d forgotten I said that;
but I will keep my word."
15 He asks for a thousand,
the King gives him five.
Through the gate of Elvira
the great army rides.

¡quánto del moro hidalgo,
quánta de la yegua baya,
quánta de la lança en puño,
quánta del adarga blanca,
quánta de marlota verde,
quánta aljuba de escarlata,
quánta pluma y gentileza,
quánto capellar de grana,
quánto bayo borzeguí,
quánto laço qual esmalta,
quánta de la espuela de oro,
quánta estribera de plata!
Toda es gente valerosa
y experta para batalla;
en medio de todos ellos
el Rey Chico de Granada.
Miran los las damas moras
de las torres del Alhambra;
la reyna mora, su madre,
de esta manera hablava:
"¡Alhá vaya contigo, hijo,
Mahoma vaya en tu guarda,
y te vuelva de Jaén
con mucha honra a Granada!"

So many fine nobles,
20 riding bay mares!
So many strong lances
and shields are held there!
So many green tunics
and cloaks of bright red!
25 So many red helmets
with plumes, on their heads!
So many red boots
adorned with fine bows,
stirrups of silver,
30 spurs shining gold!
All valiant knights,
all skilled in the field,
and there in among them
is King Boabdil.
35 From the Alhambra
the women look on,
and the Queen of Granada
shouts down to her son -
"May Allah preserve you,
40 Mohammed defend
and bring back your honour
safe from Jaén!"

(Pérez de Hita:165-66; S29, M72)

60. ANTEQUERA

De Antequera partió el moro
tres horas antes del día,
con cartas en la su mano
en que socorro pedía.
Escritas yvan con sangre,
mas no por falta de tinta.
El moro que las llevava
ciento y veynte años avía;
la barva tenía blanca,
la calva le reluzía;
toca llevava tocada,
muy grande precio valía;
la mora que la labrara
por su amiga la tenía;
alhaleme en su cabeça
con borlas de seda fina;
cavallero en una yegua,

Three hours before dawn
the Moor leaves Antequera,
with letters for help,
he is their bearer,
5 written in blood,
though they've got ink in plenty;
the messenger Moor
is a hundred and twenty,
his beard shining white,
10 his baldness all glowing,
though he wears a fine cap
of worth beyond knowing,
finely embroidered
by his own Moorish lover;
15 a veil with silk tassels
his face also covers.
Instead of a stallion,

102

Ballad 60

que cavallo no quería;
solo con un pagezico
que le tenga compañía,
no por falta de escuderos,
que en su casa hartos avía.
Siete celadas le ponen
de mucha cavallería,
mas la yegua era ligera,
de entre todos se salía.
Por los campos de Archidonia
a grandes bozes dezía:
"O buen rey, si tú supiesses
mi triste mensajería,
¡messarías tus cabellos
y la tu barva vellida!"
El rey que venirlo vido
a recebir lo salía,
con trezientos de cavallo,
la flor de la morería.
"Bien seas venido, el moro,
buena sea tu venida."
"Alá te mantenga, el rey,
con toda tu compañía."
"Di me, ¿qué nueva me traes
de Antequera, essa mi villa?"
"Yo te las diré, buen rey,
si tú me otorgas la vida."
"La vida te es otorgada,
si trayción en ti no avía."
"Nunca Alá lo permetiesse
hazer tan gran villanía,
mas sepa Tu Real Alteza
lo que ya saber devría;
que essa villa de Antequera
en grande aprieto se vía,
que el infante Don Fernando
cercada te la tenía,
fuertemente la combate
sin cessar noche ni día;
manjar que tus moros comen,
cueros de vaca cozida.
Buen rey, si no la socorres
muy presto se perdería."
El rey, quando aquesto oyera,
de pesar se amortecía,
haziendo gran sentimiento
muchas lágrimas vertía,
rasgava sus vestiduras

he's riding a mare,
and except for his page
20   alone he rides there,
though hundreds of soldiers
are home unprepared.
Seven times he is ambushed
by Christian knights,
25   but his mare is so quick
they escape all the fights;
they go past Archidona,
he cries out these words:
"Good King, once my message
30   of hardship you've heard
you'll tear out your hair
and your free-flowing beard!"
The King sees him coming,
and rides through the doors,
35   with three hundred knights,
the best of the Moors:
"Greetings my friend,
a fine welcome be yours!"
"Allah preserve you,
40   My King, and your men!"
"From my town, Antequera,
what news do they send?"
"I'll tell you, Good King,
if my life you will spare."
45   "I'll spare you your life
unless treachery's there."
"May Allah forbid
I commit such a sin!
My King, you should hear now
50   the news that I bring
of your town Antequera,
the danger it's in;
for the regent Fernando
your town is surrounding,
55   all night and all day
the defences he's pounding,
and all we now eat
are cooked hides of leather –
if you can't help us soon
60   we'll be lost altogether".
When the King hears this
he faints in his horror,
and then he starts weeping
in pain and in sorrow,
65   he's tearing his clothes

con gran dolor que tenía.
Ninguno le consolava,
porque no lo permitía,
mas después en sí tornando
a grandes bozes dezía:
"¡Tóquense mis añafiles,
trompetas de plata fina!
Júntense mis cavalleros
quantos en mi reyno avía,
vayan con mis dos hermanos
a Archidona, essa mi villa,
en socorro de Antequera,
llave de mi señoría."
Y ansí, con este mandado,
se juntó gran morería;
ochenta mil peones fueron
el socorro que venía,
con cinco mil de cavallo,
los mejores que tenía.
Ansí, en la Boca del Asna,
este real sentado avía,
a vista de él del infante
el qual ya se apercebía,
confiando en la gran vitoria
que de ellos Dios le daría.
Sus gentes bien ordenadas,
de San Juan era aquel día,
quando se dio la batalla
de los nuestros tan herida,
que por ciento y veynte muertos
quinze mil moros avía.
Después de aquesta batalla
fue la villa combatida,
con lombardas y pertrechos
y con una gran bastida,
con que le ganan las torres
de donde era deffendida.
Después dieron el castillo
los moros a pleytesía,
que libres con sus haziendas
el infante los pornía
en la villa de Archidonia;
lo qual todo se cumplía.
Y ansí se ganó Antequera
a loor de Santa María.

(1550:244-46; S30, M74)

at the news he's been told,
and noone can calm him,
he won't be consoled;
but then he recovers
70 and shouts to those round:
"Let the pipes and the trumpets
of silver now sound!
Let all of the knights
of the kingdom come down
75 and go with my brothers
to Archidona, my town,
and help Antequera,
the key to my crown!"
And at this command
80 a great army is found,
eighty thousand on foot
are gathered around,
with five thousand knights,
the best he has there.
85 In the "Boca del Asna"
their camp they've prepared;
Fernando has seen them,
he's not unawares,
he's trusting in God
90 that the fight will be won;
his forces are ready;
it's the Day of St John;
in the battle we lose
a hundred and ten
95 but the Moors lose some fifteen
thousand of men.
After the battle
the town becomes ours,
battered by cannon,
100 and with the siege-towers,
we've captured the walls
where fought the defenders,
then the army of Moors
their castle surrenders.
105 Fernando agrees
without any dishonour,
they can take their possessions
to Archidona –
Antequera is ours!
110 To Our Lady's great honour.

61. THE DUKE OF ARJONA

En Arjona estava el duque
y el buen rey en Gibraltar.
Embióle un mensajero
que le uviesse a hablar.
Malaventurado duque   5
vino luego sin tardar;
jornada de quinze días
en ocho la fuera a andar.
Hallava las mesas puestas
y aparejado el yantar.   10
Desque uvieron comido
van se a un jardín a holgar;
andando se passeando
el rey començó a hablar:
"De vos, el Duque de Arjona,   15
grandes querellas me dan;
que forçades las mugeres
casadas y por casar,
que les bevíades el vino
y les comíades el pan,   20
que les tomáys la cevada
sin se la querer pagar."
"Quien os lo dixo, buen rey,
no vos dixo la verdad."
"Llamen me mi camarero   25
de mi cámara real:
que me traxisse unas cartas
que en mi barjuleta están.
Vedes. las aquí, el duque,
no me lo podéys negar.   30
¡Preso, preso, cavalleros,
preso de aquí lo llevad!
Entregaldo al de Mendoça,
este mi alcalde el leal."

(1550:317; M70)

The Duke was at home in Arjona,
the King was away in Gibraltar,
when the King sent a messenger saying
"Hurry on back and don´t falter."
The unfortunate Duke of Arjona   5
set off for the King straightaway
and travelled the road in a week
which usually takes fifteen days.
He found there the banqueting tables
all ready prepared for a feast;   10
they went out for a walk in the garden
when they´d eaten their fill of the meat,
and as they were strolling together
the king then started to speak;
"Many people have come to complain   15
of your conduct, my Duke of Arjona,
that married and unmarried women
by you have been roughly dishonoured,
that you have been drinking their wine,
that you have been eating their bread,   20
that you have been taking their barley
and leaving them nothing instead."
"Good King, whoever has said this
has been telling you lies and no better."
"Call for the steward to come here,   25
the one who´s in charge of the letters,
and tell him to bring us the ones
that are there at the top of the pile –
you can see the complaints here before you,
my Duke, which you cannot deny;   30
Noblemen, put him in chains,
lead him out as a prisoner royal,
take him straight to my Duke of Mendoza,
for the Duke of Mendoza is loyal."

62. ABNÁMAR

"Abenámar, Abenámar,
moro de la morería,
¿qué castillos son aquéllos?
altos son, y reluzían."
"El Alhambra era, Señor,
y la otra la Mezquita,
los otros los Alixares
labrados a maravilla –
el moro que los labró
cien doblas ganava al día –;
la otra era Granada,
Granada la noblescida,
de los muchos cavalleros
y de gran ballestería."
Allí hablara el Rey Don Juan,
bien oyréys lo que diría:
"Granada, si tú quisiesses
contigo me casaría;
darte he en arras y dote
a Córdoba y a Sevilla
y a Xerez de la Frontera,
que cabe sí la tenía.
Granada, si más quisiesses,
mucho más yo te daría."
Allí hablara Granada,
al buen rey le respondía:
"Casada so, el Rey Don Juan,
casada so, que no biuda,
el moro que a mí me tiene
bien defenderme quería."
Allí hablara el Rey Don Juan,
estas palabras dezía:
"Echen me acá mis lombardas,
Doña Sancha y Doña Elvira;
tiraremos a lo alto,
lo baxo ello se daría."
El combate era tan fuerte
que grande temor ponía,
los moros del baluarte
con terrible algazería
trabajan por defenderse,
mas fazello no podían.
El rey moro que esto vido
prestamente se rendía,
y carga tres cargas de oro,
al buen rey se las embía;

"Abnámar, Abnámar,
Moslem and friend –
what are those towers
so shining and splendid?"
5 "That's the Alhambra,
that's the Mezquita,
that's Alixares,
with beautiful features;
the Moor who designed it
10 earned hundreds of doblas –
the rest is Granada,
Granada the noblest,
with many fine horsemen
and many fine bowmen."
15 King John then cries out
these words of good omen:
"If you're willing, Granada,
please be my bride;
I can offer you Córdoba,
20 Sevilla besides,
and also the town
of Jerez can be yours –
if you want it, Granada,
I'll give you much more."
25 But the breeze from Granada
this answer has carried:
"I'm married, King John,
not widowed but married;
my husband the Moor
30 will fiercely defend me."
King John in reply
these orders is sending,
"Bring up the siege-guns,
Sancha, Elvira,
35 let's aim at the top
to bring it down nearer."
The fighting grows fierce,
the Moors are in fear,
the ones on the walls
40 shout louder and stronger,
they try to resist
but can hold out no longer;
when the King sees that
he cannot go on,
45 he loads up three carts
with gold for King John

prometió ser su vassallo
con parias que le daría.
Los castellanos quedaron
contentos a maravilla;
cada qual por do ha venido
se bolvió para Castilla.

(Silva:177-78; M78)

and promises service
and gold from now on;
delighted and proud
50　the Castilians feel,
and all return richer
home to Castille.

63. ÁLORA

Álora, la bien cercada,
tú que estás en par del río,
cercóte el adelantado
una mañana en domingo;
de peones y hombres de armas
el campo bien guarnescido;
con la gran artillería
hecho te avía un portillo.
Viérades moros y moras
todos huyr al castillo;
las moras llevavan ropa,
los moros harina y trigo,
y las moras de quienze años
llevavan el oro fino,
y los moricos pequeños
llevavan la passa e higo.
Por cima de la muralla
su pendón llevan tendido;
entre almena y almena
quedado se avía un morico
con una ballesta armada,
y en ella puesto un quadrillo.
En altas vozes dezía,
que la gente lo avía oýdo,
"Treguas, treguas, adelantado,
por tuyo se da el castillo."
Alça la visera arriba
por ver el que tal le dixo;
assestara le a la frente,
salido le ha al colodrillo.
Sacólo Pablo de rienda
y de mano Jacobillo,
éstos dos que avía criado
en su casa desde chicos;
llevaron le a los maestros

Down by the river,
Álora town
one Sunday morning
Don Diego surrounds,
5　in the fields are his soldiers,
good warriors all,
and the fire from their guns
makes a hole in the wall.
You'd have seen all the Moslems
10　retreat to the tower,
the women with clothes,
the men with the flour,
the girls with the gold
and the jewels and money,
15　the boys with the figs
and the raisins and honey.
They're flying their banner
on top of the walls;
between the top turrets
20　stands one of the Moors,
he holds up his crossbow,
an arrow instals,
and shouts out aloud
so they hear as he calls:
25　"Don Diego, a truce!
The castle is yours!"
He lifts up his visor
when he hears what was said,
and the arrow that strikes him
30　goes right through his head.
Jacobillo and Pablo
support him at once,
the two that Don Diego
had raised as his sons,
35　they go to the doctors

por ver si será guarido;
a las primeras palabras
el testamento les dixo.

(Praga, 2:105-06; S34, M79)

and look to their skill,
but as soon as they see him
he gives them his will.

64. THE DUKE OF NIEBLA

"Dad me nuevas, cavalleros,
nuevas me querades dar,
de aquesse Conde de Niebla,
Don Henrrique de Guzmán,
que haze guerra a los moros   5
y ha cercado a Gibraltar.
Veo hoy lutos en mi corte;
ayer vi fiestas muy grandes.
O el príncipe es fallescido,
o alguno de mi sangre,   10
o Don Álvaro de Luna,
el maestre y condestable."
"No es muerto, Señora, el príncipe,
mas ha fallescido un grande;
que veredes a los moros   15
quán poco vos temerán,
que a éste sólo temían
y no osavan saltear -
es el buen Conde de Niebla
que se a anegado en la mar   20
por acorrer a los suyos,
nunca se quiso salvar;
en un batel donde venía
le hizieron trastornar,
socorriendo un cavallero   25
que se le yva a anegar.
La mar andava tan alta
que no se pudo escapar,

"Give me news now, my knights,
give me news, if you can,
of the Good Duke of Niebla,
Henrique Guzmán,
who´s besieging Gibraltar
at my command.
You rejoiced yesterday,
but now you are crying,
the Prince must be dead,
someone royal is dying,
or the Constable, Álvaro,
Maestre of mine."
"The Prince has not died,
but a great man is dead,
for you know that the Moslems
are rarely afraid,
yet they´d not attack him
but stayed quiet instead.
The Good Duke of Niebla
has drowned in the waves,
he was helping his men
when he could have been saved,
for the boat he was in
was turned upside-down
as he reached for a knight
just about to be drowned.
The sea was so rough
that he couldn´t survive,

:eniendo quasi ganada	when the Rock of Gibraltar
.a fuerça de Gibraltar.	30 was nearly his prize.
.loran le todas las damas,	The women in tears,
¶alanes otro que tal,	and so are the men,
lórale gente de guerra	he was such a fine captain
)or ser tan buen capitán,	the soldiers lament,
lóranlo duques y condes	35 the nobles are mourning
)orque todos sabía honrrar."	their leader and friend."
"O ¡Qué nuevas me traedes,	"Oh the news that you tell me
:avalleros, de pesar!	is painful, my knights!"
Vistan se todos de xerga,	We must all dress in mourning!
10 se hagan fiestas más,	40 No rejoicing tonight –
/aya luego un mensagero,	let a messenger go,
venga su hijo Don Juan,	bring his son here to Court,
:onfirmalle lo del padre,	I'll confirm his inheritance,
1ás le quiero acrescentar;	I'll give him some more,
y de Medina Cidonia	45 of Medina Sidonia
1uque le hago, doy más,	I'll make him the Count –
que a hijo de tan buen padre	but so great was his father
)oco galardón se da."	that's no great amount."

(Silva:324-25; S36, M80)

65. FAJARDO

Jugando está al axedrez
el rey de Granada un día
con aquesse buen Fajardo
con amor que le tenía;
Fajardo jugava a Lorca,
el rey moro a Almería.
Xaque le dio con el roque;
el orfil que le prendía.
En esto dixo el rey moro:
"¡La villa de Lorca es mía!"
Allí respondió Fajardo,
bien oyréys lo que dezía:
"Calles, calles, Señor Rey,
no tomes la tal porfía;
que aun que tú me la ganasses
ella no se te daría.
Cavalleros tengo dentro
que te la defenderían."
Allí hablara el rey moro,
bien oyréys lo que dezía:
"No juguemos más, Fajardo,
ni tengamos más porfía,
por ser tan buen cavallero
contigo paz offrescía."

(Timoneda, RE:59; S37, M83)

The King of Granada
is playing at chess
with Pedro Fajardo,
the one he likes best;
5 they've bet Almería
and Lorca as stakes –
the castle says "check",
the bishop then takes.
The Moslem starts shouting
10 "Now Lorca is mine";
but now you will hear
Fajardo replying –
"Be quiet, my Lord King,
and don't be so sure,
15 even though you have won her
she will not be yours,
my knights are inside it
defending my cause."
The King answers back,
20 you will hear what he's said –
"Let us play no more chess,
nor start fighting instead,
for you're so good a knight,
we all hold you in dread".

66. MORAIMA

"Yo me era mora Morayma,
morilla de un bel catar.
Christiano vino a mi puerta,
cuytada, por me engañar:
hablóme en algaravía
como aquel que la bien sabe:
"Abras me las puertas, mora,
sí Alá te guarde de mal."
"¿Cómo te abriré, mezquina,
que no sé quién te serás?"
"Yo soy el moro Maçote,
hermano de la tu madre,
que un christiano dexo muerto;
tras mí venía el alcalde;
si no me abres tú, mi vida,
aquí me verás matar."
Quando esto oí, cuytada,
comencéme a levantar,
vistiérame un almexía,
no hallando mi brial,
fuérame para la puerta
y abríla de par en par."

(1550:290; S59, M132)

"I am Moraima,
a beautiful Moor,
I was hurt by a Christian
who knocked at my door,
5   speaking good Arabic
to deceive me the more.
"Come open, Moraima,
Allah keep you from harm."
"But how can I open?
10   I don´t know who you are."
"I´m a Moor and your uncle,
your uncle Mas´ud,
and I´ve just killed a Christian,
the law´s after my blood -
15   if you don´t let me in
I´ll be finished for good."
To my grief, when I heard him
at once I went down,
threw a shawl on my shoulders
20   instead of my gown,
I ran straight to the door
and I pulled it right round."

67. ALHAMA (1)

"Moro alcayde, moro alcayde,
el de la vellida barba,
el rey te manda prender
por la pérdida de Alhama,
y cortarte la cabeça   5
y ponella en el Alhambra,
porque a ti castigo sea
y otros tiemblen en miralla;
pues perdiste la tenencia
de una ciudad tan preciada."   10
El alcayde respondía,
de esta manera les habla:
"Cavalleros y hombres buenos,
los que regís a Granada,
dezid de mi parte al rey   15
cómo no le devo nada.
Yo me estava en Antequera
en las bodas de mi hermana.
¡Mal fuego queme las bodas,
y quien a ellas me llamara!   20
El rey me dio la licencia,
que yo no me la tomara.
Pedílla por quinze días,
diómela por tres semanas.
De averse Alhama perdido   25
a mí me pesa en el alma;
que si el rey perdió su tierra
yo perdí mi honra y fama.
Perdí hijos y muger,
las cosas que más amava;   30
perdí una hija donzella
que era la flor de Granada.
El que la tiene captiva
Marqués de Cádiz se llama;
cien doblas le doy por ella,   35
no me las estima en nada.
La respuesta que me han dado
es que mi hija es christiana,
y por nombre le avían puesto
Doña María de Alhama.   40
El nombre que ella tenía
Mora Fátima se llama."
Diziendo assí el buen alcayde
lo llevaron a Granada,
y siendo puesto ante el rey   45
la sentencia le fue dada:

"My noble Lord, fortress commander,
bearded and handsomely dressed!
For the loss of your fortress Alhama
the King puts you under arrest;
he´s ordered your head to be taken   5
and placed by Alhambra´s main door
as your punishment and as a lesson
which others will tremble before -
for you lost to the Christians Alhama,
the town you´re responsible for."   10
The commander replied to the envoys
and these are the words that he said;
"My noble Lord knights and good soldiers,
All you who Granada have led,
please say to the King as my answer   15
that I owe him nothing instead,
for I was elsewhere, Antequera,
where one of my sisters was wed -
now I call down a curse on the wedding,
may our Christian hosts there fall dead!   20
The King to me granted permission,
it wasn´t a favour I´d seek,
I´d asked for a fortnight off duty,
he gave me another full week.
Alhama was lost in my absence,   25
I know to my sorrow and shame;
the King has lost part of his country,
but I´ve lost my honour and name.
Yes, I lost my wife and my children,
the ones I loved best in the world,   30
and among them the flower of Granada,
my daughter, my beautiful girl.
The one who now holds her as captive
the Marquis of Cádiz is called;
I offered a copious ransom   35
but he didn´t accept it at all;
I know from the answer they sent me
that my daughter a Christian became -
my daughter now calls herself Mary,
adopting a new Christian name,   40
instead of her Moslem one, Fátima -
putting me and Alhama to shame."
They took him away to Granada
despite all the words that he said
and there in the King´s royal presence   45
the appropriate sentence was read;

que le corten la cabeça
y la lleven al Alhambra.
Executóse la justicia
anssí como el rey lo manda.   50

(Pérez de Hita:256-57; S38, M84A)

---

68. ALHAMA (2)

Passeava se el rey moro		The King of the Moors
por la ciudad de Granada;		at home in Granada
cartas le fueron venidas		is given the news
cómo Alhama era ganada.		of the loss of Alhama –
Las cartas echó en el fuego	5	the messenger´s killed,
y al mensagero matara;		the letters are burned,
echó mano a sus cabellos		he tears at his hair,
y las sus barbas mesava.		he pulls at his beard,
Apeóse de una mula		he´s got off his mule,
y en un cavallo cavalga;	10	to his horse he has turned;
mandó tocar sus trompetas,		he orders the trumpets
sus añafiles de plata		of silver to blow
porque lo oyessen los moros		so the Moslems can hear
que andavan por ell arada.		out at work far below;
Quatro a quatro y cinco a cinco	15	in fours and in fives
juntado se ha gran batalla.		they gather around,
Allí habló un moro viejo		then speaks the old Moslem
que era alguazil de Granada:		who governs the town,
"¿A qué nos llamaste, el rey?		"Sir, why did you order
¿A qué fue nuestra llamada?"	20	the trumpets to blow?"
"Para que sepáys, amigos,		"Alhama is lost,
la gran pérdida de Alhama."		I want you to know."
"Bien se te emplea, Señor,		"Then here´s the result,
Señor, bien se te empleava,		here´s the reward,
por matar los Bencerrajes	25	you put Bencerrajes
que eran la flor de Granada.		all to the sword,
Acogiste a los judíos		you welcomed the Jews
de Córdova la nombrada.		from Córdoba town,
Degollaste un cavallero,		you cut off the head
persona muy estimada.	30	of a knight of renown;
muchos se te despidieron		and many deserted
por tu condición trocada."		since you changed around."
"¡Ay, si os pluguiesse, mis moros,		"But I hope you´ll agree
que fuéssemos a cobralla!"		to recapture Alhama!"
"Mas si, rey, a Alhama has de yr,	35	"Sir, if you have to go,
dexa buen cobro a Granada;		leave defence for Granada;

his head should be cut off and taken
and placed by Alhambra´s main door.
The sentence was then carried out,
as decreed by the King and the law.   50

---

y para Alhama cobrar
menester es grande armada;
que cavallero está en ella
que sabrá muy bien guardalla."
"¿Quién es esse cavallero
que tanta honrra ganara?"
"Don Rodrigo es de León,
Marqués de Cáliz se llama;
otro es Martín Galindo
que primero echó el escala."
Luego se van para Alhama
que de ellos no se da nada.
Combátenla prestamente;
ella está bien defensada.
De que el rey no pudo más
triste se bolvió a Granada.

(1550:178-79; M85)

though to capture the fort
a large army needs sending,
for the Christian who won it
40 will fiercely defend it."
"And who is the Christian
who´s captured it all?"
"Rodrigo, the Marquis
of Cádiz, he´s called,
45 with Martín Galindo
who first scaled the wall."
They´ve gone straight to Alhama
but it´s no good at all;
they attack it at once,
50 but it´s too well defended,
so the King has retreated,
the skirmish has ended.

69. THE CAPTIVE

Preguntando está Florida
a su esposo plazentera,
en un vergel assentada
junto a una verde ribera:
"Digas me tú, esposo amado:
¿De dónde eres? ¿De qué tierra?
Y ¿a dónde te captivaron?
Libertad, ¿quién te la diera?"
"Yo hos lo diré, dulce esposa,
estad atenta siquiera.
Mi padre es cierto de Ronda
y mi madre de Antequera.
Captivaron me los moros

The young man is lying
with Florida, his bride,
alone in a garden
by the green riverside -
5 "Please tell me, my husband,
where your home used to be?
Where were you captured?
Who set you free?"
"I´ll tell you, sweet bride,
10 listen to me.
My parents from Ronda,
and from Antequera;
the Moors made a raid

entre la paz y la guerra
y llevaron me ha vender
a Vélez de la Gomera.
Siete días con sus noches
anduve en el almoneda;
no huvo moro ni mora
que por mí una blanca diera
si no fuera un perro moro
que cien doblas offresciera,
y llevara me a su casa;
echara me una cadena,
dava me la vida mala,
dava me la vida negra,
de día majava esparto,
de noche molía civera.
Echóme un freno a la boca
porque no comiesse de ella.
Pero plugo a Dios del Cielo

and took me from there
15 to be sold as a slave
at Vélez de la Gomera;
seven days, seven nights,
I was there to be sold,
but no man or woman
20 would part with their gold
till a Moor came along
and offered a hundred.
There´s a chain at his house,
and I suffered under it.
25 My life was a torture,
I thirsted and hungered,
I crushed his esparto,
I ground out his wheat,
on my mouth was a muzzle
30 so I couldn´t eat.
But praise be to God,

---

70. THE CAPTURE OF BOABDIL

Junto al vado de Xenil
por un camino seguido
viene un moro de cavallo,
en polvo y sangre teñido,
corriendo a todo correr   5
como el que viene ahuydo.
Llegando junto a Granada
da gran grito y alarido,
publicando malas nuevas
de un caso que a contescido;   10
"Que se perdió el rey chiquito
y los que con él han ydo,
y que no escapó ninguno,
preso, muerto o mal herido,
que de quantos allí fueron   15
yo sólo me he guarescido
a traher nueva tan triste
del gran mal que ha succedido.
Los que a nuestro rey vencieron,
sabed, si no havéys sabido,   20
que fue aquel Diego Hernández,
De Córdova es su apellido,

que tenía el ama buena;
quando el moro se yva a caça
quitava me la cadena,
echava me en su regaço, 35
mil regalos me hiziera,
espulgava me, y limpiava,
mejor que yo meresciera;
por un plazer que le hize
otro mayor me offresciera. 40
Diera me casi cien doblas,
en libertad me pusiera,
por temor que el moro perro
quiçá la muerte nos diera.
Assí plugo al Rey del Cielo, 45
de quien mercedes se espera,
que me ha buelto en vuestros braços
como de primero era."

(Timoneda, RA:62-63; M131)

for his wife saw my pain,
and when he went hunting
she took off my chain;
I lay in her lap,
she told me kind words,
she cleaned me and gave me
more than I deserved;
for one favour I gave her
she gave me a greater,
for afraid that the Moor
might kill us both later
she gave me some money
and sent me home frec;
so to God it was pleasing,
whose mercies we see,
that I´m back in your arms,
where I used to be."

Coming up by the pathway that crosses
the ford of the River Genil
is riding a Moslem who´s bleeding
with wounds from his head to his heels -
he´s driving his horse at its fastest 5
in wild and precipitate flight,
and when he gets close to Granada
he starts to cry out in his fright
of the fearsome disaster that´s happened,
the bitter result of the fight; 10
"Our leader, King Chico, is beaten,
with all of the army he led,
and no-one at all is returning,
they´re captured or wounded or dead,
and of all the brave men in our army 15
the only survivor is me,
and I´ve come back to tell you about it,
the news is as bad as can be.
The soldier who beat our King Chico,
the one who has brought us so low, 20
is Diego Hernández de Córdoba -
I´ll tell you if you didn´t know -

alcayde de los donzeles,
hombre sabio y atrevido,
y aquel gran Conde de Cabra   25
que en su ayuda avía venido.
Éste venció la batalla
y aquel trance tan reñido,
y otro Lope de Mendoça,
que de Cabra havía salido,   30
que andava entre los peones
como león bravo metido.
Y sabed que el rey no es muerto
mas está en prisión rendido,
yo le vide yr en trahilla   35
en acto muy abatido.
Llevan lo drecho a Lucena,
junto a donde fue vencido."
Llorava toda Granada
con grande llanto y gemido;   40
lloravan moços y viejos
con algazara y ruydo;
lloravan todas las moras
un llanto muy dolorido;
unas lloran padres, hijos,   45
otras hermano o marido,
lloran tanto cavallero
como allá se huvo perdido;
lloravan por su buen rey,
tan amado y tan querido,   50
prometen todas sus joyas
para que sea redemido,
sus exorcas y texillos,
atutes de oro subido.
Con esto y otras riquezas   55
fue rescatado y trahido
el rey chiquito a Granada
y en su possessión metido.

(Timoneda, RE:67-69; M91)

a member of their royal household,
he was skilful and brave as he fought,
and with him the Count too of Cabra   25
who´d come up to give him support;
and they were the victors in battle,
the furious fight we had then,
and with them was Lope Mendoza,
who´d come out from Cabra again,   30
who fought like the savagest lion
among our brave infantrymen.
I can tell you our King isn´t dead though;
I saw him, a sorrowful sight,
with a lead round his neck as a captive,   35
a prisoner in pitiful plight;
they´ve taken him back to Lucena,
the town near the place of the fight."
The whole of Granada is weeping
in shouting and wailing and tears,   40
the young men and old are all crying
and loudly expressing their fears,
all the women and girls of Granada
are spreading their cries through the air,
weeping for fathers or children,   45
lamenting for husbands or brothers,
for all of the Moslems defeated
are grieved for by all of the others.
They mourn for their ruler King Chico,
the king that they love and revere,   50
they promise they´ll give all their jewels
to ransom and bring him back here,
they give up their belts and their bracelets
and all their adornments of gold –
and for these and for many more riches   55
the King of Granada is sold;
so they welcome him back to Granada
and still their King Chico they hold.

71. RODRIGO TÉLLEZ DE GIRÓN

Por la Vega de Granada
un cavallero passea
en un cavallo morzillo
ensillado a la gineta,
adarga trahe embraçada   5
la lança trahía sangrienta
de los moros que havía muerto
antes de entrar en la Vega.
Los relinches del cavallo
dentro en el Alhambra suenan;   10
Oýdo lo havían las damas
que están vistiendo a la reyna;
salen de presto a mirar
por allí a ver quién passea,
vieron que en su lado yzquierdo   15
trahía una cruz vermeja,
conoscieron ser christiano,
van lo ha dezir a la reyna.
La reyna quando lo supo
vistiérase muy de priessa,   20
acompañada de damas
assomósse a una açutea.
El maestre la conosce,
baxado le ha la cabeça.
La reyna le haze mesura   25
y las damas reverencia;
con un page que allí estava
le embía a dezir qué espera.
El maestre le responde:
"Amigo, dezí a Su Alteza   30
que si cavallero moro
huviere que lo merezca,
que por servir a las damas
me venga a echar de la Vega."
Oýdo lo ha Barbarín,   35
que quiere tomar la empresa.
Las damas lo están armando,
mirando lo está la reyna.
Muy gallardo sale el moro,
cavallero en una yegua;   40
por las calles donde yva
va diziendo: "¡Muera, muera!"
Quando fue junto al maestre
de esta suerte le dixera:
"Date por mi prisionero   45

Up through the plain of Granada
a horseman is here coming by,
he´s riding a dusky red charger
and keeping the stirrups up high;
he´s holding his shield in position,   5
his lance shining red in his hands
with the blood of the Moslems he challenged
before he came into their lands.
Inside the Alhambra, the palace,
the maids are all dressing the Queen,   10
when they hear the knight´s horse neighing loudly
confusion comes over the scene -
They rush to the dressing-room window
to see who´s been daring to ride
and they notice he´s wearing a cross   15
shining red on his left-hand side,
so they realize he must be a Christian
and say to the Queen he´s outside;
when the Queen hears the news that they tell her
she finishes dressing at once,   20
and all of the maids go out with her
as onto the terrace she runs;
Rodrigo, the Christian, salutes her
by bowing his head to the Queen;
the Queen has acknowledged his greeting,   25
the serving maids show their esteem.
A page who is waiting there with them
is sent to find out what he wishes;
Rodrigo replies to him, saying:
"My friend, will you please tell your Mistress   30
that if any of your Moslem horsemen
has the strength to obey her commands,
for the sake of the ladies he honours
he should try to drive me from your lands!"
Barbarín, who has heard the proud challenge,   35
is wanting to take on the fight,
so the ladies are fitting his armour
while the Queen watches, proud of her knight;
then the Moslem rides out, strong and splendid,
and so is his valiant mare,   40
and he vows as they go through the gateway:
"He will die, I will kill him right there!"
Barbarín comes up close to Rodrigo,
and these are the words that he´s said:
"I have vowed to the Queen and her ladies   45

que a las damas y a la reyna
he dexado prometido
de llevarles tu cabeça.
Si quieres ser mi captivo,
les quitaré la promessa."   50
El maestre le responde
con boz alta y muy modesta:
"Cumple ser buen cavallero
si tú quieres tal empresa."
Apártase uno de otro   55
con diligencia y presteza,
juegan muy bien de las lanças,
arman muy buena pelea.
El maestre era más diestro,
al moro muy mal hiriera.   60
El moro desesperado
las espaldas le bolviera.
El maestre le da bozes,
diziendo: "Covarde, ¡espera!
Que te affrentarán las damas   65
si no cumples tu promessa."
Y él, viendo que se le yva,
a más correr le siguiera,
embiándole con furia
la lança por mensagera.   70
Acertado le havía al moro,
el moro en tierra cayera.
Apeado se ha el maestre
y cortóle la cabeça;
con un page se la embía   75
a la reyna que la espera,
con un recaudo que dize:
"Amigo, dezí a la reyna
que pues el moro no cumple
la palabra que le diera,   80
que yo quedo en su lugar
para servir a Su Alteza."

(Timoneda, RE:66-67; M87)

to cut off and bring them your head,
but if you surrender at once now,
and come as my prisoner instead,
I´ll abandon the promise I made them
and take you alive and not dead."   50
Rodrigo replies to the Moslem,
in a voice that is calm but is loud:
"If you are a noble of honour,
carry out what you have vowed."
At once they retreat from each other,   55
preparing their lances with care,
and then they charge straight at each other
to start a fine struggle out there;
but Rodrigo´s outwitted the Moslem
and wounded him deep to the bone,   60
so the Moslem in his desperation
turns round to escape and run home,
but Rodrigo calls out to him loudly:
"You coward, you ought to remain,
for you´re not going to stick to your promise   65
and you´ll run to your ladies in shame!"
He sees that the Moor is escaping
so chases him fast as he can,
reinforcing his furious feelings
by hurling his lance at the man.   70
The lance has arrived at its target,
the Moslem falls off his horse dead,
and Rodrigo gets down from his own horse
to cut off his challenger´s head;
he sends off the head with the pageboy   75
to the Queen, who´s expecting his own,
and he tells him: "My friend, tell your Mistress
it´s something she ought to have known;
her knight Barbarín was unable
to stand by the words that he´d said,   80
but here I am ready and willing
to fight for Her Highness instead."

CHRONOLOGICAL TABLE

711	Moslem invasion of Spain from Africa.
	Death of Rodrigo, the last Visigothic King.
778	Roland defeated by Basques at Roncesvalles.
792–842	Alfonso II ('The Chaste') of Asturias-León.
866–910	Alfonso III of Asturias-León.
951	Fernán González declares Castilian independence.
1000–35	Sancho the Great of Navarre.
1035–65	Fernando I of León-Castille.
c.1043–99	Ruy Díaz, 'El Cid'.
1065–72	Sancho II of Castille.
1072	The Siege of Zamora.
1072–1109	Alfonso VI of Castille (of León from 1065)
1085	Alfonso VI captures Toledo.
1090	Invasion of Moslem Spain by the Almorávides from Africa.
1094	El Cid captures Valencia.
1140(?)	Composition of the Poema de Mío Cid.
1158–1214	Alfonso VIII of Castille.
1207(?)	The surviving version of the Poema de Mío Cid.
1212	The battle of Las Navas de Tolosa.
	(The main turning-point of the 'Reconquest').
1217–52	Fernando III of Castille ('San Fernando').
1252–84	Alfonso X of Castille ('El Sabio').
1312–50	Alfonso XI of Castille.
1348–50	The Black Death (and later recurrences).
1350–69	Pedro I of Castille ('El Cruel').
1353	Marriage of Pedro I and Blanca de Borbón.
1361	Death of Blanca.
1368	Siege of Baeza.
1369–79	Henrique (de Trastámara) II of Castille.
1406–54	Juan II of Castille.
1410	Siege of Antequera.
1431	Battle of La Higueruela (Granada).
1436	Death of the Conde de Niebla.
1454–74	Henrique IV of Castille.
Mid 15th c.	The earliest written ballads (Rodríguez del Padrón).
1474	Accession of Isabel of Castille.
1481–92	The final Granada campaign.
1482	The Christian capture of Alhama.
1492	The Christian capture of Granada.
1548(?)	The first Romancero printed, at Antwerp.
	(For subsequent bibliography, see Introduction).

NOTES

1. BLANCANIÑA

1. Critics are often impressed by the way that several ballads open with direct speech, without the speaker being identified; in practice, however, performers tend to explain such details to the audience beforehand.

Blanca: white skin is prized in much early Spanish literature, partly as a sign of nobility (not having to earn a living out in the fields) and partly because it fitted the stereotype they had for female beauty. Here it also serves to contrast with the dirtiness of the soldier.

Soys: before the general adoption of "usted" as a polite second person form, the distinction was normally made as in Modern French, with the second person plural pronouns and verb forms also used as the respectful singular form. The ballads are liable to use either singular or plural, sometimes choosing for metrical rather then linguistic or social reasons.

3. La: i.e. the night.

5. Avía: the ballads often use an imperfect tense where we might expect a present (and vice versa).

7. Negras: not negro, nor Moor, but dirty. He has not taken his armour off for seven years, neither to wash nor to make love; his faithfulness to her memory outweighs his present unattractiveness in her response.

10. Dormilda: i.e. "dormidla" (a common sixteenth-century transposition).

11. The Count is her husband. The audience will have already guessed that she´s noble from her white skin. He is thought to be miles away in León, so this is probably set in Castille. It is a cliché of ballads that huntsmen often find something other than what they were searching for.

12. Montes: not necessarily mountains, for "el monte" is any wilderness area.

13. There is no punctuation in any of the original texts, so it is unclear who says lines 13-16; Foster assumed the wife says it, which might well be right, even though most critics have taken the speaker to be the soldier. If it is the soldier, we have to assume that he has hated the Count vividly enough for it to burn still fierce over seven years. The performer, of course, would make clear who was speaking.

14. Halcón: hunting included falconry, and often in the ballads specifically means that.

16. Morón: "Moro", as applied to a horse, means "piebald"; the "-ón" means that it is large.

17. This line is a cliché, sometimes merely meaning "meanwhile", but in ballads dealing with sex it is often the way of inexplicitly saying that they were making love. They are certainly making love when they are found, or else the wife's reaction is not explicable.

18. Que: This is understood as a remark from the performer, introducing a new character he is about to imitate: "Here is the husband, who .."

20. The traitorous father, in this short ballad, is slightly baffling; unless it is mere padding, it seems to be more than mere antipathy between in-laws, and it suggests that those modern versions of this ballad which have a continuation giving considerable prominence to her father may have inherited something from an older form of the story. The fact that they are on bad terms makes the suggested gift all the more improbable.

21. She is in the bedroom: he is still down in the hall. Rogers has suggested that combing might have been understood as a symbol for being sexually available; if so, she is trying to placate him at once.

23. Dexéys (dejéis): this is subjunctive after "dolor" ("sad that..").

25. He's coming upstairs ("baxo", 28, shows he's now above the horse).

27. The sequence of three questions all beginning with "Cuy-" is the kind of sequence that the ballad performers enjoy; they can ham it up with ever higher emotion, more furious the husband and more desperate the wife.

30. The text prints here "embios" and in 36 "aquella"; I've assumed "envió os" and "aquí la" to be what is meant.

31. Now he's coming along the corridor ...

35. He´s now coming through the bedroom door. The lance is not (as has been suggested) a phallic symbol (not here, at least); "la" in 37 refers to it. So far, it would have been possible for the performer to play the scene for laughs, but the ending shows that it is not meant to be so seen. For an errant wife to be killed with her lover´s lance is a variant on the traditional theme of many ballads, in which a woman kills an assailant with his own dagger (see no.4, below).

40. It is normal for an audience to identify psychologically with the characters they have first had presented to them, so the audience are probably expected to be upset by this ending. It would have been possible to present the whole episode from the opposite viewpoint, that of the wronged husband, in which case this ending could easily be made to seem thoroughly deserved. This sense of identification with the lovers probably explains why a large number of the modern versions of this ballad continue the tale in such a way that the wife survives with her life. This happens for humanitarian reasons rather than aesthetic, for several of the longer versions seem a bit rambling and prosaic compared with the quick tense presentation as we have it here.

2. THE UNHAPPY WIFE

1. La: the article was often included in direct address (cp. "el cavallero" in 15). In addition, it may also imply here "the most beautiful that I have seen". I have kept "the" in the translation in an attempt not to imply that this is the speaker´s wife.
    The two lovers address each other with "tú"; husband and wife call each other "vos" (31-39) until she becomes hysterical (40 on).

7-12. It looks as if for the purpose of this ballad we have to assume that he is here telling the truth, although in other ballads (e.g. nos.22 and 23) such tales are false and designed to test the wife´s fidelity.

12. "The harm he would do": i.e. to you.

15-16. "Saca" is imperative and "sacasses" past subjunctive. The different forms are chosen probably for metrical reasons only. In 40-47 she instructs her husband with the present subjunctive. This is not just poetic licence; the subjunctive could be used instead of the imperative at the time, and the point of the past (12) may be the implication that it is unlikely to happen. Lines 18 and 19 have a conditional (apparently implying unlikeliness), but "guisaré" in 19 is a simple future (implying intention), so here too the requirements of the metre override consistency of sense.

17. Fueres: a future subjunctive (now obsolete), "wherever you go".

19-20. Indirectly accepting the proposition of 6.

23. Not actually turkeys but capons.

26. Sufrir: "tolerate".

29. In this case the cliché is vaguer than it was in the previous ballad, and we may not be meant to assume that they have actually been found making love.

30. Helo: "He" (from Arabic), "here is ..", as the performer introduces the next character to the audience.

31-32. Hazéys (hacéis), habedes: the old form of the second plural in "-des" gave way eventually to the form in "-is", but for a long time both survived together, being equally acceptable and intelligible, and the performer could choose whichever suited the rhythm of the music best. Now that "-des" has fallen from Castilian, the modern performer has lost that option (although "-des" is still used elsewhere, e.g. in Galicia). This choice is made by the performer, not his character: not even an angry husband would have been likely to switch forms so obviously in reality.

31-40. The sense of these remarks depends heavily on stressing some of the personal pronouns. I have translated in such a way that the rhythm and the sense both require the following pronouns to be stressed: "you" (31), "me" (36), "he" (37), "me" (38) and "me" (40). The successive uses of "a mí" at the ends of the couplets (36-44) has the same effect in the Spanish.

40. Açotes: the switch to "tú" here is probably accompanied by a louder and more frenzied performance, as she stops being guarded and polite (with "vos") and starts to express more violent feelings.

41-42. This is slightly peculiar. Why silk and gold, and where from? It may be that the original tale had the husband as a rich merchant or nobleman, with the original implication of the line being that this is all that his wealth is going to be good for.

49-54. The proposed inscription inspired musicians with its romantic sentiments; but the clichés here have become slightly mixed, since being killed by a jealous husband does not inspire the same audience reaction as dying of a broken heart from unrequited love. This ballad, though popular, is consequently less gripping than the previous one, and the performer will have to gain effects from romanticization rather than than drama and tension.

3. GERINELDOS

   This version of this very well attested ballad has come to be the best known, even though it was recorded in the early nineteenth century prose work of the Romantic travel writer Serafín Estébanez rather than in old or new collections. It is included verbatim in his account of a dance in Triana, the gypsy quarter of Seville; yet even though that account is likely to be coloured, he was a scholar, and we know him to have carefully transcribed real performances before finding a prose frame to insert them in.

1. The girl takes the initiative, as often happens in the ballads. Many of the girls in the love ballads are Princesses; this increases the emotional content for reasons other than mere royals-worship, since for political reasons the love life of a Princess has to be arranged carefully by her father. Dynastic marriages were one of the few moderately successful methods of ensuring alliances.

3. Quién: this is not a question but an exclamation, "If only ..". Before the common use of "ojalá", from the sixteenth century on, "quién" and a past subjunctive was the normal way of expressing such a wish (cp. for example the start of ballad no.20). Grammarians usually explain the verb as being in the first person ("If only I could be the one who .."). This is a nineteenth-century version, however, and in this case and several others it is fascinating to see how old and otherwise obsolete grammatical expressions can survive by being handed on from performer to performer; this could only happen if it were still intelligible to the audience. (It is; we can all usually understand antiquated expressions which we no longer use.) "Ojalá" is rarely used in ballads, even now.

4. "You" should be stressed.

6. The Princess, revealing her real desires, uses "tú" to Gerineldos until after they have been discovered (51-54); Gerineldos always uses "vos". Even so, we can tell that his use of "vos" is politeness rather than unwillingness, from 10.

12. Esté: subjunctive, i.e. "as soon as the King is asleep." Gerineldos will know, because he sleeps in the King's room (which is why his absence later seems treacherous, 35).

17. Castillo: the central fortress in the palace. Gerineldos is checking to see if soldiers are following him, in case this is all a trap.

20. Cuerpo garrido: the Spanish is more explicit about what is to be opened than the English translation.

21. She is checking who it is with the formal form ("vos") used when we do not know who we are talking to. Foster suggested that this hesitation shows she is changing her mind, but that is unlikely, for she is still taking the initiative in 25-26.

29. Recordar: now means "remember", but once also meant "wake" (also in 49 and 51).

30. Despavorido: this applies to the King ("frightened"), with "sueño" probably meaning "sleep" (as in 47) rather than "dream".

31. Kings and nobles normally slept with pages or maids in the same room, or at least in easy earshot.

33-4. These are the same lines as 1-2, in a different mouth, and to be performed with a different tone of voice, to show the change in emotional gear that happens here, halfway through the ballad.

35-6. It is not clear whether this a simple conditional or a question. Estébanez prints it without a question mark, but other editors (of this and similar versions) see this as a question introduced by "si" (which is not unusual: cp. the start of ballad no.1 here). Betraying the King´s dynastic plans for his daughter is treachery as much as handing the keys to the central fortress of the palace (the "alcázar") to an enemy outside; this reaction is not merely that of a jealous father wanting to interfere in his daughter´s love-life. The emotional centre of this ballad is eventually inside the King rather than either of the lovers, as he battles in his mind between his love (for them both) and his duty, so the performer must find a way of presenting and acting him as a sympathetic figure.

37. It looks as though he had already had a hint of their mutual affection, for him to assume this at once; sexually adventurous Princesses in the ballad tradition are far more likely in general to be with a noble than with a page. The tenses used from 35 to 38 (present, imperfect and perfect) show again how the resourceful performer has a variety of verb forms at his disposal, from which to choose one to fit into the rhythm; there´s no distinction in the time of the suggested actions meant to be understood here, and in real life no speaker would be so inconsistent.

43. This is the crux; the conflict between his feelings of affection (as a human) and what is thought to be his duty (as a King). The ballads have a humane attitude in general, tolerant of human weaknesses and suspicious of excessive morality (quite unlike the usual image of Spain abroad); so the husband in ballad no.1 comes over as the villain, and the King here as a hero, for having quelled his initial angry impulse to attack Gerineldos ("quisiéralo matar", but he didn´t).

44.   I.e., he wasn´t actually his son; but it was common in the Court for the King to adopt deserving children such as a cousin´s orphans, etc. (There is no consistency between "lo" and "le" in this version; this is not particularly surprising.)

46.   Next to: i.e., between them. This is a famous symbolic action in several European tales.

49.   The parallel between 49 and 29 is the kind of structure that the performers like, to keep a mental hold of the shape of the plot.

51.   "Recordad" in Estebanez; Smith transcribes this as if it were a misprint for "recordar", with "recordar heis" being a variant spelling of "recordaréis". This could be right; although the future for the imperative is not usual, "heis" by itself is even less so. The use of the "vos" forms here can be exploited by the performer to show that this is no longer a scene of intimacy and she speaks to him formally as Princess rather than personally as a woman.

54.   Yerro: this might mean "sin", although there´s no other hint of a moral or religious attitude being taken, or that she regrets it at all. I prefer to see this as "mistake", a practical matter (perhaps in that he should not have fallen asleep, 28), but the translation is deliberately indeterminate here.

56.   Between: i.e. between the Princess´s room and Gerineldos´s.

59-63.   This is in fact an admission; "picking roses" implies defloration and the garden is the usual place for making love in the ballad tradition. Gerineldos knows he cannot seriously pretend not to have been with her.

66. Castigo: a warning rather than a punishment. The ballad stops here in most versions; the emotions of the participants, which the audience has been inspired to feel as well if the performance has had any aesthetic skill, are the point, rather than the plot, and we cannot tell whether their love is meant to be thought to be going to continue or not. In most comparable tales, it does, eventually with the King´s blessing (cp. ballad no.9 here, for example).

4. RICO FRANCO

This is an unsatisfactory ballad in several respects, although if it
was originally an episode of a longer tale some of the details would
have once been clearer than they are now. We should envisage the
performer setting the scene in advance in any case.

1. Several ballads start with huntsmen. They are usually unsuccessful
in the hunt and end up finding something unexpected (as Rogers has
examined).

5-6. Castle Maynés is not a real place; Mainés is usually a name
available for a person. Nor is the ballad apparently meant to be
situated anywhere in particular.

8. Cortés: this is a term of praise (more often found in courtly
poetry than in popular).

9-10. These improbable suitors are one of the clichés available for
a performer to dredge up when wondering what to say next. The ballad
would be better without them.

11-12. Rico Franco is generally taken to be the man´s name; the
version reprinted here has "Rico franco", which might mean "a Catalan
called Rico", but the use of capitals in these texts is sufficiently
haphazard for that to indicate little. He is in any event the victim
here of anti-Catalan prejudice on the part of the Castilian performer:
Catalans (who lived in the "Corona de Aragón", hence "aragonés":
"Aragón" in the English should have the stress on the "-ó-") were
disliked for being capitalists, "rico".
    Who he is meant to be, and the connection between the huntsmen and
the rest of the episode, is not clear. Bénichou suggested that the
ballad can only be understood if we take Rico Franco to be one of the
huntsmen, with the apparent pluperfect in "robara" (11) being
positively misleading: i.e. when the huntsmen, including him, entered
the castle, he grabbed her. "Robar" is in any event an odd word; he
has not robbed her, nor stolen her, nor, apparently, does he want to
upset her, since in 15 he is presented as cajoling her. "Robar"
originally meant "to capture booty in battle", which might just be the
point here. The translation is as vague as possible, on purpose.

15. Halagar means "flatter" or "cajole": if this is his intention,
his words are extraordinarily ill-chosen. That incompetence may be the
point, though, for he is extraordinarily stupid later, in contrast
with the girl, who is cunning, "artera". The simplicity of the ´goody
versus baddy´ theme here is another symptom of this ballad´s weakness:
the same plot mechanism (the assailant dying with his own dagger) is
presented with more skill in ballad no.18.

17-19.   "Tú" in 17 and 19, but "vos" in 18; an extreme case of the grammatical flexibility allowed by the genre leading to the performer making the character say something impossibly inconsistent.

23.   "Ventura"; "what is to become of me".

24-25.   There is no logical train of thought connecting these lines; we are just being still clumsily manoeuvred to the attractive ending.

26.   "Lugués": from Lucca in Italy, known for its sharp knives. Catalans were halfway to being Italians anyway, from a Castilian perspective.

29.   There might just be some intentional irony here; though crass, he´s also well-mannered and this is his downfall. But he can hardly be being praised for "cortesía" if he has perpetrated the unexplained massacre of 19-20. "Cortese" is a very ancient or Italianate form of "cortés", and might here be a misprint.

32.   The climax. Emotionally satisfying, but spoilt by being a rather clumsy ten-syllabled line, and also ambiguous, since the immediate meaning - that which would come to mind a split second before the real one - seems to imply that she stabbed herself ("se": "se lo" is grammatical for "him" as well, of course).

5. THE PRISONER (1)

This is a neat ballad, structured around the relationship between the narrator and birds.

2.   Calor: this seems like a cliché at first, until we discover that he is in a cold dark prison-cell unable to see out (in a windowless tower, 37, rather than a dungeon).

3-4.   Songbirds meant to typify early summer. "Calandria" is always feminine, and "ruiseñor" always masculine; Foster suggests that the two are meant to be thought to be in love, but this seems unlikely. That motif comes next.

6.   "Servir" is a standard euphemism for making love; a matter much on any prisoner´s mind.

7.   "Yo": "I" suddenly appear, a personal voice in the apparently clichéd setting. Not only that, the audience find that the foregoing are phenomena I cannot see, rather than ones I can; this is a real coup de theâtre in the hands of a skilled performer, giving the audience a mild jolt.

8.   "Esta": the place is also made clear, and the audience should suddenly feel they have come into the cold, dark and damp.

11.   "Cantava": the imperfect tense here is to be taken seriously. It used to sing, but does no longer. "Me" (12 and 13) is included as if it were "my" bird.

13.   "Ballesteros" are archers (not golfers), using a crossbow, "ballesta". How does he know that it´s been killed by an archer? In the short version of the ballad, which stops here (no.6), this is inexplicable; here, in the longer version, he presumably finds out on his release.

15-20.   Three neat parallel expressions to show us visually that he has been there a long time.

21-24.   I.e., if the cruelty with which he is being treated is the King´s decision, fair enough; but if, as he suspects, the jailer is laying it on thicker than he is meant to, then the jailer can be criticised, not so much for cruelty as for disobedience, "trayción". It is as well that he phrases his complaint this way, in view of the fact that the King turns out to be listening. Kings tend to be forgetful rather than sadistic (cp. Virgil, no.24).

25.   "Quién" for "ojalá" again (cp. the start of no.3). The grammar can hardly involve a first-person in "diese" here, though; the grammarians may not have understood this usage, in the event.

26.   The bird that can talk is the third in the aesthetically satisfying structural progression from those that sing unheard (3), to the one that was an unintentional herald of the dawn (12), to these that might be active accomplices.

28.   There is no "hawk" in the Spanish.

30.   Is the implication that women are specifically skilled in training birds to talk? "Razón" is a vague word, not necessarily implying the ability to think: a parrot-fashion repetition would suffice here.

32.   The "a" is not in the text. Menéndez y Pelayo assumed that to be a misprint (or merged into the final "-a" of the preceding word), and so do I. Otherwise the "me" of the previous line is actively confusing (it would mean "to me" rather than "for (and from) me").

34.   "Empanada": visualize this as a kind of fish pie.

37.   The pick, presumably to help him climb down the outside of the
tower after escaping, is probably meant to be seen as a potential
crampon rather than a chisel. It should even so be more "tajador",
"sharp", than his fingernails (20).

39.   So indirectly the bird idea has helped, since it has impressed
the King into releasing him. Kings are often given the role of setting
things right at the end of a ballad (as they also often do in plays of
the time), at least partly as a hint to any King who might indeed be
listening. (The shorter version is uncharacteristically miserable – or
"lyrical", as critics tactfully tend to say). The husband and wife are
now able to see the delights mentioned at the start, which rounds off
the structure.

6. THE PRISONER (2)

This shorter version of no.5 is taken not from one of the
mid-sixteenth century "Romanceros", which contain only ballads, but
from the "Cancionero General" of 1511. The Cancioneros are cultured
anthologies of many metrical forms, which largely ignore the ballads
(presumably for not being cultured enough); this one is probably only
included to precede the "Glosa" composed for it by Nicolás Núñez.
Such "Glosas" are complex rhyming stanzaic poems, usually of ten lines
per stanza ("décimas"), with the last two lines being taken in
sequence from the ballad being "glossed" or expanded. In this way the
literary historian is sometimes able to find evidence for a ballad
text from a time before it became acceptable to print them.

1.   The repetition of English "now" is intended to match the
repetition of "por mayo". In this ballad these scenes of early summer
are merely imagined (rather than seen subsequent to his release); and
the birdsong structure is absent, since the lark and nightingale are
not here either. Instead the structure is: 1-4 Nature, 5-8 misery,
9-12 Nature and misery combined. Menéndez Pidal tended to assume that
the longest versions of a ballad were the earliest, with evolution
usually implying pruning; others prefer to see performers extending
their text at times; but Bénichou is probably right to suggest that
shorter and longer texts coexist, as the singer can always decide how
much to include from his stored resources to suit the time and place.

2.   "Cuando" with a noun is acceptable Spanish ("at the time of").

2-3.   Between these two lines Menéndez Pidal (in the best minstrel
tradition) added to his Flor Nueva version the lark and nightingale of
no.5, plus a nineteenth-century attested couplet: "cuando los trigos
encañan/ y están los campos en flor" ("when the wheat and flowers

are blooming in the fields"); apparently in order to have the prisoner
introduced at exactly the halfway point of the ballad. Subsequent
scholars have at times been misled into thinking this amalgam to be an
attested version. The birds have a literary point, but the flowers are
just unnecessary Romanticism, weakening the tension and increasing the
sentimentality. Such additions in nineteenth-century versions are
quite common, and usually ignored by the literary scholar.

6.   Prisiones: plural, so here we probably visualize an underground
row of dungeons rather than a tower.

9-12.   These four lines hardly vary from version to version. The
climax would be known by heart, but the performer can lead up to it as
he feels best. The performer is in control. So is the translator; this
translation has deliberately different rhymes from no.5.

7. MARIANA

This ballad is first attested only from the nineteenth century, but
seems certain to be much older; several of the ballads that deal with
individual tales of lovers were not included, perhaps intentionally,
in the early collections.

3.   Alonso: an older form of "Alfonso".

4-5.   There is a stress on the English "me" (4) and "my" (5). She
assumes that it is his own wedding; this turns out to be correct (43),
so the performer has to make their reactions here indicate as much to
the audience.

8.   Escaño: originally a "stool". The Cid had one, so it is a
suitably ancient-sounding word. It is not clear whether the stool is
in some way magical; Alonso might just have fallen asleep ... This air
of possible rather than threatening supernatural influence gives this
ballad its strange charm. Is she a witch or not? Does "florido"
perhaps imply the presence of some kind of natural potion? Spanish
tales in general rarely include witchcraft (it´s more an obsession of
countries further North), but enough of an original audience might
half-believe for the men to get a frisson of apprehension from this,
and the women a frisson of envy. The stool, and the ingredients of the
cocktail, originally had more point than mere local colour, in any
event.

10.   Alonso fails to catch a sinister implication, that this is a
stool for punishing those who let her down. The performer can probably
indicate this to the audience, however.

13.   Como discreta: not "discreet" (she isn´t) but "practical-minded". This is a common word in Spanish literature, used to imply "skilled in the ways of the world"; usually opposed to "necio", but here merely to "joven" (27).

14.   Part of her practicality seems to lie in having these ingredients readily available, as if she is indeed a practising witch just going to her store cupboard. The garden, usually a scene of love in the genre, is "florido", as the "escaño" is, but stocked with anti-traditionally malicious elements.

15.   Solimán: a corrosive compound of mercury and chlorine, used as a disinfectant.

18.   Juan Menéndez Pidal printed <u>largato</u>, in italics, presumably to imitate the voice of his informant.

19.   Espinilla: this is ambiguous, but probably means a "wart" or "pimple".

21.   A variant version explains this invitation by having Mariana suggest drinking a toast to the happy couple; a pleasantly gruesome touch.

22.   A stress on the English "you".

24.   Alonso is not here suspecting any trickery; he is characterized as being still young enough to rely on social customs instead of being wary for potential traps.

25.   Line 13 repeated; introducing the incantatory atmosphere exploited in 33-37.

26.   It is not clear what Mariana has actually done, apart from emptying her glass somewhere other than in her mouth.

29.   Veneno: poison, not magic. Indeed, such a mixture in one´s wine would not do one any good, so the uncertainty about whether it has been magic remains.

33-37.   These lines repeat 15-19; in the English, 33-36 repeat 15-18. The original list sounded a bit eerie, but the repetition makes it seem like a chant to accompany the casting of a spell over a magic brew (as in Macbeth).

40.   Well, Alfonso has got the point now. So he did have a guilty conscience from the start.

42.   The subject of this sentence (in the Spanish) is "vino"; "the wine is breaking your heart". Foster suggested that this is meant as a counterpoint to the way he had metaphorically broken Mariana´s heart; this is possible, although Spanish does not have exactly this cliché.

43-44.   Alonso is bidding farewell to his bride, who is now waiting at the church for him. These lines reassure the women in the audience that Mariana´s assumption was right.

46.   Since this is a nineteenth century version, it is possible to take the subject of "quedaron" to be "ustedes" (for use when talking to an older generation). "Quedasteis" would have been metrically equivalent.

48.   Pío: "piebald", of a horse, although the connection between the homonym "pío", "religious", and the church of the next line may not be accidental.

50.   They are all waiting at the church for his wedding, but it is going to turn out to be his funeral. The neatness of this ending, and the grammatical precision of his dying eight lines, combine with the eerie atmosphere created in the central part of the ballad to make this one of the most attractive of all.

8. FONTE FRIDA

1.   Fonte Frida: "Fonte" is a very old form of "fuente", "spring" (Latin FONTEM), and "frida" of "fría", "cold" (Latin FRIGIDAM). It is quite common for placenames to preserve pronunciations that have otherwise become archaic in the language as a whole, which is one of several reasons for suggesting that the ballad (not necessarily in this precise form) is very old indeed. In practice, editors have taken "Fonte Frida" to be a placename, although it could be taken as simply meaning "(there is a) cold spring". There is little textual authority for the modern habit of printing it as one word.

2.   Cold running water is associated with love in the popular traditions (including Galician "cantigas"), so this line sounds more natural in Spanish than it might seem.

3.   Avezicas; "ave" is feminine whether the birds are male or female. This is the place where the young of either sex meet. Foster´s suggestion that it is only the meeting-place for the females cannot be sustained; the male nightingale has every right to be there.

5. The turtledove is there, but does not find any "consolación" in the general company. The tradition of having animals and birds to represent human characteristics was well-known in Spain, despite being only rarely exploited in ballad form. Thus the mention of a turtledove would bring to the audience´s mind an image of fidelity, and the nightingale that of a dashing but untrustworthy lover. The birds can be used as symbols of these attitudes, and the audience will react to them as to humans. We all know that nightingales do not court turtledoves, but that is not the point; as in most ballads, the interest lies in strong human emotions. Real humans have mixed feelings and express in their words veiled versions of their emotions, but the emotions of the representative animals and birds can be presented direct and stark.

7 and 13. Aý: i.e., "allí", "there".

10. Traycíon: the poor nightingale may not have realized it, but his casual proposition will touch a raw nerve, as he encourages her to be unfaithful to her husband´s memory.

12. Servidor: this word tends not to imply anything permanent (cp. 25).

15-18. I.e., "I´m not returning to life" (by looking for a lover). The green branch and the flowers represent returning vitality. The water, of the fountain, is not going to give her pleasure – by muddying it before drinking she will see to that. In this way a traditional idea, that doves muddy their drinking water (which isn´t true), is neatly tied in with the idea that the spring water represents the joys of love.

19-22. It isn´t just sex that she´s renounced, but any kind of consolation in other people´s company. "Porque" (20) is followed by a subjunctive: "in order not to have children .."

23-26. The hectic vehemence of her response is out of all proportion to the nightingale´s offence, and it is unclear from the printed version whether we are supposed to sympathize with the widow´s determination to be miserable or not. In real life we could react either way, and a performer might have the opportunity to sway us through his skill, either to admire her fidelity or feel distaste for her prickliness.

9. CONDE CLAROS (1)

There are several very long ballads in the Romanceros, of which this is generally thought to be the best. It is not clear whether such a long ballad would ever be performed whole.

1. Por filo: on the dot.

3. In the ballad tradition it is more often the woman who is in this nervous state; this one depends on our realizing that Claros´s affections are real.

7. Clara Niña: "Bright Girl". Again, the proper name is also a description. Clara is a Spanish name, but Claros is not.

9. Mañana: specifically, once it is light. (Before dawn, "morning" is "madrugada").

12. Gavilán: the likeness to a falcon is in his decisiveness and determination, as he sets off hunting his prey.

15. Much of this ballad is presented in direct speech, which gives the performer an excellent series of opportunities to act the several characters, with a wide variety of tones of voice and intended effects on the audience. This variety prevents the ballad from becoming monotonous, despite the very high proportion of "-ar" infinitives at the ends of couplets.

20. Cordobán: leather from Córdoba, that is, the very best. Córdoba, the former capital of Moslem Spain, in northern Andalucía, is still a leather centre.

22. "Striped silk lining" can either be performed in English as three stresses, or with an atonic syllable on the "-ed".

24. Apreciar: i.e. it is priceless, too valuable to have a price set on it.

26. 300 is a formulaic number in the ballads, often used to express any large number, and not always meant to be taken literally (it would be absurd to do so here or in 31 or 41: cp. ballad no.16). Once the two lovers meet, such formulae disappear.

28. I.e. the King´s Court, which he is not at at the moment.

38. The palace is specified, because Claros lives in a different one.

41. The absurdity of this cortege of 300 (this is the last such absurdity) is heightened by their apparent sudden collective absence after 45, as the meeting of the lovers is supposedly secret. Performers could well skip 41-44.

44. Todos: masculine. All men find her beautiful, but realize they have little chance of approaching a Princess; hence they "penan" ("suffer"), since in the literary traditions of the time men afflicted by unreturned passion suffer great torments.

45-46. Luego (que): "at once (on ..)" in the 16th century; not just "some time later", as now.

51-52. It is not clear whether Clara´s words are intentionally seductive here or not. The performer will have to decide and act appropriately. E.g., if they are, there could be a pause at the end of 55.

60. Holgar: this can just mean "rest", but in the case of a man and a woman it has a more explicit sense, so the English is not inappropriate here (cp. "bel holgar", 106). Claros is behaving like a "gavilán" here, remember, hunting his prey.

63-66. This is a cliché, taken from other ballads, in which men used to like to prove themselves by some such chivalrous feat of arms (cp. no.71). This ballad, though, is making slight fun of that tradition, as Clara just laughs at the fatuity of such a promise (67-72).

68. I.e. "if you want to make love, just say so".

75. Claros still has not quite got her point, and feels he has to go through more of the rituals. Saying that one has been suffering in love for seven years is another cliché, and known to be one (e.g. it is also exploited by the Cid´s daughter in ballad no.50).

79-80. She compliments him on his practised skill at the conventional art of chatting up, and returns to practical arrangements.

81-83. This seems to mean that she was on her way to the baths when they met, and that she still wishes to do so first; it is also possible to take it to mean "let me wash first".

88. Real: "royal" (not "real"). The English proverb corresponds closely here.

92. As usual, love is consummated in a garden. This was traditional in literature, but probably also in real life. There was almost no privacy indoors, even Kings and Princesses had pages or maids sleeping

and living in or very near their bedroom, and most other people did not have a room to themselves.

98.   This is included to cheer up the audience; but it has also been essential to make clear that this is not rape, for she was as keen as Claros was. If the audience did not know that, they would not feel the appropriate emotions over the next ten minutes.

99-100.   This was precisely the function of Fortune. The Wheel of Fortune was conceived of as being like a water-wheel, which lifts water up from a river at the bottom and pours it out (into irrigation channels) at the top. Fortune does that to mankind: just when Claros and Clara think they are at the height of their good fortune they are to be tipped out. There is at first sight no main verb in this couplet; it could be an invocation ("Oh Fortune!"), or a case of a missing verb "to be" in 99.

101.   This is an actual huntsman, in neat contrast to the successful metaphorical hunt seen hitherto. As usual, a huntsman finds something unexpected.

102.   He should not be there because this is the private royal palace grounds.

109.   The Count addresses Clara with "vos" and the huntsman with "tú", choosing according to social status.

111.   Claros assumes (rightly) that the King would not approve.

118.   Montalbán: the Count´s titular home. There is a place in the province of Teruel called Montalbán, but he is not to be taken to be referring to that here.

121.   Sin ventura: "cursed", immediately for his refusal to keep quiet, but also, it turns out later, bcause he is about to die himself (142). Under normal circumstances the huntsman would probably have kept quiet, but the special circumstances of the political implications of the love life of a Princess, particularly if she is the heiress, (as in Gerineldos, no.3) lead him to see his social duty in telling the King. He´s not just being an odious busybody, at least.

126-31.   The huntsman keeps stressing the crown, because his news may have repercussions on who will be going to inherit it.

133.   The huntsman assumes that it was rape. In a way, it was more honourable to do so, and Clara had not said anything to him in the garden to indicate otherwise.

134.   Comportar: "turn a blind eye to".

142.   The huntsman was unfortunately unaware of the literary tradition of killing the messenger who brings unwelcome news. The King´s brutality, though, also serves to assure the audience that Claros was earlier right to be fearful of the King´s reaction.

145.   As with the King in Gerineldos (no.3), he is not merely a jealous father; it is his duty to his kingdom and royal line to supervise his heiress´s love life.

153.   The palace gardens are inside the city walls.

162.   Presumably we are expected to have forgotten the detail of his 300 precious stones (25).

163.   Mule; the high nobility ride horses (cp. 129-30).

166.   Dark, because there are no windows (cp. no.5). Palaces often had fortresses inside, with such towers at the corners.

168.   A stress on the English "with".

169.   So: i.e., "so that" ("him" being Claros, and "his" the King´s).

173.   This is briefly set specifically in the fantasy France of the Carolingian tradition (the Court of the Emperor Charlemagne). Oliver and Roland were known as the two finest knights, and the twelve "pares" (175) were the equivalent of the Knights of the Round Table. Claros, we are told later (383), is one of the twelve.

182.   It is not clear if this line refers to one person or two.

184.   The moral of this tale, which is for the most part implicit but inescapable, is that people in positions of power should listen to other people´s advice (cp. 122, 240, 378). When the King eventually does, the obvious solution to the episode (marriage) is at last allowed to occur. But before then, the audience is to be inspired to a wide range of emotions and involved in several dramatic confrontations. (If the performer is not exhausted at the end of it all, he is not doing his job properly.)

193.   Claros, like Gerineldos, was brought up at the Court. The King reacts as if to a kind of incest.

198.   Reynard was known to be a hero in the Carolingian tradition.

205.   He assumes it is rape, because the huntsman did. The audience know that he is wrong; the dramatic irony heightens the tension.

209.   On this occasion he is not taking but giving advice, and put
this way his subjects have no option but to agree.

212.   Buen rey: this formulaic phrase often occurs on occasions where
the King is doing something undesirable. Subconsciously this tends to
assure us that the ballad is not a subversive tract; usually the King
is under a misapprehension of some kind, or been swayed by wicked
advisers.

217.   Denunciar: not "denounce", just "report".

225.   Over the next few minutes we have a sequence of dramatic
conversations and hurried journeys from one place to another. The
phrases with "Ya .." serve to switch scene, and perhaps the performer
takes the chance to act (as if to say "and now I´m being the ...").

237.   It is an archbishop´s duty to forgive all sins anyway, but this
is not intended to sound like a formula; it is to be said with
sincerity.

238-39.   Between these two lines the Silva´s text prints twenty
others, which are two complex and rhyming "décimas" from a "Glosa" on
this part of the ballad (for a further explanation, see the notes to
no.5). Menéndez y Pelayo rightly omitted them, but it means that the
line numbers hereon are 20 fewer than in the original edition (which
can cause critical confusion). This prison-scene section of the ballad
was particularly prone to extraction and interpretation: no.10 here is
one such reworking.

245-48.   Incautious lovers are often harshly punished if they are
nobles in ballads, but the Count can be forgiven for not knowing he
was in a ballad. In real life, Courts seem usually to have taken
sexual freedom for granted. The modern image of "Mediaeval" times
having been ones of sexual oppression is diametrically mistaken; for
example, if a mediaeval monarch had no illegitimate children, it was a
matter for startled comment. (The word "Victorian" is usually more
appropriate to refer to such repressiveness).

250.   The Count replies like a martyr who has been asked to renounce
his faith to save his life; and saying this to an Archbishop makes the
parallel all the more striking. It was common, in fact, to present,
and even feel, the emotions of love and of religion in the same
terminology.

253.   The word "no" in the Spanish has emphasis (sufficient to stop it
eliding with "ama"). Part of the attitudes sometimes called "Courtly
Love" involved the (rather unpleasant) idea that only nobles could
feel real love.

256. English "them" should be stressed.

259-74. These sentiments are genuine; a young page has been chosen to say them, presumably because he is still young enough to be convincing if he is prepared to say what he actually feels. They sound a bit odd now, so a modern performer will have to use his skill to stop the audience reacting inappropriately.

267. The huntsman called it "deshonra" (133); the use of "honra" here, essentially referring to the same thing, is intentional. The audience is being manoeuvred into seeing Claros as not only forgiveable, but even honourable.

275. This phrase is going to be repeated several times; it is the signal that one speech has stopped and another started, in the hope that the audience can keep track of who is talking to who.

283 and 285. English "her" is to be stressed.

287. As in 225, "Ya .." signals a scene-change.

297. This is the first time that the Princess has heard of his arrest; he was arrested alone on leaving the garden, and she was not one of the people in the queue for intercession (171-84).

298. Muerta: applying to the Princess, not the ground. She has fainted rather than died. Her reaction further reinforces the audience´s necessary understanding that her love for Claros is genuine.

299. Damas, dueñas y donzellas: from old to young. She has 300, remember.

304-05. The Princess has a problem because if she intercedes for Claros she is admitting her complicity; should she keep quiet and not admit that she had encouraged him?

309. Old women in the ballads usually advise young women not to be shy but to act on their love.

311. Ya ..: the scene changes again.

313. Fuese: i.e. "se fue", "she went off".

317. The same line as 299, but not the same people. These are the general public.

321. Pregoneros: town criers, part of whose duty was to accompany

criminals to the place of execution and proclaim to the public what
was their crime (as a deterrent to others).

326.   "Me" in the English should be stressed. The Princess has some
authority over the soldiers, of course.

331.   Al conde: both Menéndez y Pelayo and Smith print "el", but the
original is "al"; it is Clara who reaches Claros, by forcing her way
through the armed guard, not vice versa.

333.   Esforçá: a variant of "esforçad". She does not know, what the
audience do, that he has already acted with impressive "esfuerzo"
(250). Both are reacting heroically.

335-36.   "Your" and "mine" need stress in the English. "Aunque" with
subjunctive means "even if"; she is not suggesting a swap.

337.   Not surprisingly, the guards do not know what to do. The
"alguazil" may also be the executioner.

341.   Second person address to "Your Royal Majesty" must have been a
great problem. Here, although "Vuestra" is used, the verb-form is the
polite third person singular imperative. When he uses "tu" in 347 the
confusion is complete. Metri gratia, but an audience might have been
slightly taken aback even so.

346.   Enforcar: i.e. hang on the gallows ("horca").

347-48.   The constable, despite having the King´s orders, feels he has
not got the power to overrule the Princess.

359.   This line is ambiguous. It may mean that if he had had a son he
would have burnt Clara Niña and Claros; or it may mean (as
translated) that he will punish them with death if she is in fact
pregnant with an heir (after the birth). Either way, the Princess is
currently the heiress, and all Kings are very anxious to have someone
of their own line succeed them.

362.   Vivos: burned alive.

363-88.   Clara´s reaction, a magnificent set-piece of great courage
and directness, is the first time she has spoken to her father on the
subject. She seems to succeed by convincing him that she is in no way
angry with Claros for what happened (although still not quite
admitting that she encouraged him), as much as through the argument
that his death could easily start a civil war.

366. Él: "you". Even before "usted" became normal usage a third-person verb could be used for polite second person meaning (as in 341); and occasionally this would be accompanied by such an "él" as this.

367. Claros´s father died defending the crown and the royal line; the argument is that Claros can hardly be killed for wanting to join it.

373. Mal querer: a noun meaning "malice".

376. She points out that if he is killed for rape, that is a confirmation of the existence of a rape; and to be a rape victim was considered dishonourable rather than a cause for sympathy.

378-80. The moral is here stated explicitly.

387. Revolver te hían: i.e. "te revolverían", a split conditional. Future and conditional tenses in Spanish were originally two words, the infinitive plus the relevant form of "haber"; they coalesced into one word very early, but when a pronoun intervened (here, "te") the split form could be used until the fourteenth century (as it still can in Portuguese). It is a surprisingly archaic use for this ballad, though, which on the whole is not an archaizing composition.

389. The King at last is prepared to listen. This is the moral of the whole ballad, but shorter extracts saw the main point rather more crudely (that sex is its own justification: see no.10).

396. As the archbishop thought all along; he is there, so perhaps we are supposed to assume he has been influential in this new advice.

398. Afamar: to restore the Princess´s "fama", good reputation (in sexual matters); by the Count´s death, and the implicit proclamation that she had indeed been raped, she would have been "disfamada" (376). Women in fifteenth and early sixteenth century literature are often presented as being preoccupied with their "fama", a far more potent inhibition than any consideration of morality. This probably corresponds to reality, being evidence of practical sense rather than of hypocrisy.

403. This recapitulates the decree of the King, who had not realized that they were in love before. If he had, much sorrow would have been saved, but it would have not been such a magnificent literary work.

405. Ya..: "and now .."; the performer has led the audience to share every emotion, and now presents the happy ending.

408. Desposar: "marry" (rather than "take the handcuffs off", the "esposas" of 159).

409.   Secret marriages could be legal until the twelfth century, but subsequently some kind of Church or civil public ceremony was thought desirable. For a Princess some kind of publicity at a wedding was thought essential (then as now).

411-12.   This phrasing neatly picks up 99-100 and rounds off the ballad.

10. CONDE CLAROS (2)

This ballad recreates the prison-scene of the former ballad, lines 235-56, at slightly greater length. The focus is exclusively on the emotions, rather than the drama and the narrative of the original. We probably have to assume that the longer tale is the original, even though this shorter extract is earlier attested; this version is (perhaps wrongly) attributed to Juan del Encina (1469-1529), who set it to music.

1.   As often, a short ballad starts with direct speech without naming the speaker.

2.   The assonance is "-á", as in the previous ballad; yet the lines here not only rhyme, all in "-ar", but are all verbal infinitives. The audience could well notice such a striking structure, but rather than inspiring monotony, in a song this probably seemed a skilful achievement.

15-16.   Claros has broken his trust as bodyguard. Since the plot mechanism leading to this emotional summit is omitted here, some explanation of the illicitness of their love needs to be inserted. There is no comparable comment in ballad no.9, naturally, for the audience know what´s happened. Independent ballads on the same theme have independent existence, and can easily acquire internal details that have a function in that one ballad but might be contradictory to other details in another on the same theme.

20.   Valiera: "it would have been better .."

23-24.   The contrast between these lines and 3-4 shows that there is no ideal of poetic justice here; unpleasant consequences can easily follow actions that do not deserve them.

25.   There is no textual sign of a change in speaker. Even in song, the performer will have to indicate it somehow. There is no Archbishop here; this is merely an uncle.

26 and 28.   Stress on "agrée" and "be".

31-32. These would be dishonourable deaths; dying for love is not.

34. Que: i.e. "lo que", "which cannot cause me pain".

35-36. Recalling 3-4, in English as in Spanish.

11. DEATH CONCEALED

300 attested versions of ballads on this theme (the majority, surprisingly, in hexasyllabic verse) have been collected together recently by Beatriz Mariscal de Rhett; yet although this is a widely-spread theme of probable great antiquity, the earliest attestation is only late nineteenth-century.

1. The protagonist in this tale is usually not a King, nor called Pedro; there is no connection between this ballad and those on the only King Pedro there has been in Castille (1350-69). But he stars in several ballads (here, nos 54-58) and his name consequently sounds appropriate for use in the genre.

3. This is illness, not accident. In several other versions, he is wounded from war.

6. The shepherd is often absent from the tale, also; maybe he too is brought in here from a vague association with one of the Pedro ballads (no.55).

10. Alda is known to be a name suitable for a royal wife whose husband dies tragically (coming from the tradition represented here by no.16).

20-21. There is probably no contrast intended here between "de mi vida" and "de mi muerte". The former is a cliché for "dear" (cp. 36). He hopes not to upset his wife further at an already traumatic time (death in childbirth being common); after forty days she should have recovered - indeed, she does, for she is once again "delgada", "thin", in 29 - and be able to take the shock.

25. I.e., not since the birth.

27. Suegra, "mother-in-law"; in English verse that would sound even more awkward than "Queen Mother".

29-30. This is an obvious non-sequitur. Perhaps this is also some kind of echo, of the original Alda (ballad no.16), one of whose servants tried to protect her from bad news by misinterpreting a dream in a kind but illogical manner.

31. Linda: "pretty", but also implying that she wishes to celebrate the birth.

37-38. The Spanish repeats the same phrase; the English tries to achieve the effect with "again and again".

45 and 47. The English explicitly contrasts the behaviour of the two mothers. The Spanish does not. The immediate reaction of Alda on hearing the news is that she is wearing the wrong clothes, for she has come brightly dressed as befits the mother of a new-born child; this seems likely to be a nineteenth-century addition to the ballad, at a time when keeping in with neighbours and worrying what they will think is a major preoccupation of both life and literature. The fifteenth century was generally less petty and trivial, and more likely to end without this comment. Several modern versions have the wife drop dead from shock at the end, or even commit suicide, despite the thoughtfulness of the husband´s delaying tactics (22); this is a more artistically satisfactory, less humane and (probably) a more ancient dénouement than the mere sorrow at a social faux pas we have here.

12. THE LADY AND THE SHEPHERD

This is still a well known theme in both ballad and lyric poetry; many modern versions are collected in Vol. X of the modern Romancero Tradicional ("La dama y el pastor"). This sixteenth-century "pliego suelto" version is also reprinted there. The ballad has achieved fame in that it was for long thought to be the earliest attested in written form, since a Majorcan Catalan version has survived, apparently dated to 1421; but Aubrun has recently shown that that was probably written down in c.1470 (which gives the written priority to Juan Rodríguez del Padrón in mid-century).
    The theme is a variation on a common Medieval motif, the "pastourelle", in which a knight seduces a shepherdess in a garden. Here the noble lady tries and fails to seduce a shepherd. Thus the original versions had a resonance now largely lost, playing on the expectations aroused by a genre the audience already knew. This could well have been treated humorously as a result. Without this implicit

comparison, the ballad seems slightly untypical now, in that the man is not only unwilling but even angry.

2. There is no ambiguity in her invitation. In ballads the "vergel" is the scene for love-making.

7-8. Gentil: not a compliment but a statement of fact, she is a noble; so there is no contradiction between the words and the anger.

11. Pastorcico: the diminutive is a sign of affection, not of youth (the shepherd has a family).

13. Siesta-time is a normal time to rest, and typical in the pastourelle.

15. Posada: "posarse" is to lie down.

17-24. The invitation strikes the narrator as a bit suspicious; we should see him partly as a practical soul too wary to get involved with an apparent neurotic, but also as a low-class individual insufficiently refined to appreciate what he is being offered. His reasons for refusing are, of course, practical rather than moral.

21. Sierra: the text has "cierra", but in this case I have emended it for clarity´s sake.

25. The use of "pastorcillo" here sounds patronizing.

31. Her skin is as white as paper (cp. Blanca Niña, no.1); but not the modern shiny whiteness of photocopy paper. Paper then was pale but still brownish.

33. The medieval taste was for firmness rather than size, so the diminutive in "teticas" is not inconsistent with the fantasy ideal we are being presented with.

35-36. Garça: "heron". Her neck is like a heron´s in delicacy rather than length. Esparver: "sparrow-hawk". Her eyes are like a hawk´s in brightness rather than in fierceness. The point of the images, which were hackneyed rather than original at the time, is immediately clear in the Spanish, but might not be so in English; hence the translation has lost the bird comparisons, for the sake of avoiding unwanted implications.

40. The man continues to refuse and has the last word. This might imply that he was right to do so; perhaps the noble lady is supernatural, or the lure for a trap ...

13. THE WHITE-FOOTED DEER

At first sight this ballad seems to be structurally as incoherent as
Rico Franco, no.4; the King at the start is equally unidentified,
there are unexplained references, and we are not told what happens at
the end. This is, however, adapted from near the start of a much
longer tale which we know in full from its survival in France (cp. the
study by Entwistle); and on the assumption that the audience know the
whole tale - Lancelot succeeds in the quest -, this ballad works well.

1. Despite the mention of Lancelot, this king is not to be taken as
King Arthur but as some unspecified King of some unspecified land. The
use of "haber", rather than "tener", for "have", was normal.

5-6. The transformation of humans into animals is not common in
Spanish tales, but this one comes from France, where it seems to
happen all the time.

6. Can: now usually a hunting-dog, but once a normal word for any
dog.

8. Passó ..: this might merely mean he crossed the sea (to Morocco,
the home of the "moros").

9. The connection between the rest of the ballad and the first eight
lines is never made clear. Presumably the stag of 5 is the same as the
white-footed one that turns up later; yet this is surprising to the
literary historian, since the white-footed stag is not usually thought
to be a transformed Prince.

10. The assonance changes here (from -á to -á-o), which supports a
suspicion that the first eight lines have been printed in the wrong
ballad.
      This is Lancelot´s usual occupation at this stage of his legend;
as another ballad puts it at the start (S57, Ml48): "Nunca fuera
caballero / de damas tan bien servido / como fuera Lanzarote .."
("Never was a knight so well looked after by women as was Lancelot
..").

18. Aquel: "that", implying that we all know which one she means. In
the French tale, the knight who captures the deer´s foot will thereby
win the Queen´s hand (the Queen not being Guinevere); the speaker
here, however, is not royal.

23. Ya ..: indicating a change of scene, as in Conde Claros (no. 9).

25. He takes hounds, because that is the way to catch deer.

27.   Hermita: not necessarily a "cave", just somewhere barren in the middle of nowhere. Hermits were common only before the sixth century; subsequently, holy men tended to band together in monasteries. But the type survived in literature for centuries after they were rare in practice. They were thus a useful standby for plots set in the wilds (cp. no. 30 here).

29.   As usual, the text has no inverted commas or other indication of speech, so it is not clear who is speaking here. Smith takes this line to come from Lancelot, and I have deferred to his judgement; but it might seem more natural for all of 29-32 to be the hermit´s.

35.   Esse: cp. "aquel" (18), everyone knows it.

44.   The cubs aren´t in the Spanish, where "parida" means "having recently given birth" (as in no. 11). In the French legend, the lions are the stag´s bodyguard.

47.   The hermit switches here from "vos" to "tú", as he changes from giving news to offering personal advice.

48.   Do quier: modern "dondequiera". "Fuer(e)" is a future subjunctive.

50-54.   It is unclear whether these four lines are part of the hermit´s remark or a cry from the narrator; it may be more likely that the narrator rather than the hermit knows about Quintañona (as she is usually called). In the Arthurian tradition she is Queen Guinevere´s maid, usually on Lancelot´s side. Within this ballad the implication is that Quintañones is the girl of line 11, who sent Lancelot off on his wild deer chase, but in the longer tale she is not. The ballad stops here, before the long story has really got under way, and the result seems now rather peculiar (to those who do not know the full tale).

14. ROSA FRESCA

This ballad is extremely vague in its reference. We have no idea now of how this scene arose nor of what happened next; it is as if we had ballad no. 10 on Conde Claros and no more. Probably, once upon a time, a further context was known to the audience. If so, the reason why this scene survived the loss of the longer tale lies in the recognition of the emotions involved.

1. As with other names, it is not clear whether her name is Rosa
Fresca, Rosa, or something else with "rosa fresca" being a
description. Either way, she is young and attractive.

2. Garrida: there were two words "garrida" in Old Spanish, meaning
"pretty" and "silly". The inconvenience of the potential confusion is
probably what led to the loss of both words.

5. "Now that I am prepared to love you properly"; naturally, the
audience reaction is to wonder what he has learnt in the meanwhile.

7-8. "Your" and "mine" carry stress.

13, and 19-20. León is "over there" ("allá"); nor are we in
Castille (19), which suggests that the tale is set in Aragón;
probably no further East, or the text would be likely to be in
Catalan.

19-22. It isn´t his being in León that upset her (in 13) but his
being married; the man can deny the whole story because of the
inaccuracy of this detail, but his evasion of the question of his
marriage is equivalent here to an admission that he has indeed got a
wife and family. The immorality of adultery is not considered very
relevant in ballads (see the first two here), but this deviousness
probably leaves the audience on Rosa´s side, even though it is normal
for us to assume that the character we first meet is the one we are
meant to identify with.

15. THE PRINCESS AND GALVÁN

1. Buena: in the context of a ballad Princess, as we have often
seen, to be good implies to be prepared to let her love life be
arranged by her parents for political motives; and as usual, our
sympathies in these circumstances are meant to be with the girl. This
plot is more far-fetched than that of the Claros ballad (no. 9), so I
have only chosen to include a short episode concentrating on one of
the emotional highlights of the longer tale. (In an even more
improbable scene, M160, Galván is arrested while smuggling out a
newborn baby; but there is, as often, a happy ending with the marriage
of the lovers.)

4. Parido: three children had actually been born, apparently with only her maid knowing about it.

9. She: i.e., the maid (was angry). "Enojo", "pique" is often postulated, and rarely explained (e.g. at the start of no.13), to aid the plot.

14. Castigar: "warn", rather than "punish".

15. Still: i.e., now.

16. A Queen needs legitimate children to be the heirs; illegitimate children cause problems. The present Queen may, in addition, be feeling that her daughter should not be allowed to avoid making patriotic sacrifices she had made herself. Castilla: the setting has been transposed, since this is another tale that came from France and was originally set there.

18. The word "mal" suggests that this is probably a curse ("may you be struck by lightning") rather than a threat to burn her at the stake; but in view of the King´s threat at the end of no.9, it is possible that the latter is indeed intended.

20. "As the day I was born". This is, of course, a lie, but rather than be offended by her mendacity we are expected to be full of admiration for her inventiveness (if she is never to have a husband, her condition may never be discovered).

24. "Servir", the common euphemism, can be used of a woman making love to a man as well as the other way around.

The translation has been given the same assonance throughout, to see if that sounds as acceptable in English as it does in Spanish. That decision is a question of taste, but it may be that the assonance pattern is already sounding obtrusive after only 24 lines.

16. DOÑA ALDA

1. Alda: this is a Hispanization of the French "Aude".

2. The ultimate origin of this tale is in the French <u>Chanson de Roland</u>. Roland is the leader of the rearguard of Charlemagne´s army as it retreats through the pass of Roncesvalles from a campaign in Spain (for further explanation, see no.31); the audience for the ballad might not know all the details of the <u>Chanson</u>, but they are likely to know that Roland died. We can thus be sure from the start that there is to be an unhappy ending, and the tension of the ballad is heightened by the dramatic irony, giving the formulaic 300 maids of 3-8 a poignancy they do not have elsewhere when they are merely a cliché to indicate great wealth.
Esposa: it becomes clear later (48) that she is not yet his wife.

5-6. The maids wear uniform, as if they too, like Roland, were in an army.

7-8. These two verses refer to the same thing, with the difference in tenses purely arising for metrical reasons.

9-10. Sino: "except". What Alda is an exception to is ambiguous: she may be in different clothes eating an individual meal, but the English has chosen to understand it to mean that she is not eating at all (which seems most likely in view of "acompañar", 4). If so, it adds to the sense of foreboding.

12. Cendal: a fine gauze or silk.

13-16. It would make better sense in English if there were only three maids, only one of which was playing music. In Spanish noone in the audience will be disconcerted by the hundreds (the number 300 is a cliché), but in English the performer will have to be quite skilful to prevent the audience wondering how a whole vast orchestra of a hundred players could possibly lull her to sleep.

17. If dreams are mentioned, it is usually to indicate some kind of parallel between the content of the dream and real life; but the parallel may be in the emotions aroused rather than the practical details. There is no contradiction between Alda´s being scared stiff by the dream, knowing it needs explanation, and not knowing what that explanation is.

32.   An "azor" is probably a goshawk, which is - despite some
uncertainty among recent critics - smaller than an eagle (even a
little one, "aguililla"). The problem is, what do the two birds
represent? Animal life, in dream and fable, tends to represent human
attributes in general (as in no.8), but in this case the hawk goes
where only Roland has any right to go, under her dress, so both the
audience and Alda´s maid can interpret the hawk as representing
Roland.

37.   El aguililla: the eagle is the subject of this sentence. (Much
confusion has been caused by the misprint as "al" in Smith´s edition.)
Alda proves unable to save him from the eagle.

42.   The old maid has the wisdom to understand it, but also the
kindness to offer her a more optimistic interpretation in the hope
that her understanding might be wrong. The audience appreciate this
attempt at a brave face, but nobody is meant to be convinced by it.

46.   The Pyrenees are not, of course, over the sea from Paris; this
detail comes in as a reminiscence of tales of other anti-Moslem
crusades, in the Holy Land, which is often described simply as being
"over the sea".

47.   This is a desperate remedy; Alda can hardly be the eagle when
she´s already in the dream as herself, and whatever the eagle
represents is tearing her husband to pieces.

49.   Equating the wilderness with the Church is hardly convincing
either; as before, this is intended to seem improbable.

51-52.   Alda is not taken in, but is touched by her maid´s
considerateness.

53-58.   The tension has been made so great that the horror at the news
is none the less for being at second hand and presented through the
grief of a surviving relative; this is a technique that preserves the
strength of the distress without giving us crude details of the gore.
The eagle represents not the human enemy (Moslem or Basque) but the
aggressiveness of war.

58.   The English translation is unable to capture one detail of the
Spanish, the use here of the word "caza", "hunt". Hunting involved
falconry, in which goshawks were used (and eagles were not); this is
the connection between the symbolism of the dream and the event.
      In some versions, Alda here dies of shock.

17. ROSA FLORIDA

1. The jingle of the first line is intentional, a variant of the several first lines that contain a name repeated (e.g. no.8)

2. There are the ruins of a castle near Montiel, on the River Guadiana, said to be Rocafrida; with a spring nearby said to be Fonte Frida (cp. no.8); and a cave nearby said to be Don Quixote´s "Cueva de Montesinos". All the tales are fiction, of course, but the setting and its name are old and deeply rooted in the traditions.

2-3. The text printed says "Rocha" twice, but this is presumably a variant of "Roca", "Rock".

3-4. The Spanish literally means "They call the castle ´Roca´ and they call the spring ´Frida´". Unfortunately, it is impossible to say the latter line in English without bursting into laughter, so the translation has rephrased it. Their names are only intended to indicate their most obvious quality anyway.

6-10. This provides a magic setting, and it is not at all clear why, since the rest seems rather basic in comparison. It also indicates her wealth, which is relevant, since she can afford to turn down the ten noble suitors of 13-14.

12. She is a flowering rose, "Rosa Florida" (two words in the texts), in the bloom of youth. "Florida" is stressed on the "i". (The south-eastern section of what is now the United States was known to the original Spanish explorers as "La Florida", "The Flourishing (Province)"; modern Florida is only a small part of that.)

13-14. These rejected suitors are another cliché of the genre, available for establishing a girl´s desirability. It is inappropriate to argue that there are unlikely to be three Dukes of Lombardy at once, since the phrase is taken for its indication of this desirability without the audience necessarily even noticing its literal meaning.

16. There is stress on the English "be".

17. Montesinos is a Spanish name, but a French Count whose name is often used in these tales.

18. Medieval love tales quite often hinge on one person´s obsession for someone they have never met. In real life Princesses would often be betrothed to foreigners they had never met, but this was a dynastic convenience that rarely connected with the individual passions of the participants.

21. This what a "camarero" literally is: someone who serves in the "cámara".

23-24. This pair of phrases recur in several ballads. "Aqueste" and the less common "aquese" have fallen out of use since, unlike "aquel" and their Catalan cognates.

25-26. The Spanish phrase is very colloquial here, so the English is appropriate.

27. She is denying the illness, rather than the love.

29 and 31. Past subjunctives being used as imperatives; in 33 the metre permits a present imperative ("di").

30. Bien guarnida: "well endowed by Fortune", another set phrase of no obvious relevance used merely to fill the line.

32. Cosa: here used of a beloved person. "Prenda" was also so used in no.11; neither seems to have sounded odd, but we can hardly translate as "thing".

36. It might appear presumptuous and arrogant for her to make this claim (how could she know?); but this is not our intended reaction. Rather than a remark of Rosa´s this is a comment by the narrator, to tell the audience in an aside what a good deal Montesinos is being offered.

37-38. In variants of this tale (and in the ultimate French source) this reference to her sister is rather less enigmatic than it seems here. "Sea" is a third-person imperative, as in a curse.

42. This ballad more than most requires some thought from the performer; depending on his tone Rosa Florida could either be made to seem mad or admirable for her determination. There is something a bit unconvincing about this text anyway, for at least five and probably seven of the lines only have seven syllables, two have nine and one has ten (17).

18. MELISENDA

This ballad is well known to critics now, but is only preserved in a
"pliego suelto", and then only to precede the "Glosa" made on it (by
Francisco de Lora: for Glosas, see the comment on no.6).

4.   The start of this tale is similar to that of Conde Claros (no.9)
with the roles reversed. The King is here an Emperor. It is thought
that the ultimate French origin of this tale is the same as that of
Rosa Florida (no.17), although here the lovers have met before and are
in the same place.

9-10.   I.e. these are flimsy night-clothes only.

17.   She is asking for advice from those who know about it from
experience, rather than just heard tales.

25-26.   Old women (apart from girls´ mothers) are always presented as
being in favour of acting on desire.

33.   Naturally, there are royal bodyguards on sentry duty. Fernandillo
is the same person as is later called Hernando.

37-39.   Mal: "illness". Irrational love was often seen as a mental
illness by doctors, but more kindly by singers.

41-46.   Her explanation is transparently ridiculous and not meant to
be thought to be able to fool Hernando. "Letrán" is the Lateran, the
Basilica in Rome where Papal Councils are held; which sounds
impressive, since a vow made there can hardly be ignored later, but it
can hardly explain why she is half-naked and on her way to the spare
bedrooms.

50.   Her impatience is so great that she changes tack and resorts to
violent deceit.

51-54.   This is a better excuse than was given to Rico Franco (no.4),
although she is not in fact dressed for the street either. But the
victim here, unlike the unmistakeably evil Franco, is a poor sentry
just doing his job; and even so, the audience ought to have been swung
onto her side, into seeing her deceit and even his murder as to be
applauded. Our sympathy for her feelings are supposed to override any
distaste at her actions (murder, lies, deceit, taking religion in
vain), so the performer needs to be more than usually skilled at
playing on an audience´s emotional response here.

63-64. A modern audience might feel that the revelation that she can
cast spells detracts from the sympathy for ordinary human weakness
that has kept our attention so far; even in the ballads, occasional
resource to supernatural abilities on the part of women does not
usually get attributed to sympathetic characters (Gallarda, in no.26;
even Mariana, no.7, is a bit frightening).

67-70. Every noble has enemies; that is a fact of life.

71. Like Mariana, Melisenda is "discreta", but not in the least
"discreet"; she can think on her feet of practical ruses.

76. I.e., from over the sea ("moros" are from Morocco).

77. He recognizes her and responds favourably; cp. Clara, near the
start of the Conde Claros ballad (no.9); and, as her many maids in
that ballad, his soldiers are not there in the plot once the lovers
have met.

81-82. They go to make love in the generically appropriate place, the
garden, where the laurel has a shadow even at night. The formula is
more important than the logic, of course.

19. THE PRINCESS IN THE TREE

This ballad is often called "Romance de la Infantina", the diminutive
expressing desirability rather than size.

9. Her hair has not been cut for seven years (cp. the prisoner in
no.5).

16. Such supernatural intervention in human affairs is common further
North, but unusual in the Spanish tradition.

24. Alone: i.e. only.

25. This situation is more disconcerting than most, and the knight
can be forgiven his hesitation (although Rogers, aware that most men
in the genre are ever-eager, finds it incomprehensible). A similar
unwillingness to risk a possible trap in no.12 is, after all, seen as
sensible. But the moral of this tale is the opposite to that of no.12:
"do not hesitate". For unfortunately, despite what she said in line
20, she can´t wait to find a man (or men), and whereas the shepherd in
no.12 was stolid and not fully appreciative of what he was turning
down, this knight realizes only too well.

28.   This line (in the Spanish) is an exceptional example of how clumsy use of traditional line-fillers can make a character´s speech sound ridiculous. (All the line needs is something meaning "from my mother".)

35.   As usual in the genre, old women advise direct action in love when the young are not so sure. This may conceivably be connected with the fact that the ballads are often sung - indeed, nowadays, almost exclusively sung - by old women, probably regretting and romanticizing their own lost opportunities when young.

38.   The Spanish says "he could not find the hill" that she was on. This is quite intelligible, if the whole place was under a spell; but modern editors have tended to prefer "no la hallara en la montiña", "he did not find her on the hill". The English is indeterminate.

40.   Caballería: this can be a collective noun for "caballeros" (as e.g. "morería" for "moros").

41.   This is a ten-syllabled line; either the result of clumsy performing or inappropriate editing (both of which are equally plausible). Ten-syllabled lines are found in modern versions, but usually only if there is a group of unstressed syllables at the start which can be treated as initial grace notes in the music. A modern performer could omit "desque".

45-46.   This is a rare case of a ballad finishing with an explicit moral.

49-50.   He isn´t actually proposing to do this to himself; Islamic justice was not approved of. The function of these lines is to show the strength of his self-annoyance.

20. ARNALDOS

The function of literary criticism is that of illuminating the texts; rarely can a simple text have been so confused by the critics as this ballad of Prince or Count Arnaldos. There is even confusion over the attestation of the text printed above. In the sixteenth-century corpus a version of this ballad ends at what is here line 20, and another at what is here line 26; since the sailor´s song in the latter version is not rendered verbatim, but is on the other hand said to be magical, this variant acquired great critical acclaim for its enigmatic and mysterious atmosphere (since the plot, participants and atmosphere are not made clear by that point, and the good fortune mentioned at the start is not yet specified). Then Ramón Menéndez Pidal, the deservedly) most respected of all Spanish medievalists, delivered a lecture in Oxford in 1922, subsequently printed, in which he implied that the above text had been recently discovered in Morocco (Poesía popular y poesía tradicional en la Literatura Española, Oxford U.P., 1922). He gave no further reference there to his text, and when the lecture was reprinted in his Los romances de América (Buenos Aires, 1939) he gave a reference to his own "Catálogo del romancero judío-español", no.143 (in Cultura Española, 5, 1907, 198-99); which is not this text at all, although it does continue beyond this line 26. (He can hardly be blamed for misremembering, given his circumstances in 1939). We can be sure that the dénouement is accurate in essentials, for Bénichou subsequently found a similar version in Morocco (in 1946), but not in detail, since Menéndez Pidal liked, in the best editorial and juglaresque tradition, to adapt the sources to suit his purpose; he often did this in his Flor Nueva, as in our ballad no.6. Accordingly, since it seems quite likely that both longer and shorter versions have always been available, for the performer to choose the length required for any audience and circumstance, the sense of enigmatic mystery beloved of critics for the last 150 years was created by their own ignorance of the dénouement, an ignorance which earlier audiences and contemporary Moroccan sephardim do not share; yet modern critics still tend to prefer, and even sometimes only to print, the short version. (These questions are discussed with admirable sanity in Caravaca´s study). Obviously, any work of literature will seem enigmatic and mysterious if only the first half is printed as if it were the whole story. Menéndez Pidal preferred the short version, inspiring Spitzer to start a long critical polemic´ by saying he preferred the long one. We do not presume to arbitrate, but it seems only sensible to print the long one, and if performers want to stop at line 20 or line 26 (or anywhere else) they are naturally at liberty to do so.

This is in fact a standard tale, the one about a lost or enchanted Prince(ss), as in both the previous and the subsequent ballad in the present collection.

1. Ventura: "good fortune", rather than "adventure". The nature of the fortune is only clear in the long version; he was captured and about to be enslaved when his captors realize he is the lost Prince they have been looking for. In the shorter version, it seems just to be his luck at hearing a soothing piece of music, which is hardly as striking.

2. Sobre: again, he is only "on" the sea in the long version, but as Foster rightly observes, "sobre la mar" can occasionally mean "at the sea-side". La mar: actual sailors tend to use the feminine for "mar".

3.   Infante: i.e. Prince.

4.   St John (the Baptist´s) day is June 24th, Midsummer´s Day, and a traditional time from pre-Christian ages for magical and mysterious events; or, indeed, significant events of any type (cp. no.60).

5.   As usual, a huntsman finds the unexpected. Here he is on the shore, or, at least, in sight of the sea.

7.   A "galera" has both sails and oarsmen; the oarsmen were usually enslaved prisoners of war. This detail is crucial later, and it could be that many in the audience would be aware that galley-masters were always liable to press-gang the unwary into service and realize that the song is a kind of bait. If so, the words "ventura" and "galera" give contradictory hints as to the dénouement, which the audience will be interested to see resolved.

8.   Alta mar: i.e. from out to sea, rather than coming along the coast.

9-10.   These improbable details indicate wealth (like the gold, silver and sapphire of Rosa Florida in no.17, or the servants of Alda in no.16, and elsewhere) and are not expected to be taken literally. Critics often have, though. Everyone knows that medieval tales are liable to mix the literal and symbolic-supernatural, and the audience was sophisticated enough to understand what was literal and what was not; but in this case critics have tended to lose hold of what they know.

12.   Cantar: a song of any length. In modern usage "cantar" tends to be used only for huge epics, but the eight-line verse sung here was a "cantar" too.

13-20.   The most famous short variant includes no words for the song, but states that it calmed the seas and the winds, and attracted the fish and the birds to come and hear it: "que la mar hacía en calma / los vientos hace amainar, / los peces que andan al hondo / arriba los hace andar, / las aves que andan volando / en el mástil las hace posar." This was the effect of the music rather than the words, and, indeed, in the long version also it can only be the music that has the magnetic effect on Arnaldos, for the words are unexceptional. He is ensnared by a kind of reverse-siren technique. (Smith implies that the longer versions also include the details of the magic song´s effects on nature, but this seems not to be accurate.)

16.   Fortuna: at sea, these are storms. There is no thematic connection between this and the "ventura" of line 1.

17. A Moroccan would be more likely than a Castilian to use this phrase, which, although plural, may be meant to refer to the Bay of Biscay.

19. Fustas: literally "whips". This might be intended literally, since galley-masters whipped their slaves to action.

27. Here starts the section unknown to critics till this century. The 'navío" is the galley, and the "barca" the rowing-boat being sent to capture the willing victim as a galley-slave.

31. I.e., the noise made by the ship going through the water.

34-35. Spitzer thought there was a gap of seven years between lines 34 and 35, and Smith agreed with him. This seems to me very improbable. The point of the ballad is that his captors discover that they have found the object of their search - this is his "ventura", otherwise he would have been enslaved. The seven years mentioned in 41-42 are from an earlier time, as Arnaldos explains to them and to us why he was on a Spanish shore in the first place. Sailors rescuing a Prince lost at sea are a standard plot mechanism, also exploited in the next ballad here (no.21). (Besides, if the Prince had not already been lost for some time, the expedition would not have been organized in the first place.)

35. The hammer that clamps the irons on him, as he is to be taken to the galleys, not only wakes him up: it may be implied that it has the effect of reminding him who he' is, as if the seven-year absence had also been a loss of memory - or, indeed, an enchantment, as with the 'Infantina", the Princess of no.19.

39-40. The English here is clumsy, unfortunately. This is a rare occasion when the short line chosen is hard to reconcile with all the information included in the Spanish. There should be stress on 'French" and "grand" in 39.

45. Nuestro: this identifies his captors and explains why they are there in the first place. No mystery is intended in this ballad - at least, no bewilderment as to the plot - and the "ventura" of the start is neatly explained at the end as a remarkable and fortunate coincidence. Without such coincidences, there would be few tales to tell.

50. There have also been proposed religious and erotic interpretations of this tale. The religious is unlikely; a few nineteenth-century versions are indeed Christian in attitude, but the religiosity there is explicit, and lacking from the more ancient tradition, which is that attested in Morocco, since the singers there

are Sephardic Jews. The erotic is possible, because Juan Rodríguez
del Padrón, whose three poems in "romance" form are probably the
earliest ones we know of (mid-15th century), composed a variant in
which the song explicitly attracts Arnaldos to his lost lover (that
being his "ventura"); yet, as with religion, if a ballad is about sex
it usually says so, and it is very much simpler to assume Rodríguez
to have been using the common and admired technique of reinterpreting
an old theme in a new way. This poor ballad really does deserve to be
left alone to mean what it says.

It is to be hoped that the Johnsonian view of the criticism of
this ballad taken here is not seen as dismissive of the ballad itself;
this is an excellent ballad, for reasons quite different from those
usually attributed to it, with attractive structure, neatness, drama,
emotion, plot, character and direct use of language.

As an experiment, the translation (of this one only) has been
devised without any full rhyme at all.

21. ESPINELO

This ballad was used by Catalán as his sample ballad for critical
commentary.

1. Espinelo: he is named after a plant, which is a mystery that his
girl and the audience want resolved through the narrative.

3-10. The details of his luxury may here be meant literally: he turns
out to be a Sultan, although this too waits to be revealed.

8. Literally, the sheets are invisible in water.

11. Mataleona: the stresses are on the first "a" and the "o". This is
a vaguely oriental-sounding name, which could mean "lion-killer"; she
has similarly exotic peacock-feathers, but no further role in the
plot.

14. I.e. she uses the feathers as a fan.

18. ¡Cómo nasciste en buen día!: this is a cliché, implying "how
successful your life has been!", often used in the epic Poema de Mío
Cid. The cliché is here exploited for constructive effect, however,
for despite the routine flattery of the good omens mentioned in 19-22
(with their astrological hint of the exotic East) it turns out that
his birth was about as inauspicious as possible.

19-23. This is a "captatio benevolentiae", a device to win the
addressee´s goodwill before making a request.

25.   Catalán makes two assumptions here, both plausible but neither
necessary: that Espinelo is actually on his death-bed, and that this
is the first time he has ever told anyone of his origins.

27.   This is the flashback technique: to start at the end of the story
and then explain how that position was reached. This device is
surprisingly capable of producing suspense in an audience even though
the eventual outcome is known.

30.   So this is yet another "lost royal heir" story. Catalán points
out that many of the modern versions have Espinelo's speech in an
"-ó-a" assonance, which in his view is embryonically visible here,
suggesting that Timoneda has drastically rewritten his source to a
different assonance. This is not really very likely, if only because
some modern versions also have the same assonance as this.

36-38.   Part of the point of the tale is to show the falsity of the
belief that the production of twins is a consequence of a woman having
had two lovers. 36 and 37 are two methods of judicial execution, the
latter probably implying being thrown off a high cliff, as in the
Classical tradition.

41-42.   It is not clear from the text whether the Queen had in fact
been adulterous, or whether her despair lies in the assumption that
people would wrongly think she had.

44.   Loca fantasía; the implication of this remark is unclear; maybe
it is merely thought mad to ask a captive Moor for advice, maybe the
Queen is being driven mad, or maybe the decree itself is being
described as mad.

45.   The Moorish girl, presumably a political prisoner, connects with
the Eastern astrological theme announced earlier. The Spanish Moslems
were experts in astrology, that is, the art of interpreting human
nature and the future from the stars; thus her advice is not only a
womanly wile, but assumed to be based on her ability to see what is
going to happen in the long run. Nor is she bound by the same laws and
social mores as the Queen, so feminine solidarity will keep her as a
silent ally.

51.   The trick, as in many tales (Snow White, etc), is to send away
the unwanted child while keeping a chance of its survival.

52.   Ambiguous, in Spanish as in English: either "the son you prefer"
or "the one you would prefer to lose".

53.   This almost meets the requirements of 37, that the offender
should be thrown in the sea ...

55.   Embetumada (sic):   covered in tar ("betún"), to make it waterproof.

57.   Porque: with subjunctive, "so that ..". The jewels are to pay whoever finds him for his upbringing.

59.   Me: stressed in the English, as "mí" is in Spanish.

60.   I.e., out in the open sea, away from her subjects´ eyes.

65.   In this ballad we can see how he knows where his name comes from, but we do not know how he knows of the circumstances of his birth. In modern versions he often tells this tale back in his original kingdom, whereupon the King, who is either his father or twin brother, recognizes the jewels, realizes who he is and all is forgiven in a happy ending. Here we have to take the truth of his account on trust.

67.   Por esso: "that´s why".

73.   This adoption was indeed fortunate; Mataleona was right to assume good fortune came in somewhere.

74.   The questions at the start are answered; how he achieved his name and how he achieved his royal status. Thus the ballad exploits the flashback mechanism to achieve a neat and artistic structure.

22. THE HUSBAND'S RETURN (1)

Menéndez y Pelayo´s comments on the early variants of this are a bit confusing; this text has come from the "pliego suelto" of Juan de Ribera, as reprinted in 1821 by Boehl von Faber. The plot is a common one; a husband, returning from a long absence, tests whether his return is welcome before revealing who he is (the "Yellow Ribbon" theme).

1.   Lejas: that is, "lejanas".

8.   In Spanish this theme is known as "las señas del esposo". Knights in armour were often unrecognizable, so in war they would carry some identifying mark ("seña") on their armour or weapons.

11.   The "tablas reales" were a variant of draughts played using dice.

16.   In fact, the inside of the cloak, rather than the vest.

17.   Cabe: "near".

24. Valencia, in the Catalan part of Aragón, had close links with Italy (cp. the comments on no.4), and a different culture from Castille. The cosmopolitanism of which Catalans are proud seems a bit outlandish to the Castilians, including the wife here.

33. You: to be stressed. I.e., your husband had a lover, so why not you?

36. The wife is of the same type as the turtledove in Fonte Frida (no.8), the faithful widow.

40. She could not become a nun because she is not in fact a widow. This comment prepares her for the final revelation; indeed, if the performer is skilful, the ending could be as much of a coup de theâtre for the audience as it is for the wife, since this tale plays on the audience´s previous experience of tales of both faithful widows and adulterous wives.

This poem is almost in rhyme, if we admit the colloquial [s] at the end of "ajedrez" (12); then the first three and the last five couplets end in "-éis", with only the semivocalic [j] sound distinguishing that ending from the "-és" at the end of the intervening thirteen.

23. THE HUSBAND'S RETURN (2)

This is the same theme as the previous ballad, in a version first recorded towards the end of the last century. The wife here is the first person protagonist, which makes the happy ending more personal, and is appropriate for the fact that more recently attested ballads are usually found in the mouths of women.

4. The Sierra Morena is the large and sparsely populated hilly area that separates Andalucía from New Castille; although this ballad was collected in Asturias, it is probably set to the south of this Sierra, where it descends quite abruptly.

5. En: the original version prints "n´".

11. Entrugar: an Asturian word for "ask" (Menéndez Pidal suggests that it descends from Latin INTERROGARE, which is plausible).

14-15. As usual, seven years is a phrase used for "quite a long time".

16. Why has he sent no message? This detail increases the value of her faithfulness, but makes the man seem insincere. (Maybe a man would omit this detail in performance.)

19.   She said earlier (5-6) that he seemed like her husband from the armour and the horse; with these on, he cannot be fully recognized, even with the visor up to talk.

22.   Perhaps we are to think that she had made the horse's coverlet herself; she is capable of it (see line 1).

28.   A cliché in both the Spanish and the English.

30.   Prieto is still a normal word for "black" in America.

31.   In the previous version she mentions no children, rejects advances and aims for the convent; here she has three sons, has not been propositioned, and aims for military revenge; in other versions she has three daughters. The details of the tale can be manipulated by the female performer (probably subconsciously) to suit the kind of woman she has in mind, or wishes to seem like as she sings.

38.   Acordoje is not standard Spanish: I have taken it to be either a variant or a misprint of "acongoje".

24. VIRGIL AND THE VIRGIN

This ballad collates several readily available motifs, including the forgotten prisoner (as no.5), the overeager court lover (as no.9), the seven-year absence (as no.23) and the nature of the happy ending (as no.18).

1.   Yes, Virgil, and the name really does ultimately connect with the great Roman poet. He was sometimes seen as a Christian prophet, and was chosen by Dante to be his guide in Purgatory; but until the general rediscovery of his poetry (in the early fifteenth century) he was in the general imagination the star of improbable tales centring on his lustfulness. In Juan Ruiz's fourteenth-century Libro de Buen Amor (261-68), for example, he represents the dangers of lust, in a tale which ends with him hanging helpless in a basket on a rope outside the walls of his lover's house. Here he is transferred, as seems to be the fate of so many love-ballad protagonists, to the generalized King's Court.

4.   Surprisingly, Isabel is not made the Princess; perhaps because, unlike Claros, this really is a case of rape, and the pardon will seem less believable if the King is the father of a rape victim.

10. The phrase would normally be "él le vino a las mientes", and the grammar has become somewhat convoluted by the need to juggle the "él" to the assonance position at the end. The singer´s art consists largely of such juggling.

21-22. The Queen is afraid that he might forget or change his mind.

24. Es: now this would have to be "está", but "ser" had once many of the functions now exclusive to "estar".

27. Rogers´s suggestion that combing hair is a powerful symbol of sexual interest in a woman may also apply here; that Virgil has not forgotten his old habits. But it may not. Supposed symbols that can just as easily be taken as circumstantial details cannot be proven to have a further point.

30. Encanecer: become "cano", "white", only used of hair.

33-34. The King stops Virgil complaining, on the grounds that he was sentenced to ten years as it was. Virgil catches the implication, and is quick to affirm that he was not complaining at all.

33-43. There is a succession of couplets in alternate mouths here, with no narrative at all between the speakers; the performer will have to act skilfully to stop the audience getting confused.

46-50. It is not clear whether we are supposed to think it was not rape anyway (as with Conde Claros, no.9), or that the experience had left even so a memory of pleasure she wished to repeat. Either way, the garden, now a marriage-bed, represents doing in an acceptable context what was previously a "traición", a deed of treachery, so the structure of the ballad has been neatly rounded off.

25. THE SPECTRE

This ballad is a variant on the "husband´s return" theme, with the husband in the first person returning to find that his wife has died. It was printed in no early collection, nor does it seem to be widespread now; Menéndez y Pelayo was the first to print it, having been given it by the folklorist F. Rodríguez Marín. That version is in a peculiar (and inconsistent) spelling apparently intended to be phonetic, but which is unhelpful enough for me to have regularized it except where the text offers some real difference from standard Spanish (as e.g. "pa" for "para", line 33).

1. The speaker is some unspecified person met as the husband returns

home. (S)he addresses him as "usted", since this is a
nineteenth-century version.

7.   The word "señas" has dropped from Spanish by this time,
"señales" being used instead here.

14.   That is, "more noble than me".

17.   Here is the first indication that this is first-person narrative,
introduced at the same time as the supernatural element; a combination
that suddenly makes the tale twice as personally involving for the
audience.

21.   Ghosts are rare in Spanish tales. This one is even friendly. Her
first imperative uses "usted" ("siéntese"), but when she identifies
herself and starts talking intimately she switches to a consistent use
of "tú".

25.   The absurdity of Rodríguez´s transcription is well exemplified
by his spelling "abrasaban" (which would normally mean "singed"),
merely because his informant pronounced [s].

26-28.   The popular imagination tends to see death in terms of such
images, with none of the Christian redeeming features.

26. GALLARDA

Here as elsewhere the attractive girl summons the knight; he agrees
and this time finds himself in mortal danger. However, unlike Alonso
(no.7) but like Rico Franco´s victim (no.4), he escapes through the
thematic device of killing his attacker with her own dagger. Juan
Menéndez Pidal´s transcription is admirable, but I have taken the
liberty of spelling the protagonist as Gallarda rather than Gayarda;
it makes no difference to the pronunciation, and her name is probably
one of those intended to indicate her main quality ("gallarda",
"spirited")

2.   Florida: this is like Mariana´s seat (in no.7), which was also the
prelude to near-supernatural aggression. There are several
similarities between these two ballads.

8.   The knight hesitates (as did the shepherd in no.12 and the
huntsman in no.19); and we can now see why hesitation might be wise.

10. There is great scope for the performer here, as in the last ballad, when the frightening detail suddenly intervenes into the initially low-key text.

18. Like Mariana, Gallarda uses her garden, the usual place for love, to aid her own perversion of love. "Montisa" is not a standard Spanish word, and the knight´s reply suggests that this might be a misprint for "montiña".

21. Si sabes: probably "if you know what they really are", rather than "if you know how to speak politely". Cortesía: she is complaining at his swearing, "diantre".

25-27. He has more sense than Alonso, who drank Mariana´s potion (no.7) - but then, he´s seen the heads.

38. Gallarda, like Rico Franco (no.4), is stabbed to death with her/his own dagger, as one of her/his former victims has his death avenged by his son/daughter. There are two other "Gayarda" ballads in Menéndez Pidal´s collection, in which they go to bed, she puts her dagger under the sheet, and he takes it while they make love, without her realizing.

39. Portera: female, the concierge.

42. Por mi vida; more than a mere formula, she would really be risking her life.

49-50. There is stress on "in" and "out". This exclamation at the end is similar to that at the end of the Lancelot ballad (no.13), except that here the story is now over.

51. Dirme: i.e. "irme". Él: i.e. "you".

27. KING RODRIGO AND LA CAVA

This ballad shows the rape. A shorter version was much commoner, but this one seems better in that it gives La Cava a character of her own. It only survives in the now rare Barcelona Silva; Díaz Roig states that it is in the 1550 Zaragoza Silva, but it is not.

2. Descubierto: not "discovered", but "revealed" to La Cava.

3. Julián had a daughter at Rodrigo´s Court, but she could not have been called La Cava, which is apparently in origin an Arabic word for "whore". The ballad-singers cannot have known that, though, for it is essential to the plot that she is neither Arabic nor in any way to blame for what happened.

7. White skin, as usual, is a symptom of nobility as well as
desirability.

13. She is "discreta" in that she fears a trap; such directness in
ballads can be a trap, though it is usually in that case coming from
the woman. It need not be a trap, of course, and what we have here is
essentially the start of "Gerineldos" (no.3) with the roles reversed.
This is one of several details in this ballad which connect with the
general traditions but in an unusual, and at times perverted, manner,
to indicate that she is indeed an unwilling victim. For very few girls
in the ballads are actually unwilling to make love; even Isabel, the
victim of Virgil (no.24), married him cheerfully in the end.

20. Siesta: this is the afternoon.

23. Muy descuidada: she is not at all "discreta" here.

25-32. It is true that the ballads of these cycles depend for total
comprehension on a knowledge of the longer tale, but the focus of the
ballad's attention and the audience's interest is still going to lie
in the human emotions strongly felt by the individual participants, in
these ballads as in any others. So they can be successful even if the
audience know nothing of the longer tale. Indeed, a modern knowledge
of the actual history sometimes seems to lead critics to an irrelevant
irritation at historical inaccuracy, and occasionally to the attitude
that the more accurate history makes for a better ballad. This is not
the case. Literature has its own standards of plot, theme, logic,
intelligibility and structure, of a neatness that never occurs in real
life (and any history book that deals in plots, trends and themes is
misrepresenting the inconsequential and chance nature of real life in
order to attain literary values).

33-36. Since it is almost unknown in the ballad tradition for the
woman actually to dislike making love, a ballad audience used to
sexually aware heroines will indeed be shocked by what has happened to
her, for having their expectations of the genre denied as much as for
Rodrigo's behaviour itself. Nor is it set in a garden. Here also is a
rare case of the audience's sympathy not being with the one who feels
the sexual obsession, and whose emotions we are introduced to first; we
are usually meant to identify and sympathise with the infatuated, and
see those who frustrate the obsession as opponents (most dramatically
in the Melisenda ballad, no.18). Elsewhere, of course, the feelings
turn out to be mutual, if only because whenever possible ballads about
love like a happy ending. Here, on the other hand, the function of the
tale is precisely to lead up to a previously known unhappy ending
instead, the invasion.

35-36. She is wondering which is more "discreto" in her plight, since both revealing and concealing her rape might be very dangerous.

39. Her friend; i.e., a girl friend.

44. Engañado: her friend complains that although they are friends, La Cava has not explained why she is upset. La Cava here is presented as unequivocally deserving of sympathy; other, shorter, ballads omit this scene and call her "malvada" ("evil") or "maldita" ("cursed") for having told her father (as an echo of other well-known tales in which a man is indeed falsely and maliciously accused of rape).

55. Her father: that is, Count Julián.

60. A "doncel" is a young man, older than a page.

61. Tarifa is the southernmost point of the Iberian Peninsula, so this is not a long journey.

70. This is not a case of a "mysterious" ending, since the end of the tale, the successful invasion, is known to be what it all leads to.

28. JULIÁN IN CEUTA

1. The Moslem Conquest of North Africa had proceeded largely by a process of conditional surrenders and treaties rather than war. Howell's study has established that Julián was a Visigoth who ruled a mainly Berber area including Tangier, Ceuta, and on the Northern shore of the Straits, Algeciras; he owned the only four merchant ships to carry trade over the Straits, so that when he and the Moslems made an agreement in 709 that they could hire his ships, the sight of them would be in no way suspicious. This agreement preceded the presence of his daughter at the Court in Toledo (from 710), so cannot have been caused by any mistreatment of her there; but in any case, as Howell points out, if Julián expected the Moslems to think a rape was worth taking military action against, he would have found them merely laughing in response.
    Ceuta is still Spanish, and still a garrison town.

3. Aliende (allende): "over there", as this ballad is seen from Spain.

5. I.e., the Count checked it.

6. Messengers are killed by the recipient in the tradition if they

bring bad news, rather than by the sender; Foster suggests that this murder is to preserve secrecy. The action also characterises Julián as ruthless.

13.   I.e., if the King of the Moors gave help to the Count.

15.   At this point the ballad changes in character from a simple narrative to a more complicated lament. It may be that a later writer has lengthened a brief pre-existing ballad. The eulogy of Spain´s virtues (15-22) was no more than the truth; Visigothic Spain had been the most civilised part of the world in the preceding century. But the memory grew out of proportion into a myth of a golden age, and the Northern Christians (particularly in León) liked to think of themselves as "Goths" and the rightful rulers of the whole peninsula. It becomes clear from the comments of lines 27 ("hoy", "today") and 50 that the later sections of the ballad come from a time when Moslems were still powerful in the peninsula; that is, long before the 1550 date of this collection, and quite possibly from the thirteenth century or earlier, although not necessarily in exactly this wording.
      The lament has its ironic side, though; Moslem Spain was also a shining civilization, the outstanding civilisation of Western Europe in the tenth century.

22.   Proeza, borrowed, like English "prowess", from the French in (probably) the twelfth century, is a chivalric term, appropriate to the time of performance rather than the time set. This is not at all surprising, since the Late Middle Ages saw previous times much as if they were like their own.

23-24.   Julián is a traitor to his country, but also a traitor to his religion. Here his desire for revenge is not approved of; it is still seen as the reason, but not as a justifiable excuse. Indeed, the implication of 47-48 is that one measly deflowered virgin was hardly worth bothering about.

28.   Nuestra; "we" are to blame, i.e. the performer (and audience, if this was ever performed like this) are to identify with all Christians, of whatever time.

29-30.   This comment only strictly applies before the eleventh century, and there is no reason not to suppose the thought dates from as early as that. The Christian area of the North-West was largely dominated by the kingdom known as the Asturias until 914, and as León after the capital was moved to the city of León then. These Asturians were proud of being Asturians, but later ballads, the surviving versions of which more often tend to come from Castille than León, do not share this view; indeed, in the very Castilian "Santa Gadea" ballad (no.48) Asturians are regarded as the lowest class of all people. Asturiás is very "brava", mountainous and rough, but the implication of line 30 seems to apply to the people as "brava" rather than to the land.

31. Triste: "sad", but also "causing sadness".

34. Campal: that is, a pitched battle between whole armies on a battlefield, "campo".

37. There is little shame in losing to superior numbers ... but how can an invading force outnumber the local inhabitants without gross mismanagement from the latter? (This is not the sort of thought that is meant to occur to an audience or reader, but the use of the phrase shows how an established cliché can be used regardless of implications that would be awkward if it were all to be taken literally.)

42. "Orpas" is a civil opponent of Rodrigo, whose reality is now lost in the mists. It is thought that there was a civil war going on in the Peninsula at the time of the invasion anyway, mainly with the armies being away in the North-East. This may be true.

47-48. This is unintentionally ironic. The popular imagination seems only able to comprehend such enormous geopolitical events by personalizing them into the emotions and experiences of individuals involved (this is still true), and has thus reinterpreted this invasion as a tale of personal emotion; but the creator of this later part of the ballad assumes that the personal tale is true, and criticises Julián for thinking his own personal affairs warranted such a catastrophic course of action. This gives an almost academic air to the final comment. Yet it must come from a time when there was still a strong Moslem presence in the peninsula, so "academic" is meant to imply "intellectual" but certainly not "irrelevant".

48-50-52. These lines in the English rhyme in effect; Spanish [a] is very similar to English [ʌ] as in "cover". So the similarity between "Cava", "recover" and "discover" is a mild joke in the English.

29. RODRIGO'S RETREAT

There has not survived a ballad on the actual battle; the emotional response of the defeated Rodrigo appeared more gripping.

1. Huestes: from Latin HOSTES, "enemies", but the word had come to mean any army, hostile or not.

2. Desmayaban: literally, "were fainting".

3. Some national pride is saved by the device of having resistance for seven battles first.

6. Real: this is a noun meaning "(royal) camp".

7. Desventurado: "ill-fated", a theme expanded later in 51-56.

7-20. Many of the couplets in this section are structures based on the technique of saying the same thing twice running in different words.

16. Velle: i.e., "verle", "to see him". We are being presented with a visual, almost cinematographic, picture of the defeated King.

17. Tinto: this word now normally means "red", of wine, but in origin meant "tinged". Here it is both at once, "stained red".

19-20. This probably means that the jewels that were once in his armour have been knocked out, leaving just their hollow settings behind.

21-22. Another visual image; the sword is like a saw because the number of blows it has given and taken on its blade makes it seem serrated. "Sierra" originally meant saw, with the meaning "mountain range" coming from the same visual imagery applied to a row of mountain peaks seen in the distance.

25-26. Rodrigo has lost the battle and can now be presented for the audience's pity; here he is not a villain but a sympathetic character. Indeed, this ballad does not mention La Cava, and it is legitimate to wonder if it may descend from a tradition of the story into which the rape had not been inserted at all. (The existence of competing versions of legends is quite likely).

27-40. The visual technique continues, but becomes more personally involving; having seen the picture that Rodrigo presents to an onlooker, we are now taken behind his eyes to see what he sees himself.

29. We see this from ("dende", that is, "desde") above. Such a panoramic picture of a battlefield is rarely available to the

combatants, so this is probably meant to be taken as the first time that Rodrigo fully realises how catastrophic is his defeat.

31-32.   The standards and banners carried by his troops are potent symbols of who they are and what they represent; their abandonment in the mud represents the loss of his kingdom, civilisation and religion rather than being mere local colour.

38.   Both the Spanish and the English have in this line, unusually, four full word stresses. This makes the line longer to say, and the slowness could be seen as representing his horror at the sight.

40.   This is a kind of stage direction to the audience as to how they should react; with pity.

43-48.   These are famous lines. The parallel structure technique of lines 7-20 recurs, but here the two halves of a couplet are in strong contrast. Such concision of presentation is direct and dramatic. The non-literalness of the tenses is striking here; present and past are specifically being contrasted, yet for reasons of metre and assonance lines 46 and 48, referring to the present, include an imperfect (technically past) tense form.

49.   He hasn´t even got the smallest bit of any fort, a turret.

51-54.   He suggests that this ill fortune was pre-established by the stars he was born under, a standard idea in astrology and also in ballads (cp. Espinelo, no.21). This works well, picking up the word "desventurado" of line 7, but jars sharply with the theme of the other Rodrigo ballads; there he is punished for sins committed through his free will, but if the stars are to blame then he is not. So it may be that we are supposed to see Rodrigo here as deluding himself in a vain attempt to excuse his sin. But it seems preferable to ignore the other ballads, and assume that though they may all perhaps have been connected at some time, they are separate works in the sixteenth century (and probably much earlier also), so that a ballad-singer can insert stock idioms and themes from the common arsenal of such resources where it fits a particular presentation of part of the story regardless of the implications for the collective theme. Whether anyone believed then that their future could be affected by their birth sign is hard to say; but some people seem to take this idea seriously even now, when it is known to be nonsense, so at least a fair number of an audience might well be moved to sympathy by this exclamation rather than to scepticism or derision.

55.   Había: "I was bound to" lose it, because of my stars at birth.

56.   En un día: "in one day". This may be to be taken literally, in view of the "ayer", "yesterday", of lines 43, 45 and 47.

57-60. His men have died, and he sees it as an extra punishment for
him to have to live on. Ironically, "mezquino", "poor", is an Arabic
word (borrowed after the Conquest), whose use here shows how the
Arabic invasion indeed changed Spanish culture ...

30. RODRIGO'S PENANCE

The style and tone of this ballad - complex grammar and religious
presentation - mark this as not a "popular" composition. This does not
mean it is unsatisfactory, and indeed it was "popular" in the sense of
being well-liked, appearing in four separate printed early versions.
Its more "erudite" approach has led me to put all the translation in
the past, in an equivalent attempt to increase the narrative aspect at
the expense of the dramatic.

1-2. This opening immediately sets the scene; there is only one King
Rodrigo.

4. He has no horse here. He is specifically on foot (as in line 45).

6-7. I.e., the most impenetrable mountains, where the Moors would
find it hardest to follow. This seems successful in that pursuers are
not mentioned again; the interest is not in war but in Rodrigo, and in
particular in whether he will make it to heaven. "Porque" with the
subjunctive (modern "para que") means "in order that".

9. If Kings are to receive deflating news it tends to be shepherds
who give it; cp. ballads no.11 and 55. This is a reasonable plot
device; apart from hermits and outlaws, only shepherds were likely to
be found in the vast unpopulated areas of Mediaeval Spain, since they
would go out for months on end with their flocks into these wild and
unowned territories.

18-22. Truly oral ballads tend not to have indirect speech like this
but offer everything in direct speech, for the performer to act
(drama) rather than report (narrative); cp. here lines 56, 83-84 and
99-100. The words of Rodrigo, however, being the focus of interest,
are always presented directly.

19-20. Desierto: this word meant originally "uninhabited" (as in a
desert island) rather than "desert". This is not a desert, since it
supports sheep. An "ermita" is where a hermit lives; not necessarily a
"cave", as in the English, but usually. This word was derived off
Latin EREMUS, which gives Spanish "yermo", "barren land", so the
hermitage, unlike the shepherd, is by definition usually in

semi-desert. This is part of the point of being a hermit, to live in barren places far from human society and thus, so it was assumed, be closer to God. (There is no connection at all between La Cava and a cave, Spanish "caverna").

24. Rodrigo´s wounds are not mentioned, but the episode is easier to follow if we assume that he is suffering serious wounds and likely to die anyway. This explains his urgency to find somewhere to do the right penance and thus be absolved of his sin before he dies; for if he does not, he will not go to heaven.

28-29. The author explains carefully that the shepherd usually only had bread in his knapsack, but today happened ("a caso") to be a meat day. The purpose of this detail is unclear.

31. The browner the bread, the rougher the corn used, so the less it was supposed to suit refined taste.

36. Manjares: fine foods, including white bread. A farinaceous equivalent of the "ayer/hoy" theme of the previous ballad.

41-42. These are jewels he had on (the chain probably around his neck). His armour had lost its jewelry in the previous ballad, but we may not be expected to know that here. They will be no good to him now, so this donation symbolises the way his priorities have changed from material to spiritual. This religious attitude is quite unlike the ethos of the traditional ballad (which regards sexual satisfaction as more important than, and even as excusing abuse of, religion, as in no.18), but it makes for good literature even so.

48. If the English seems convoluted, the Spanish is even more so, as well as being deliberately archaizing.

49. He gives thanks that he has found a place in which to expiate his sin. La Cava is not explicitly mentioned in this ballad, but her rape is in the background all the time (unlike in the last ballad), and it becomes clear later that we are all supposed to know exactly what sin he has on his mind.

63. Literally, "don´t be upset".

70. The translation is not quite accurate; the immediate need is for pardon rather than grace.

74. Convenía: not exactly "convenient", but "appropriate". The hermit is not seeking for the most unpleasant punishment, but for the one that can take him towards heaven rather than hell.

75-76. God sent a message; hermits could receive such visions, so this is not meant to sound as odd as it does to a modern ear.

82. The hermit is a kindly soul, pleased not at the pain Rodrigo will suffer but at the way God has granted him a manner of penance and absolution. That is why the King is also delighted (in 85).

92. The hermit is trying to sound encouraging.

100. I.e., the King is afraid that the snake will not bite him, rather than that it will; if the snake does not, then the appropriate penance has not been done.

107. The King is "good" now that he has been saved.

109-12. If we did not before see why the snake was chosen (being similar to his sexual organ), we do now. Such prurient bad taste often accompanies in literature a disapproving attitude to sex; in contrast, the many ballads that celebrate and hinge on sex do so unambiguously but usually in good taste. It is this part of him (rather than his stars) that has in this ballad caused the loss of Spain, so for it to suffer the final penance provides poetic justice.

115-16. These two lines are rather unfortunate, and it is easy to see why Timoneda omitted them in his version. It is, of course, the point of the whole ballad that Rodrigo leaves this life in the direction of heaven rather than hell; but all men and women should expect a long time in Purgatory before they get there. Only saints go straight to heaven without spending time purging their sins first, yet the last line seems to imply that Rodrigo is a saint. This is absurd. The crux of the ballad is that it was touch and go whether he was even to be heading that way at all, and that if he was eventually to creep through the Pearly Gates it was a sign of God´s infinite capacity to forgive. Perhaps this is just a case of a ballad cliché subsequently turning up and overriding the original perspective.

  The nineteenth-century Belgian writer Leclercq composed a delightful variant of this episode, in which at the end the hermit turns out to be Julián in disguise, rubbing his hands at the revenge he has taken and the pain he has given Rodrigo.

31. THE FLIGHT OF MARSÍN

  This ballad recounts the battle and the flight of the Moslem commander. It only survives in a "pliego suelto", but a shorter ballad corresponding closely to lines 67 onwards (S42, M183) is known elsewhere. It seems quite possible that the editor of this "pliego"

amalgamated more than one preexisting ballad (to fit neatly onto the
two sides of one page), or even perhaps composed some of it himself.
The assonance changes after line 6, but returns to its original
pattern after line 35; 1-6 plus 35-66 make sense as a ballad on their
own; so, perhaps, do 7-30, though these may represent only a part of
some other version. This suggestion seems to be marginally more
tenable than the opposite hypothesis, that the short ballad is a
fragment of the long.

1-2. These two lines set the scene unambiguously.

6. Baldwin and Reynard are two of the twelve chief knights; cp. the
end of Conde Claros (no.9), where Claros is said to be Reynard´s son.

13. Roland is the leader of the rearguard, some way behind the main
army which has gone on ahead to the top of the pass unaware of what
has happened behind; the only communication, to ask for
reinforcements, is on a large mountain-horn. One long note would be
understood as a cry for help.

16. Puertos: the pass. Roncesvalles itself is on the southern side,
with the watershed being the border between Spain (Navarra) and
France.

18. It is seen as a weakness to have to ask for help. This view is
absurd, but the performer and audience need to share it to follow the
arguments here and in 25-30.

23. Battles were often seen in personal terms as the success or
failure of the leader rather than of the whole army, as if they were
single combats.

31. Reynard is not going to be the weak one either.

35. The French nationalism survives even in the Spanish version; not
all Spaniards could stomach this (see the note to no.33).

46. Pan: i.e. the fields of wheat. This picks up the dismissive
phrase of line 42.

49-50. Roncesvalles, in the English as well as the Spanish, is four
syllables. Fleeing that way will merely lead the Moslems to the main
French army, so that will not help them.

51-52. Perro: rather than a term of abuse, this is almost a statement
of fact, a technical term for "someone of another religion". His
actions were preordained by his stars - even those who were sceptical
of the Moslem science of astrology were sometimes prepared to admit

that maybe it was valid for Moslems themselves - so the tone of line
52 is as of another statement of fact.

53. Nykl established that this is Arabic "Al-qāri´a", a much-used
introductory exclamation literally referring to the Day of Judgement.
This seems right, but it shows a surprisingly accurate knowledge of
Islam; particularly when we compare it to the grotesquely ignorant
distortion of Islamic practice that turns up later (87-90). This
discrepancy could be used as an argument in favour of the view that
this text has amalgamated separate ballads.

54. Sí: i.e., "así", often used at the start of a curse, with the
verb in the subjunctive. Here, literally, "May rabies kill you!". It
cannot be "si", "if", for "si" never takes the present subjunctive.

58, 60, 62. These three lines end in an "-are" form, which seems to
be an archaizing infinitive rather than the future subjunctive. This
is probably an attempt to reproduce the "Mozarabic" Spanish spoken in
Moslem Spain, since this infinitive ending fell out from Castille by
the twelfth century, and five previous line-ending infinitives are
unaffected. The ballad as a whole, including this speech, is not
noticeably archaizing in language (e.g. "ayáys" rather than "ayades"
and "vosotros" rather than "vos" in 61).

58. Soldada: the pay given to a professional soldier, "soldado", who
has a wage rather than being a conscript.

66. Stress on "they", as the swaying back and forth continues.

67. Turpin was the archetypal crusading Archbishop of the Church
Militant of the Age of the Crusades. In the eleventh and twelfth
centuries there really were such people who saw slaughter as their
Christian duty.

73. Ya; the next scene begins, as in 43.

78. Marsín is a fictional figure, not even appearing in the French
Chanson. The defeat is presented to the audience in terms of its
effect on the survivors; here the defeated commander, Rodrigo in
ballad no.29, in no.16 the future wife of the dead Roland, in no.32
the father of one of the dead warriors. This again shows good taste
(cp. the comments on the end of the previous ballad), if the audience
can be made to experience the starkness of the emotions without the
gore (missing in the common version of this ballad that starts at
approximately line 67).

79-80. I.e., he had a horse, but chose the zebra instead (to
characterise him as weirdly oriental). It is hard to believe that

Moslems actually had zebras on Spanish battlefields, so Smith concluded that it can only have been an onager (a wild ass); but this is fiction, after all, and "zebra" does mean "zebra".

87-90.   Islam specifically forbids the making of representative idols, and usually even of representative pictures (which is why Mosques have intricate geometrical ornamentation, rather than pictures). The French (and English) knew nothing about Moslems (or "Saracens"), but it is so surprising to find this ignorance in Spain that it may be reasonable to suggest that this ballad must have been performed only in Northern Spain, away from the frontier. Further south they knew better (see nos. 59-71).

91-98.   This seems to mean literally that of an army of 105,000 he is the only survivor; but as usual, high numbers are not to be taken literally. Rodrigo, too, was the sole survivor.

95.   Mataleona: this is the name of the Sultan´s lover in no.21, apparently being a name available in the genre for any Oriental woman. ("Matar", "kill" is in origin Arabic, as "mate" in chess).

103.   Encantado: "heaven´s assistance" seems to have been with Roland, inspiring Marsín to consider becoming a Christian. Both sides tended to assume that their God was on their side as they committed mass murder on the infidel (the Crusades´ apparent legitimization of bigotry and homicide makes them a low spot in European culture; the Spaniards themselves, on both sides, were more tolerant than most).

109-14.   Marsín gets near delirious, but then has a lucid moment. Structurally, this neatly brings in Roland and Turpin at the end, and the swaying allegiances in Marsín´s mind match the sway of the earlier battle.

32. THE DEAD KNIGHT'S FATHER

After a battle, each side is usually allowed to return and collect their dead.

.   The "matanza" (dead bodies) are not identified till here; the audience is inspired to a universal sympathy for a bereaved father before the individual context is clear.

-16.   This is a flashback explaining his presence; the survivors draw lots to see who has to look for Beltrán. A variant ballad explains that they did not realise he was missing until they got to the border.

3.   He puts the reins back on his horse.

16. Xaral (jaral): the bush, off the beaten track, where nothing can be found at night.

17-18. Where a meadow ended and a sandbank began.

28. Prisoners were often ransomed; he´s literally worth his weight in gold.

29. Tienes muerto: probably not "if you have killed him", but "if you have his dead body".

31. If he´s dead, then a large ransom cannot be expected.

34. Señas; his individual recognition signs (see nos 22 and 23).

39. I.e., when hunting, the hawk scratched him.

41-46. The father´s emotions are the focus, but they are not made explicit here; the audience has been led to identify with him and can feel the appropriate response without prompting.

46. De parte a parte: right through.

33. BERNARDO'S BIRTH

1-2. Alfonso II, "El Casto", was King of Asturias from 792-842, so a suitable King to have this legend of distant times attached to. (The Kingdom changed its name to León after 914). He was known as "The Chaste" because he had no children. Indeed, this was almost the only thing later known about him, so the girl in the tale has to be his sister rather than the usual daughter; apart from that, this is a Princess-and-lover tale like so many others.

4. This Ximena has the same name as the Cid´s wife, but otherwise there is no connection.

6. Saldaña is a castle in the province of Palencia, prominent from the twelfth century (Queen Urraca died there in 1126, Alfonso VII married there in 1128), the time of origin of the legend, but in the time that the ballad is supposed to be set it was not even in Christian hands.

12-16. The plot for several ballads is encapsulated here, but this is at the start of a "cycle", a longer tale whose point comes years later. This ballad only occurs in the 1550 Romancero and is untypically perfunctory, with no direct speech and omitting all the interesting details, so it may have been composed then, as a preamble for the next one, which immediately follows it in that collection.

34. BERNARDO AT COURT

1-4. This identifies the time, place and story for us. Bernardo is now an adolescent. The "l" in "Bernaldo" is not a misprint; Spanish words that once had two "r" sounds in close proximity have often changed the second to an "l" (as in "árbol", once ARBOREM); but in proper names the changed form tends not to become the standard one.

5. Prisoners were cut off, and it would indeed be possible for Bernardo not to know (cp nos 5 and 24), even though the Count has been there for several years.

6. Gelo: this is the Old Spanish form of what would now be "se lo" (not reflexive, but instead of *"le lo").

8. Defendía: "forbid", i.e. the opposite of "defend".

10. His kinsmen: i.e. the Count´s family, not the King´s.

11-13. Velázquez means "son of Velasco", and Vasco is a western form of Velasco, so these two might be meant to be father and son.

15. They want Bernardo to know, but have been forbidden to tell.

16. Poridad: "secret", though this word does not turn up in the English till the replay in 23.

17. Fijas dalgo: the word "hidalgo" ("high noble") was originally "hijo de algo", "son of something"; "fijas dalgo" is the feminine. The women seem not included in the ban on telling Bernardo. There is probably the further implication that they are noble enough for Bernardo to think he can believe them.

19. It is optional whether or not to include a "de" before a Spanish surname, so the English translation has not cheated by inserting one. Lines 16-22 are exceptionally clumsy in the Spanish (even more than the translation).

33. The "you" is to be stressed.

37. Supo: "found out".

43-48. He wears black as if in mourning for his father´s suffering, but the King misinterprets his appearing in this way ("assí") as wearing the black of the executioner.

47-74. The direct speech in this ballad provides a wide range of emotions for the performer to simulate in the characters and to arouse in the audience; the guilty conscience of 47-48, the entreaty of 51-55, the anger of 58-64, the humility of 67-74.

67-70. The King is all-powerful, but God and Mary are even more so.

73-74. Bernardo is confirming that he is loyal to the King whatever the decision is about his own father. This humility suits the tone of this ballad, but is hardly consistent with his insubordination in the ballads set later in the cycle.

75. Con: "despite".

77. Bernardo, like Gerineldos and others, has the status of adopted son.

35. BERNARDO'S CHALLENGE

1-2. Bernardo is now older, and installed in the mountain fort of El Carpio. There is a hill called Carpio Bernardo about 25 kilometres upstream of Salamanca by the river Tormes; the story is that Alfonso had allowed him to live there.

7. Burgos is not, in fact, on the Arlanza but the Arlanzón; it is the capital of Castille, whereas Alfonso is King of León; but the audience will not mind about these details.

12. This line is most unclear in the Spanish, but the presence of a heron ("garza") ensures that there is some reference being made to hunting.

14-16. In his armour he is not personally recognizable, but his bearing is such that he must be a fine warrior; this implies that Bernardo is already known to be such. It is improbable that a Granadan champion would be so far north, but such details are not the concern of this ballad (and Granada fits the assonance).

20. I.e., his intentions are not peaceable.

32. Literally, they lie through their beard.

33-36. The story is very unconvincing; if this were true, surely they would have said so before. Yet we are not supposed to deduce that Bernardo has just made this up. Such secret marriages were legal before the twelfth century, and a common plot device for long after, but royal marriages normally required the assent (or at least the knowledge) of the King.

37. Yerros: that is, "hierros", "irons".

38. Illicitly pregnant women were often sent to nuns, as a punishment but also as protection. The nuns saw it as social work ("charity").

40. Alfonso, being "El Casto", has no direct heirs, and if Bernardo were legitimate he would inherit the Kingdom. (In real life, Alfonso was succeeded by his second cousin Ramiro I, 842-50). There was a myth, believed by the French (still, in some cases), that Alfonso II had sworn allegiance to Charlemagne. He had not; indeed they hardly had any relations at all, and Charlemagne is not even mentioned in any Leonese history until the twelfth century. Bernardo is the representative of the Spanish reaction to this claim. Thus his anti-French sentiments here are a national crusade rather than a mere family vendetta.

44. La Montaña: Santander.

45. Zaragoza was a kingdom in Moslem Spain, and had indeed inspired the whole Roncesvalles expedition. The Spanish are expected to feel more akin to Moslem Spaniards than to Christian French.

51. República: for the good of us all; this word has probably been inserted by Timoneda here.

53-54. This is the opposite of what the King said in the previous ballad (61-64), where he promised that he would never release the Count. But the desired emotions are best aroused here if he has made the opposite promise, so as usual the internal requirements of the individual ballad are taken as overriding the cohesion of the whole cycle (suggesting that they cannot have been performed in sequence). Here the King has to be morally in the wrong, and this broken promise ensures that he is.

36. BERNARDO'S INHERITANCE

1. This episode follows closely on the previous ballad.

3. Anyone described as "discreto" will be understood by the audience to be the hero; as usual, it means "practical" rather than "discreet".

4. Trayción: treachery, rather than treason (which a King cannot commit). Bernardo has received a letter asking for his presence at court, but fears that it is a trap (the same plot device recurs in the next ballad, attached to El Cid; indeed, the two heroes seem to have been merging into the same type).

7. Messengers who bring unwelcome news can be killed, but the killer is not usually the hero, so Bernardo is given enough sympathy to elude the formula.

10. Razón: a vague word, meaning here "remark".

11-14. His bluntness and rudeness are quite different in style from the Bernardo of ballad no.34.

17. The assonance pattern changes in this couplet, which might suggest that 1-14 were once a separate unit; on the other hand, another version (M13) has the "-á" assonance all the way through, including the meat of 1-14.

25-26. The rebellious vassal tends to be admired (if the King is Spanish). This cheek may explain the popularity of such episodes. It is not, however, "democratic" in spirit, as has been suggested; the feeling is in support of the nobles and their regional interests against the King and his central interests (and the peasants).

25. Mala: the noun is not specified. ("Cosa"? "Respuesta"?)

30. This line in essence repeats line 12 (with no distinction made between "son" and "están" here), which makes for dramatic irony; this is a standard greeting, but the audience know that he despises them.

31. Mal vengades: the opposite of "welcome", "bien vengades", the subjunctive of the verb having imperative function.

33. The King says that Bernardo is just a tenant in the castle, where Bernardo claims he was given it. For present purposes, we have to assume that Bernardo is telling the truth here, and this is another broken promise. (Poor Alfonso II thus has his character traduced in the general memory for the sake of literary structure; he was actually a successful and productive King, only remembered for his ill-treatment of a nephew who did not even exist in reality.)

35. Mentides: "you lie", but it is also the formulaic way of issuing a challenge to the recipient's honour, so the fact that the King eventually backs down is a sign of dishonour as well as weakness. The change from the "vos" form here to the "tú" form in "dizes", in the next line, seems startling, but as usual can only have been done to fit the rhythm - no other point is being made.

40-46. This reference to a battle at "El Encinal" can only be what is referred to in the thirteenth-century chronicles (that first attest the legend) as a battle at Benavente. "El encinal" means "the oak-grove", but it seems easiest to take it as a place-name here.

48 (and 64). Heredad: i.e. not only is it Bernardo´s, it is his to hand on to his family. He is not just a life-peer.

49-50. The release of his father is what he wants and still does not get.

52. The King complains that Bernardo is addressing him as an equal, rather than as a vassal.

54. This is line 18 repeated; the ballad has a rounded structure, as the initial precautions come to fruition at the end.

61. Hombre: medieval "omne", which became "hombre" and was earlier HOMINEM, could be used as was the related French word "on", to mean "people in general", but also as a first person pronoun.

63-64. The King backs down from what he said in 33-34, and accepts Bernardo´s claim in 47-48.

69-70. Bernardo resents being patronised, but even so his reaction is rather silly, refusing after all to accept the castle.

        Bernardo, in the legend as preserved in the thirteenth-century histories, goes on to defeat the French at Roncesvalles. Perhaps because this was less interesting than his birth and inheritance, but probably mainly because the rival version of Roncesvalles as a French victory over Moslems came to be so well known, that final victory, in origin the purpose of inventing the legend at all, fell out of the popular memory.

37. XIMENA'S COMPLAINT

1. King of Castille from 1035 to 1065 was Fernando I, and he is the King in the ballads concerning the Cid´s youth. These ballads cover much of the same ground as part of the long fourteenth-century poem Mocedades de Rodrigo - the two are clearly connected in some way; most critics see the ballads as descending from the epic, but it seems no less likely to have been the other way around.

2. Escobar, who gathered together many of the Cid ballads, chose to print the words at the end of each couplet with an extra "-e". This was merely an affectation. It is true that the general rules of Spanish assonance regard a final unstressed "-e" as optional (e.g.

"va" can be in assonance with "madre"), and that the reason for this
lies in ancient history, before the twelfth century, when many of the
words that now end in a consonant indeed had an extra final "-e". That
is the case with all infinitives, so that "fablare" (line 8) is an
archaic form of "hablar". But this delight in archaizing has led to
such absurdities as "alláe" (48), which never existed.

3. Ximena: Rodrigo´s wife in real life was a cousin of the King´s
called Ximena, but they married in 1074, and may not have met before
that year (which is long after this ballad is set), and the whole
story of their original meeting, as elaborated here, is fiction.

4. The plot hitherto (which is omitted from this selection) has been
that Rodrigo killed Ximena´s father Lozano because of a feud between
the two families; we are meant to think that his murder was
justifiable.

9-10. Ximena and her mother are dishonoured because they are unable
to take due vengeance on her father´s killer, and she is asking the
King to do his duty by them. Rodrigo is not mentioned by name till
line 31, but all the original audience would know this story well, and
understand the references.

13-22. Rodrigo´s behaviour, here and elsewhere, seems extraordinarily
unbecoming to a national hero (as well as quite unlike his character
in the long epic). The point is that, being the national hero, he has
an uncritical audience wholly on his side anyway, who will rejoice at
the way he makes everyone else seem small in comparison. For
Castilians are not only proud, they are proud of being proud (which is
why other Spaniards tend to find them irritating).

23-28. This general comment serves to point a contrast between the
self-confidence of Rodrigo and the vacillation of the King.

30. Começare: probably a misprint for "começara".

31-36. The King is here thinking to himself, not talking to Ximena.
He knows that it is his duty to arrest a murderer, but he also knows
that Rodrigo has many admirers at Court who would be annoyed.
Rodrigo´s great asset, and the source of his contemporary admiration,
was his skill as a soldier.

31. Cid: the Arabic for "Lord", a title apparently bestowed on
Rodrigo by his Moslem subjects in Valencia - i.e., after 1094, so its
use here is anachronistic.

32. Escobar´s antiquarianism has got out of control here. He means
"se revolverán", the old form of which is "revolverse (h)an", but

that was never written as a single word, and the "(h)an" never had a final "-e" after the "n" (it was originally HABENT). The result is therefore inauthentic.

35-36.   This is a way of de facto arresting him without actually issuing a warrant.

37.   This does not mean "the words were not said", but "no sooner were the words said than ..."

39-40.   An extreme case of the metrically convenient choice of tenses, since the action referred to with the present tense of "lleva" happens before the action referred to with the pluperfect of "dado había".

42.   Rodrigo cannot understand why his father has opened a letter addressed to him. (His father fears some kind of royal disapproval.) Rodrigo's rudeness to his father is also not expected to cause any surprise or offence among the ballad audience.

46.   "Me" is stressed in the English.

48.   His father is cautious and Rodrigo is brash; we are expected to admire Rodrigo, although his father is clearly acting sensibly. "Allá", "there", is Burgos, and "acá", "here", is Vivar.

53-54.   "You" and "I" are both stressed; "fuerdes" is a future subjunctive, "wherever you go".

38. RODRIGO AND FERNANDO

This ballad follows straight on from the previous one.

1.   Diego Laínez is Rodrigo Díaz's father. This is an age before surnames (which only began to be handed from father to son in the late thirteenth century). Diego's father was called Laín, so he is identified as "son of Laín", that is, "Laínez"; Rodrigo in turn is identified as "son of Diego", that is, "Díaz".

2.   Diego is going to kiss the King's hand, the symbol of vassallage; this motif is eventually to dominate the ballad.

5.   Rodrigo, the proud Castilian; the image of pride and defiance is meant to be admired by the audience, or by a Castilian audience, at least.

7. Cabalgan: this word derives from "caballo", but the verb does not necessarily apply to a horse. The contrast between the workaday mules and the noble horse is picked up again at the very end. The sequence of couplets from here to line 22 explicitly contrasts the civilian dress of the other soldiers with the practical military dress of Rodrigo, to show that Rodrigo fears a trap which the others do not. There is no hint that Fernando actually is planning a trap.

12. Daggers in ballads have golden handles, more often than not. This is a practical weapon, for earlier in the cycle Rodrigo had stabbed Ximena´s father with this very dagger.

13. Sendas: "one each".

17-20. Rodrigo is wearing his ceremonial red headgear, but underneath it is his helmet, in case of trouble (so it is not actually shining at this moment).

30. Laçano: this is presumably a misprint in the Silva, for Ximena´s father is usually called Loçano (Lozano).

31 (and 71). Como: "when", a meaning it no longer has.

38. Defend: that is, in a duel.

42. If Rodrigo is to be punished for his murder of Lozano, it will have to wait until after his death. They react in this way partly because Lozano was unpopular (his death is supposed to have been justifiable) but also because everyone - in the audience as well as in the story - knows that Rodrigo is invincible. So their cowardice looks to the King as though they all support him, and he refrains from taking the matter any further. Even so, such is the power of fiction, Ximena eventually marries him and becomes the loving wife.

43 on. There is a tension here between the general expectation of a ballad audience that a King is to be obeyed and the tradition of the spoilt brat vassal successfully cheeking the Spanish King (which happened in the Bernardo ballads, and also in those, not reproduced here, concerning the tenth-century Count Fernán González of Castille and the King of León).

57. Rodrigo is not a loyal vassal, but he has been endowed with elementary respect for his father (despite his boorishness at the end of the previous ballad). The epic Poema, however, depends crucially on Rodrigo´s unswerving loyalty as vassal (to a different King) even in exile; and how both traditions coexisted in popular memory - if indeed they did - is hard to understand.

62. Beneath: everyone else is on the ground, and Rodrigo is still above them, mounted on his horse.

63-64. As Rodrigo kneels, the dagger with which he killed Lozano slips out of its sheath; it was all ready for action if need be, and the King appreciates that fact at once.

77. Rodrigo is annoyed by his father's subservience; the theme initiated in the second line of the ballad has come to its climax.

83-86. It makes fine literary sense for the soldiers whose clothes were contrasted with Rodrigo's at the start to end the ballad by going back dressed in the practical military attire that Rodrigo has been wearing all along. Presumably they are supposed to have had it with them anyway, but the symbolism has outrun the practicalities; where did these 300 horses spring from? (a question we are not supposed to think of).

These two ballads (37-38) and no.49 (set much later) are connected with the Mocedades de Rodrigo tradition, which essentially presents the hero as a childish boor; and until the last century, that was the dominant image. The restrained and authoritative commander figure that appears in the other ballads here hardly survived in the popular traditions at all.

39. FERNANDO AND THE ARCHBISHOP

1-2. Fernando I of León and Castille died in 1065, dividing his kingdom between his three sons and two daughters; the civil war that this arrangement provoked came to a head at the siege of Zamora in 1072, the central event in the ballad cycle that includes our nos.39-48.

8. There is no firm evidence to suggest that Fernando had an illegitimate son, but if he did he certainly was not Archbishop of Toledo. (I am very grateful to Derek Lomax for his help in unravelling the events of these years.)

11. Toledo had been in Moslem hands since the Moslem Conquest, but it still remained in theory the primatial see of all Spain. Toledo was to be captured 20 years later (1085), and from 1086 the Archbishop was once again an important figure in Leonese-Castilian politics. This whole episode is all the more strange in that this is not an anti-Fernando ballad, probably not an anti-clerical ballad (though Smith disagrees with that view), and the illegitimate Archbishop introduced in such a matter-of-fact way at the start of the cycle has

no further part to play in the story at all. And yet it seems to have been a well-known ballad, notwithstanding the fact that it contradicts the rest of the well-known tale.

12.   Españas: all the separate kingdoms of the Iberian peninsula.

15-16.   It was money that was required to become Pope; this is here a statement of fact, rather than a criticism, although it would be possible for an anti-clerical performer to perform this in an anti-clerical manner.

40. FERNANDO AND URRACA

1.   The scene is still Fernando´s deathbed, but the bastard Primate is absent and his daughter Urraca (who did exist) is here instead, speaking to her father. "Queredes" is a future auxiliary ("you´re about to die"), as it sometimes is in the ballads, but even so the more normal meaning of "want" makes this phrase a bit strange.

2.   San Miguel: The Archangel Michael was the Archangel at the centre of heaven, who in early Christian tradition received the souls of the newly dead (rather than St Peter).

5-6.   Sancho received Castilla, and became King Sancho II.

7.   Alonso (a common form of Alfonso, at least before the twelfth century) received León, and became Alfonso VI.

8.   In fact, García received Galicia, which does not fit the assonance.

10.   Urraca is left literally without a "heredad", a home to hand on to her descendants. In real life there were two daughters, Urraca and Elvira, who seem to have been given some kind of lordship over all or many of the monasteries.

11-18.   Urraca chooses a canny prospective revenge; she has no divisions, but her ability to ruin the family´s good name is a stronger threat. This aspect of her personality, inserted to add interest to an otherwise dull narrative, caught the imagination (returning, for example, at the end of no.42); because she allied later with Alfonso, subsequent Castilian (that is, anti-Alfonso) chroniclers claimed she was Alfonso´s incestuous lover.

15-16.   An interesting distinction. Conflicts between Christian kingdoms at this time (and most other times) were far more bitter than anti-Moslem feeling. Apologies are offered for the Americanism in the English of line 16; it is included as a parallel to 15.

18.   "I will do good for your soul"; this is the same soul that she hoped would be allowed into heaven in line 2, so the implication is probably that she will offer masses on his behalf to speed his passage through Purgatory (as well as that he needs such help as a result of his ill-treatment of her).

19-22.   Urraca achieves her aim; Fernando does not relish this dishonour.

23-25.   In fact, Zamora is not in Castilla la Vieja, but León. At this time it was essentially a frontier town largely inhabited by Christian emigrants from the Moslem South. It seems almost certain that Urraca participated in the rebellion at Zamora, and probable that she had lordship of the town.

27.   The River Duero runs just to the south of it.

31-32.   Fernando´s curse will eventually be seen to apply to Sancho.

34.   This ending is rightly famous, and is the psychological mechanism by which the decisions of 1065 are directly connected (in the literature) to the siege in 1072, since the events of the intervening years form no part of the cycle.

41. URRACA AND RODRIGO

1.   The scene is now inside Zamora in 1072. In the meanwhile, the war has been largely won by the Castilians; Alfonso of León has run away to Toledo, and the only serious resistance to Sancho is coming from Urraca in Zamora. She is the speaker here, in a famous ballad whose circumstances seem to have been immediately identifiable to an audience from the first line.
    Rodrigo is Ruy Díaz (El Cid). What Rodrigo was actually doing in the first thirty-odd years of his life is not at all clear, but it seems certain that he was the Castilian commander at Zamora, and possibly commander-in-chief of all the Castilian forces. Zamora here is on the verge of surrender (and thus Sancho on the verge of becoming ruler of all Fernando´s kingdom); Rodrigo has come to negotiate terms. It would be normal for a besieged commander in a hopeless position to agree to negotiate and thus avoid further bloodshed, and, in view of later events known to have happened, a logical reason has to be found within this ballad for Urraca not doing so. As often, historical events are reinterpreted in terms of emotions understandable within

personal relationships. Both Urraca and Rodrigo are given feelings and remarks that work well within this ballad and explain satisfactorily the outcome of this episode. As a consequence this ballad stands apart from the main cycle, since both characters are seriously inconsistent here with their presentation elsewhere.

3.   This can only be interpreted as a confidential conversation inside the castle, given the nature of the remarks. A ´linking´ section tacked on to the end of the preceding ballad in the 1550 collection has Urraca shouting at Rodrigo off the city walls, but that is probably not meant to be the setting (that interpretation may have been inspired by the reference to the fortifications in line 29).

5-8.   There is no hint elsewhere that Rodrigo was one of the King´s adopted sons common at Court in the general ballad tradition; as we have seen in nos 37 and 38, he grew up at Vivar with his own father. This ballad cliché is inserted to explain how it was that Rodrigo and Urraca could have been lovers, for the aim of this ballad is to present their inability to come to terms with each other as the result of a lovers´ tiff. Santiago is Saint James, the patron saint of the Reconquest, whose body was thought to be at Santiago de Compostela.

13-22.   A typical Princess-and-lover scenario is inserted here. Of course, the audience knew that Rodrigo´s wife was Ximena, so a complaint that Urraca was deserted in Ximena´s favour is logical. Urraca is not making this up; the originator of this ballad was.

14.   My sins did not wish it: that is, as a punishment for my sins I lost you.

17.   The real Ximena was related to the royal family (she was sister of the Count of León), but this suggestion that he was tempted by her wealth does not work as a complaint, since Urraca must have been as rich or richer.

20.   Fueras: "you would have been".

23-24.   Rodrigo interprets her remarks as an offer to be his lover again. His response jars with the main tradition of Rodrigo´s private life, in which he is faithful to Ximena. A divorce, particularly for dynastic reasons, would have been simple to arrange and a satisfactory end to the war, so Rodrigo´s interpretation was plausible.

25-26.   Urraca in turn refuses to accept his offer, exhibiting religious scruples that were absent from her remarks to her father in the last ballad. "Ánimas" are specifically in Purgatory, suffering torments for earthly sins (in this case, adultery).

27.   After line 26, Rodrigo leaves the city, and is here addressing the troops outside that escorted him to the walls. This line is intentionally similar to the first line.

29.   Torre mocha: a flat-topped turret; we visualise Rodrigo pointing up at the city walls.

30-34.   This method of expressing the pain of a lover whose advances have been rejected is a cliché of late fifteenth-century cultured poetry rather than of genuine balladry. The suggestion that has been made, that this refers to Cupid´s dart, the pain being the pain of love rather than of rejection, seems implausibly erudite even so (yet for so many other reasons is this ballad untypical, that perhaps that is indeed meant to be the audience´s interpretation).

42. VELLIDO DOLFOS (1)

1.   Someone is shouting a warning to Sancho as the Castilian King is outside Zamora: the references in lines 1-3 identify this situation. Within this ballad it does not matter who is shouting (in the event the shout´s disembodied nature is rather effective, as we view it from the perspective of the besiegers); within the cycle it is probably Arias Gonzalo, Urraca´s army commander, who is more offended by the treachery than he is relieved by the subsequent ending of the siege.

5-10.   Who these two are and what the four other treacheries consist of is unknown; it seems probable that it was intelligible once.

12.   Sancho certainly died outside Zamora as the result of some kind of trickery; a famous but laconic Latin account of 1074 uses the word "dolose". It may even have been roughly as explained in the next ballad (this one is merely a summary).

12-14.   These are probably meant to be the words of the cry, but a performer could interpret them as a narrator´s remark.

16.   The "postigo", which is still there, is a little gate in the city walls.

19-20.   Urraca is credited with having arranged the assassination of her brother by promising herself to a known criminal as reward. In any event, it is a skilful ploy, because the war as a result comes to an abrupt end; for Alfonso, though having lost the war, now inherits the kingdom automatically.

43. VELLIDO DOLFOS (2)

This ballad explains in detail the treacherous act summarized in the previous ballad.

4.   Gonçalo: Arias Gonzalo, Urraca´s military commander. His sons try to prevent the attack because they are honourable, and they can also see the reprisals ahead.

8.   Part of the treachery is that Sancho already knows and trusts Vellido (cp. line 46).

9-10.   Vellido is pretending to be a deserter, transferring his allegiance in technical terminology.

14-15.   Perhaps the argument is that since Alfonso has surrendered, his ally Urraca ought to have done so too (rather than rebelling); but the sense in which Sancho has been deprived of what is rightly his is still rather forced.

23.   Falso: it´s a real door, but hard to see from the outside when shut.

25.   Leal: This word betrays a Castilian-centred view of the world; Gonzalo´s loyalty is to Urraca, not to Sancho, but one who betrays an opponent in the Castilians´ favour is "loyal" in Castilian eyes here.

26.   Avía: This cannot mean "had", since Vellido must have talked to the King before Gonzalo is able to warn him.

34.   Gonzalo can (rightly) foresee that the whole of Zamora is likely to suffer in the Castilians´ revenge.

37-42.   Vellido claims that Gonzalo is trying to stop Sancho following Vellido´s advice in order to prevent the attack (which he is, although Gonzalo is also trying to save Sancho´s life); and Sancho accepts this, although this acceptance implies an improbable ignorance concerning the internal politics of Zamora.

46.   Criado: the insertion of this detail looks like having recourse to a cliché of the genre in order to fill the space.

49-50.   If the audience had not guessed, these two lines should indicate what Vellido has in mind; not only will he manage to kill Sancho, he will escape.

52.   The grammar of the Spanish is wrongly elaborated here, since Vellido has the "voluntad" (the plan) not the King - yet the meaning is clear.

5-56. Venablo: this is a variant of the common motif of a man being killed with his own weapon. The "venablo" is larger than a dagger but smaller than a lance, suitable for hurling rather than stabbing. Once again the ballad´s love of a common motif has overridden plausibility; if Vellido had gone to such trouble to be alone with Sancho, he would have brought his own weapon.

9-60. He has to stand up to get enough backlift.

9-70. The Castilian King has to die (as a known fact); but why didn´t our hero stop him? The legend solves that by saying he had a very good try, but there was no time to put on his spurs.

3-74. Vellido is on foot; there is a neat structural point here, since we first saw him running from the sons of Arias Gonzalo, and now he is running back from Rodrigo, even faster.

6. Vellido gets through the gate in the walls and locks it behind him.

8. Laín Calvo was Rodrigo´s grandfather (chosen for mention here because of the "-á-o" assonance).

5. Noone dare tell him that he´s dying.

7. The Count of Cabra is old enough not to be shy. "Cabra" is a strange choice of title: Cabra is a town in Andalucía where Rodrigo was involved in a skirmish eight years later, and hence has an aura of Cid-relatedness, but the creators of a Castilian ballad such as this would have known it was not a Northern County.

02. Sancho dies for being too trusting, "confiado", in line 44. This ballad is more self-contained as an episode than several of the cycle, even being able to end with the exemplary type of death.

44. DIEGO ORDÓÑEZ'S CHALLENGE

. The murder of Sancho was dishonourably achieved, so the Castilians feel justified in challenging the honour of Zamora; Diego Ordóñez is a Castilian leader and cousin of the King.

0. The challenge as a whole is formulaically phrased, in what laymen, at least, think of as a legalistic style. "Fementidos": i.e. "fe mentidos", faithless.

7. Fish are an important part of the Spanish diet, but even so this

may sound rather silly to English ears. It is not meant to in the
Spanish, where the inclusiveness shows the depth of the Castilians´
horror.

26: Ganados: that is, the "carnes" of the challenge.

29: Consejo: if a whole town is challenged.

32. There is a genuine difference in national taste here. The English
might prefer the common-sense justice of Gonzalo´s complaint, but the
Castilians see virtue in lumping all the Zamorans in together whether
they deserve it or not, from the purity of their anger.

45. URRACA AND GONZALO

6. The men of Zamora prefer an honourable death to dishonourable
life: the French warriors´ sentiments at Roncesvalles (no.31).

7. San Millán (Emilianus) was a Visigothic hermit who died in 574.
The monastery of San Millán de la Cogolla (in the Rioja) was said to
be on the site of his hermitage. It was an important religious centre
and large landowner in the Middle Ages, although the saint himself was
not much revered elsewhere.

13. At the end of the previous ballad we discovered that there would
have to be five individual duels to protect the city´s collective
honour.

17-18. The emotions brought to the fore here are those of the father
afraid for his sons.

24. If they are in the line of Laín Calvo, they must be cousins of
Rodrigo Díaz (Calvo´s grandson) and thus able to share in his glory,
despite being on the "wrong" side in the war. Rodrigo, however, is not
mentioned in the duel scenes at all.

30-32. The winner of a duel is supposed to have won by the grace of
God and thereby vindicated his own honour and the truth of his claim;
might is right.

37-38. There are hints here of the ballad cycle on the Infantes de
Lara (not included here), in which a father sees the severed heads of
all seven of his sons in sequence.

43. Grevas: "greaves", thigh-armour.

50.   Gonzalo is commander-in-chief, but for single combat the young and agile are more suited.

52.   The war is over, but Urraca is none too sure of keeping any of her estates without Gonzalo´s protection.

57.   Hija: that is, Fernando´s daughter.

60.   Mediano: "average (in size)", not "middle"; he seems to be a fifth son, younger than the others. (In the next ballad the first knight to fight is apparently called Fernando).

69-72.   He rides out through Vellido´s gate onto the flat area outside the city walls.

73.   As in the <u>Poema de Mío Cid</u>, line 3610, the judges arrange in the judicial duels that neither side has the sun in their eyes (this was said to be part of their duty in the ancient Fueros).

74.   We don´t see the actual duel in any ballad; this one presents the preceding emotions, and the next the subsequent ones. As usual, the emotions are the focus of interest, rather than the fighting.

46. FERNANDO ARIAS

1.   Fernando Arias, who seems to have been Arias Gonzalo´s third son but here to have been the first to fight, has lost his duel, and is now being brought back dead to Zamora through Vellido´s gate. The duel scenes are seen from a Zamoran perspective; we see the lament of the surviving relatives of the dead loser (as with Alda and Beltrán´s father, nos 16 and 32) rather than either the death itself or the celebrations of the victors.

2.   Literally, the gate "had never been shut"; presumably, it had stayed open during the duels, for it had certainly been shut in the siege itself. (This ballad has been translated less literally than some others.)

3.   The Spanish here has a first person verb: "I saw ..." ("vi"). "I" turn up nowhere else, but it is not a misprint, being a constant of the variants. This has the effect in performance of the singer introducing his own eyewitness account, which is correspondingly vivid.

14.   The Spanish is even more oddly pedantic than the English; all related, if only in the third or fourth degree.

20. Urraca Hernando: that is, Urraca, King Fernando´s daughter. In the same way, Fernán de Arias has (9) his father´s first name as his own second, which was not the normal practice.

23. King Fernando had made Gonzalo her protector (cp. the previous ballad).

27-30. This sentiment is a common ballad motif, also appearing in the short Conde Claros ballad (no.10). The last two lines are a bit illogical; losing the duel ought to imply that he was in the wrong and the justice of the accusation, rather than that he has vindicated the city. He was, however, fighting with good intentions.

47. SANTA GADEA (1)

1. Alfonso, King of León, had fled to Moslem Toledo, where he was under house arrest.

2. Cuidar: a common word for "think", from COGITARE.

3. Sancho: i.e., Sancho II of Castille, in control of León other than Zamora by 1072.

9. The use of the word "Rey", "King", is enough to show him that something serious has happened; he has inherited the combined kingdom (León-Castille) automatically on Sancho´s death.

19-20. This ballad assumes that Alfonso had not incited the assassination, whereas the better-known ballad on these events (no.48) rather implies that he had.

23-24. If the King of Toledo realized that Alfonso was a King rather than a defeated exile, he might exact some unwelcome bargain as the price of his release; so their exit has to be unobtrusive. "Aquí" is the "alcázar", the fort inside the city, where he is part-prisoner, part-guest.

25. Peranzules: the stress on the "u".

27. Errados: i.e., "herrados", "shod". Reversed horseshoes are to mislead pursuers.

29. The horses are waiting outside the alcázar, but inside the city.

37-38. Rodrigo is in an awkward position. He has to accept that Alfonso is inheriting the Kingdom, but Rodrigo is the leader of the victorious army that has just defeated Alfonso. Both have great cause to be wary of the other, as a result.

43-44. If thirteen separate knights swear innocence, Rodrigo might be prepared to believe in it.

49. Santa Gadea; St Agatha´s church in Burgos.

50. Alfonso is already called "King", but it looks as though he is not crowned until after the oath. It has been suggested that Rodrigo may in fact have had some kind of status as regent in the intervening days, but there is no real proof of this, and it is likely to have been an invention of the subsequent legends.

53. The kind of bolt that is fired by a crossbow. In this ballad the bolt on which he swears is said to have been blessed ("bendito"); in the next it is not.

55. The Leonese faction in general are under suspicion.

60. The oath of non-complicity is fair enough, but it seems a bit unfair to insist that Alfonso ought not to have been pleased at his enemy´s death. The audience know that he was (line 8).

62. The strength of the oath, which is much elaborated in the next ballad, depends on what is to happen to Alfonso if he is lying; his death is to be the most humiliating imaginable, though not necessarily either immediate or painful. To be killed by Asturian peasants is the most dishonourable death that a Castilian could imagine. Alfonso (of León, which includes Oviedo, the capital of Asturias) would hardly feel the same way, however.

63-64. Ella: i.e., the death. "Solar" is a piece of land, the property of an hidalgo.

77-78. This is a threat, which suggests that Rodrigo´s fears are likely to be realized: "you have power over me today ("agora"), but I´ll have it over you tomorrow ("cras")".

80. In real life, Rodrigo seems to have served Alfonso until 1081, when he was exiled; then he hired himself to the kingdom of Zaragoza. So the Cid as mercenary, who turns up here but hardly elsewhere in the legends, is in fact realistic. But the popular motif of a Castilian hero who successfully insults a Leonese King (as in the early Cid ballad no.38, or in the tale of Fernán González, not printed here) is the reason for this attitude.

86. Verná: future of "venir".

90. One of the few things that the legendary tradition knew about Alfonso was his mistrust of Rodrigo; this episode may have been

entirely invented in order to explain it. This is unfortunate for poor Alfonso VI, whose reign was in general energetic, important and successful.

48. SANTA GADEA (2)

1. This well-known ballad covers the same ground as the second half of the previous one.

4. Rey castellano: this phrase is pointed, for the question is whether Alfonso, King of León, is fit to be King of Castille.

6. Buen rey: "good king" is a formulaic expression, but here it is probably meant to sound sarcastic.

8. Ballesta: "crossbow", the fiercest weapon of the time. The tone of the oath in this ballad is less religious and more pugnacious than in the previous one.

9-10. Villanos: the opposite of the people at Court. This ballad gets quite carried away by the details of Alfonso´s prospective punishment, even to the extent of losing touch with the context; the subjunctives of lines 9-30 are all imprecations of what is to happen if (31-34) Alfonso swears falsely. The performer has great scope for hamming the horror of the scene. And yet, despite the humiliation of being murdered by the most unsavoury of Asturian peasants, Alfonso is still not being threatened either with hell or with great pain.

11-28. The contrasts in each half of the couplet are between the civilian and unglamorous nature of the assassins as compared with high nobility; this comparison is implicit in the Spanish, but made explicit in the English for the point to be clear (lines 14, 20, 28).

13. They are to use the goads normally employed for prodding the backsides of cows, rather than gold-handled daggers of the type often used in ballads.

20. "Contray" and "frisado" are fine cloth.

22. Labrados: "embroidered".

23-24. "Caballero" (and "cabalgar") can be used for riders of other animals than horses ("caballos"); and for those who are not noble, provided they are mounted. Conversely, a nobleman is a "caballero" whether or not he is on a horse.

29-30. The left hand side was thought to be of ill omen, which is how "siniestro" came to change its meaning from "left" to "sinister".

36. The King's oath is not presented in direct speech, but his subsequent anger is. This line might be ambiguous; it could perhaps mean "who had never found himself under such an oath before".

39-40. These two lines contain four word-stresses each, making for a slow rhythm; the performer could thus make it seem heavy and menacing.

42. Will: stressed.

44. Rodrigo implies that Alfonso can hardly bestow any honour on the Cid by being his Lord, since he still feels, despite the oath, that Alfonso is lying.

45-46. These lines are almost the same as in no.38, where his father kissed Fernando's hand but Rodrigo did not want to. It seems to be Fernando that Rodrigo is referring to here also; his father was a loyal vassal of Fernando, who had not wanted Alfonso to become King of Castille, and the point seems to be that Alfonso is an unworthy successor who does not deserve to inherit such obligations.

48. "You have shown yourself to be a bad knight": this line is a cliché found in other ballads. His badness consists in his common practice (in ballads) of being cheeky to a Leonese King, which he is to accentuate in 55-56.

49-50. The nature of the Cid's departure is different in this ballad from in the previous one, but as usual in the legend the period between the death of Sancho and the exile is collapsed and the one is seen as the motivation for the other.

57. Alfonso has sworn, but Rodrigo will still not accept him as King; by not kissing his hand he has not become his vassal, so that although he is in exile he is not a rebel.

61-66. There is a contrast between the picture of the potential assassins (9-26) and the shining knights in the Cid's retinue.

65-66. Shields at the time were usually round, with a tassel on the central hub. "Colorado" now means "red", but in the Middle Ages could still have the original meaning of any bright colour.

67-68. One of the printed versions omits this couplet, and that might be best, since it looks forward to subsequent events in a way that spoils the internal structure of this individual ballad. It seems to be a clumsy reminiscence of the start of the epic Poema de Mío Cid, which begins with the newly exiled hero leaving Burgos but still being generally admired and having somewhere to camp. If so, it is confusing the issue, since the cause of the exile in the Poema was something else entirely, and the whole structure and theme of the epic depends on Rodrigo´s being a loyal vassal even in exile (rather than an ill-tempered runaway).

49. THE CID AND THE POPE

This ballad has no connection with history at all, but the idea that the Cid defended the honour of Castille against slights from the Pope is already traditional by the time of the Mocedades de Rodrigo (c.1365) where such a confrontation is that work´s climax.

3. This is the only time, other than at the siege of Zamora, when we see Rodrigo in the ballad tradition with Sancho II, rather than with Fernando I or Alfonso VI. The choice of Sancho makes sense, however, since in other ballads Rodrigo is seen as resentful of the monarch, but he is always a staunch supporter of Sancho. Chronologically this would go between ballads 40 and 41, but is no part of that cycle so has been postponed till here.

4. It was not normal practice for Kings and generals to attend Papal Councils; they were meant for bishops and cardinals. Even so, there is a grain of realism here, for it was precisely during the 1060s and 1070s that the Popes were trying to assert temporal as well as spiritual authority over the North-Western Spanish kingdoms and the land they reconquered from the Moslems. (Alfonso VI eventually managed to repel their temporal claims in 1080). This connection between the story and the history is probably only coincidental.

13. The Church of St. Peter: the Vatican. Peter was probably martyred there under Nero; his body was there, and he was the founder of the Papacy. This makes the Cid´s subsequent behaviour all the more distasteful, and the ballad´s approval of it all the more striking.

19-20. The Castilians often felt resentful at not being taken seriously enough on a world stage. This feeling was understandable in the sixteenth century (when Spain was the strongest world power, and when this ballad was printed), and common in the late thirteenth (when Alfonso X nearly became Holy Roman Emperor), but hardly sensible at the time of the Cid. Anti-French feeling, however, has always been common, and no Castilian audience would have objected to that. The idea that a display of spoilt pique will help right the wrong is one that also appears in other ballads connected with the Mocedades.

20. We are to visualize the seating as a hierarchy of height, with the Pope´s and the French King´s chair on one step higher than the Castilian King´s chair.

23-24. Even vandalizing the Vatican is seen as honourable if it is done for good patriotic reasons.

28. Savoy is in North-West Italy, near the French border.

30 and 43: Disown: "excommunicate" unfortunately cannot fit the short lines of the English. The Pope bars him from Communion (a punishment they often resorted to).

37-38. The conflict is seen by the Cid (as at Zamora) as a question of honour to be resolved in single combat, but the Duke will not accept that.

41-42. The Duke here is restrained in his response; in another version he tells Rodrigo to fight the devil instead ("¡Demándetelo el diablo!").

45-48. The Cid at least has the grace not to like being excommunicated, but still manages to be offensive even when lying prostrate; and in another variant version (M33) he even threatens to cover his horse with the Papal vestments if the Pope does not relent, which the Pope then does.

54. One ought to be "cortés" at the Court, by definition. The Cid is not at all "mesurado" ("dignified") in this ballad, and is apparently admired for not being so, whereas "mesura" is his greatest quality in the epic tradition of the Poema.

50. THE CID AND BÚCAR

The Cid´s career between 1080 and 1090 is complicated and in part unclear, although we know that he served the King of Moslem Zaragoza from 1081 to 1086; this fact is conveniently forgotten in later legends that prefer to present him as a crusader. But the height of his career was without doubt the capture of the rich and powerful Moslem state of Valencia in 1094, which he then ruled as his own kingdom. The Almorávides, Moslems from Africa, were invading Moslem Spain, and the Cid repelled them from Valencia, putting up the only serious resistance to the Africans; this increased his already impressive reputation. The capture and defence of Valencia play a large role in the early part of the epic Poema de Mío Cid. The

attacking Almorávides are led there by King Búcar (in real life not
a King but a general, Abu-Beker). This episode survives in the popular
traditions better than most of that epic, but the politics and context
are largely forgotten, and instead this tale too is reinterpreted in
terms of Búcar´s desire to seduce the Cid´s daughter – the Moslem is
identified as Búcar in Escobar´s version (M56), although his name is
not included here. (The epic also invents fictitious personal lives
for the daughters for the plot to hinge round.)

1. The "he" of "helo", as in "he aquí", is probably an Arabic word;
and as such might be intentionally chosen to apply to the Moor.

3. A la jineta: standing on the stirrups, like a jockey, as a sign
of his determination.

4. Vaya: "bay", pale reddish-brown.

5. Maroquines: that is, from Morocco, where "moros" such as the
Almorávides came from.

8. Azagaya: "assegai", mentioned because he is from Africa.

10. Bien cercada: with strong city walls, like Zamora (40) and
Álora (63).

13-14. This sets the time as that of the Cid, in case the audience
had not realized.

17. Perro: as elsewhere, a technical term, used by a member of
either religion to refer to a member of the other. The term "Cid" is
only not anachronistic from now on, since the name seems to have been
given him by his Valencian subjects (it is Arabic for "Lord").

18. The Christian heroes had preserved the Germanic insistence on
beards as symbols of power. When Rodrigo captured his Leonese opponent
García Ordóñez at Cabra in 1080 he pulled out some of García´s
beard, and in the Poema that is remembered and seen to rankle years
later. But for a "moro" to talk like this is less appropriate.

21. This ballad has hopelessly garbled the dramatis personae. The
performer of this version knows that there is an Urraca Hernando in
the Cid´s life somewhere, and has used the name as an available one in
these circumstances; but Urraca Hernando was actually Princess Urraca,
Fernando I´s daughter, the defender of Zamora. The Cid had two
daughters, and a son who died fairly young; the daughters were in real
life called María and Cristina, and in the Poema they were Elvira and
Sol.

23. This line does not seem grammatical, but is the same in all five early printed versions.

24. When he's satisfied, he'll hand her on to all the other Moorish soldiers; this detail is mentioned to ensure that we know he is a villain, since in ballads an energetic lover is usually admired.

26. The Cid has heard his shouted soliloquy, and thinks of a way to stall him until he is himself ready to attack.

27-30. Urraca is to keep Búcar there by pretending to be in love with him in return; she has to be able to put on her most attractive clothes at once. The critic Bénichou was taken aback by her acting the role here of "shameless seductress", but in fact she is speaking through a window - presumably with bars on - and the clothes she has put on are her Sunday best, "ropa de Pascua", not a bikini; attractive, but not seductive. (This scene is illustrated on the front cover of Díaz Roig's edition).

31. Perro: see the note to line 17. "Hi" is for "hijo" (as in "hidalgo", "hijo de algo").

33. Babieca is the name of the Cid's famous horse, who has a star role in the Poema (where he actually does chase Búcar) and was said to be buried with him. Babieca had been captured off the Moslem King of Seville.

35-46. This conversation is the emotional centre of the ballad, the calm between the storm of his arrival and that of his departure (cp. no.43). Urraca speaks as enamoured Princesses usually do in this genre, but this speech is sophisticated, for she is inventing emotions and expressing them in terms thought likely to intrigue her hearer, rather than saying what she actually thinks.

49. This is Búcar speaking; he knows of Babieca, which was once in Moslem Spain, and is the son of his own mare.

57-58. Talking animals are unusual except in fables, where they represent human types anyway. Here the horse is an actual horse expressing in words his frustration at not catching his mother up (he is some way behind, following the footsteps).

63. This boat with its helpful boatman was not pre-planned as an escape route by Búcar, he is just lucky to find it. (Maybe this is some kind of reminiscence of his return to Morocco with his navy?)

68. Allegar: originally ADPLICARE, to bring a boat to shore; the word "llegar" was created for intransitive use as "arrive" by removing the prefix.

71-72. It may be that the subject of these lines is the boatman rather than the Moslem.

74. Surprisingly for a national hero, the Cid is not a success at chasing people; he lost Vellido through not having his spurs (43) and Búcar through taking too long to prepare.

76. Rebentava: the Cid "burst" in grief; this was the word used in line 57 by Babieca, and we may be meant to make a connection.

79-82. Yerno: "son-in-law", which Búcar might have claimed to wish to be. This is a challenge couched in the usual terms; throwing the lance is equivalent to throwing the gauntlet, and structurally picks up Búcar´s aggressive lance of line 15.

51. THE "AFRENTA DE CORPES"

Ballads nos 51 and 52 seem to have been taken direct from the plot of the epic Poema, probably created in the sixteenth century from a prose version rather than being a continuously surviving fragment of that epic. The epic (recently published with parallel English text in this series), like most ballads, presents the Cid´s career largely in terms of his personal life; after the capture of Valencia, the plot hinges on the marriage of the Cid´s two daughters to the Leonese noble brothers, Fernando and Diego, Counts of Carrión. Carrión is in the province of Palencia, just on the Leonese side of the Castilian border. These Counts existed, but did not marry the Cid´s daughters, nor, so far as we can see, did they have any particular involvement in the Cid´s career; since they are the villains of the tale, it has been suggested that they were chosen for the part by a composer with some kind of anti-Carrión axe to grind. The central episode of the last part of the epic is the so-called "Afrenta de Corpes", "Assault at Corpes", (lines 2527-2753) which is summarized for us here. There is no connection between the Cid´s daughters in this tale and Urraca in the previous ballad, who can hardly be married.

1-3. The references in these three lines should be enough to fix the context for a reader or audience. We are in Valencia; the Counts and their wives have been there for two years since their marriages.

5-6. During all their marriage their wives have not seen their husbands´ lands in Carrión, so this request, at a time of a lull in the fighting, is a natural one.

9-12. Rodrigo had never been keen on the marriages in the epic, only agreeing because the King had suggested them and he is continually trying to return to the King´s favour (being an exile).

13-14. Breaking this promise to the Cid increases the horror of their eventual behaviour.

19-20. These celebrations are mentioned to provide a contrast with what happens next. Valencia was then, as it is now, renowned as a centre of fertile fruit orchards.

21-22. A league is about three to four miles.

27. Álvar Fáñez (or (H)Áñez) was, in real life, a more significant person than the Cid; he was a military commander under Alfonso VI, particularly renowned for his successful defence of Toledo in 1109. He died in 1114. He was not with the Cid in Valencia, and seems to have had no particular connection with him. In the epic tradition, he has become the Cid´s second-in-command; and in this ballad he has become the Cid´s nephew and even "criado" (another formula of the ballad genre that makes little sense if taken seriously).

32. Monte: not "mountain" but "wilderness". The oakgrove of Corpes is not a real place, although several scholars have tried to locate it somewhere on the route from Valencia to León. It is a kind of perversion of the traditional beautiful garden in which most love scenes are set in the genre (the "vergel"). In the epic, but not here, it is actually in the lands of a friendly Moslem ruler, who is eventually instrumental in the girls´ rescue.

41-42. It is surprising that at this emotional climax we are not given the speech of the participants directly; in the epic, they have quite a lot to say here.

45. Nor are they naked in the epic. The point of this episode has been interpreted in a wide variety of ways recently, since scholars don´t like to think that the appeal is merely pornographic. It has been likened to ancient fertility rites, since it has been suggested that the marriage was never consummated anyway; it has been seen as modelled on accounts of Visigothic tales of virgin martyrs. Within the epic structure it concentrates our emotions, epitomises the characters and provides the mechanism for the Cid´s eventual return to favour (as he appeals to the King to right the wrong here committed).

49-50. The Counts ran away in the great battle outside Valencia, and displayed great cowardice before an escaped lion. In the epic they rationalize their behaviour here as taking revenge for the contempt the Cid´s knights feel for them as a result. It increases the audience´s contempt, of course, if all they can fight are defenceless women. But the horror to be felt is not entirely at the women´s pain; it seems from line 3 that we are meant to think that this is a despicable way to treat their father-in-law, rather than their wives.

53–54.   There has been some argument over whether we are supposed to think that the Counts meant to leave the girls to die or not. I feel sure that we are, both here and in the epic, for they did not know that Alvar Fáñez was close behind and the wilderness was full of wild animals and vultures.

61–62.   In the epic they go back to the Cid at once; in the ballad there is an echo of the sixteenth-century incipient belief in the goodness of country people.

67–68.   In the ballad as it stands (where the Cid´s being an exile is not mentioned) this remark is rather anodyne, but it provides a point of high tension in the longer tale; will the Leonese King side with his Leonese protégés or with the Castilian exile? For the answer, see the next thrilling ballad ...

52. THE CID'S ARRIVAL AT TOLEDO

1.   This ballad picks up where the linking couplet at the end of the previous one leaves off. "Corte" just meant the King´s Court, but it could be summoned for special purposes to be the highest law-court in the kingdom (like the British House of Lords). The "Cortes" were not summoned as a kind of embryonic Parliament with geographical representation until Alfonso IX of León did so in 1188. When the King summoned such a "Corte" all nobles were expected to attend.

3–5.   The significance of having all three at once is that they cover all the three main areas of the kingdom; León, Old Castille based on Burgos, and New Castille, recently conquered and based on Toledo. Alfonso can hardly have been present at all three at once, and the implication seems here to be that in each centre nobles had to come from the whole kingdom; thus the Counts of Carrión could legitimately be summoned all the way south to Toledo. The Cid, being an exile, and now ruler of a separate state in Valencia anyway, could not be summoned in this way; but the Cid is (in the tale, not in real life) trying to return to Alfonso´s favour, so would be best advised to heed the summons to arrive in thirty days. Toledo is as close to Valencia as Alfonso could come within his own kingdom, so the decision to meet there shows that the King is already prepared, quite literally, to meet the Cid halfway.

8.   The weak and the strong: or, as here, the exile and the favourites, since the Cid is by now hardly weak.

9-12. It must have been infuriating for a noble to be summoned from urgent regional business to attend the Court, so such a sanction as being held to be a traitor was occasionally necessary to ensure attendance.

14. The Counts of Carrión, there to explain their attack on the Cid's daughters. The mathematics do not come straight from the epic here; there (1.2970) it is a seven-week period, and the Cid arrives five days late (1.3015).

22. It might be true that the Cid won every fight (in the twelfth-century Poema de Almería he was said to have never been defeated in battle, ab hostibus haud superatur); but here there is a further implication, that the Cid can win battles (e.g. against the African invaders) while the Counts can only beat up women. The King's remarks here are bad news for the Counts, since if the King is prepared to be as fair as this they will have no defence to the Cid's charges. (In the Poema their only defence is that they are Leonese nobility and therefore entitled to do what they like to lesser humanity: a defence that goes down badly, both at Court and among any audience.)

27. The Cid (as he did much earlier, in no.38) arrives with a 300-strong bodyguard, being naturally unsure of his reception. Here his army wear uniform, to stand out as well-disciplined, and perhaps to intimidate their former colleagues, the Counts.

32. Albornoz: a Moslem-style cape ("burnous") like a bathing-robe. This strange detail is probably included to remind the audience of the Cid's power over the Moslems in Valencia.

33. This greeting is necessary, to stress his loyalty at once.

34. It may be the King who says this line.

35-36. This excellent ending comes at the emotional climax; the ballad is inconclusive, but the audience can probably be trusted to know that the Cid wins in the end.

53. KING BÚCAR'S DECREE

Thematically, this ballad belongs in the first section; it is included at this point to show how porous the distinction is between the historically based cycles and the love ballads. Búcar´s name is given to the King here because it is available in the genre as a result of the tales of Búcar´s attack on Valencia; but otherwise there is no connection at all. (The original, even in the epic, was specifically not Andaluz but African.)

1-2. Moslem Spain was known collectively as Al-Andalús. From the early eleventh century it was often fragmented into several states. Since it is set in a cheerful but bygone kingdom, this ballad has untypically been translated in the past tense.

6-7. Kings and nobles married for dynastic and political reasons, but most also had "mancebas", concubines, women they were not married to but who they actually liked.

9-10. This is what the Cortes were for (see the note to the start of the preceding ballad).

15-18. This theme appears elsewhere, of a ruler decreeing death for facets of the subjects´ personal lives; in Espinelo´s case (no.21) the result is tragedy for the Queen, but this ballad is not at all tragic - Búcar is "sabio", "wise" enough to avoid that.

21. Sobrino: literally "nephew", but it was also the word used for a King´s illegitimate children, of which he often had several, so he might be meant to be understood as the "manceba"´s son.

20, 22, 24; also 38, 40. Given that this ballad is a clever and humorous one, the translation has permitted itself rhymes more reminiscent of Ogden Nash than usual. Such rhymes are in general too sophisticated for the genre.

30-31. I.e. she´s unhappily married to someone else; and in the ballad tradition (unlike in the dramatic traditions of the following century) the audience´s sympathies are meant to be entirely with the adulterers (as in the first two ballads here).

35-36. She has begged him to find a way round it. This is worth making clear, to stop us feeling at all hostile to the young man.

39-40. Worldly wisdom; practicality rather than the letter of the law, even for those who made the law. A pleasingly sophisticated final subversion of the audience´s expectations as to why he was called "sabio".

54. PEDRO AND FADRIQUE

1. The first-person narrator is Henrique´s twin brother Fadrique, who was killed in Sevilla on 29th May, 1358. This was a public and notorious event, and the presentation in the first person is a clever way of ensuring that the audience is on Fadrique´s side here, whichever side they may have been on politically when they first heard it. He was actually at Jumilla, not Coimbra, but Coimbra (in Northern Portugal) is better known.

5. Pedro set up his capital at Sevilla, in what had been Moslem Spain; this infuriated his more traditionalist subjects further north, who saw this move as near-heretical.

7. Maestre: an old form of "maestro" (originally MAGISTER). Fadrique was "Maestre", Commander, of the Military Order of Santiago, one of the Orders set up in the twelfth century, at the time of the Crusades, as simultaneously military and religious organizations. These Orders owned a great deal of land, and long after their original function was irrelevant their leaders were among the richest and most powerful of the nobility.

-12. They are said to be dressed in ceremonial rather than military fashion, to stress that Fadrique has no suspicion of any trap. He is the innocent victim unwittingly summoned to his doom; other ballad heroes can see such summons as dangerous and go prepared (see nos 34, 48, 52).

13-14. Doing the journey in such record time is part of the literary tradition rather than literal truth, to exemplify his keenness to be obedient. The distance from Coimbra to Sevilla could hardly have normally taken as much as 15 days on horseback (it´s just over 300 km).

15-20. They were hurrying so much that they omitted usual precautions. The death of the page presages the even greater misfortune caused later by the same loyalty.

25. The Puerta Macarena, the city entrance.

27-36. This detail is rather odd, and comes from the same source cliché as it does on the return of the huntsman Pedro in no.11. Again, the function is to stress Fadrique´s keenness, if he lets his obedience to Pedro come before baptizing his first son and his own twenty-first birthday celebrations.

35-36. He seems to have news from Coimbra, which is absurd if Fadrique has come so impossibly fast himself; and line 36 seems to mean that Fadrique himself is the godson. Perhaps performers would be best advised to omit 27-36 altogether.

37.   The Spanish has modulated to the third person here, but "I" am back in 43.

42.   Five times it is explicitly stressed, as here, that the murder is of his brother, making it even more shocking. Yet Henrique was to do the same, as revenge.

45-46.   Fadrique is expecting to come to a jousting tournament (5-6), but even when there is obviously no tournament going on the penny still doesn´t drop.

50-60.   The ballad, in emphasizing his innocence, borders on making him seem daft at this point. If Pedro was as notoriously "El Cruel" as the propagandists pretend, Fadrique might have known. The ballad may well, of course, have changed in many details between 1358 and 1550.

65-72.   Pedro´s reason for the murder is presented here as mere pique, but it soon becomes clear that his mistress María is the real villain in the propagandist tradition, being given the Salome role, asking for the victim´s head on a plate. This is an ancient cliché, of course, with no connection with reality; it seems improbable that in real life María had anything to do with this murder at all. Indeed, the history written by Pero López de Ayala, who was alive at the time and may even have been there, suggests that María might have actually tried to warn Fadrique in advance not to come. In a shorter variant ballad her viciousness is centre-stage; this ballad has the nastiness more diluted. The reason for this is probably the French support for Henrique. In 1353 Pedro had married the young French girl Blanche (in Spanish, Blanca de Borbón) but after three days of marriage he abandoned her and returned to his mistress. As a result María was to be blamed for almost everything his opponents could think of.

77-78.   This shows that it was planned all along, not just a sudden fury.

79.   I´m dead now, so the narrative has to be third-person from here; but the change, already hinted at, is skilfully done and possibly not even noticed by an audience.

83-84.   Sano: "healthy". Line 86 of the English is an invention - these longer lines often need a lot of padding.

87.   Fadrique is called a traitor for supporting Blanca de Borbón. Pedro proclaimed that his liaison with María was a legitimate marriage, but few agreed with him.

92. This line merges four vowels into one syllable, apparently ("la ha a un"); although in fact many lines in this composition (for no immediately interpretable reason) have nine syllables rather than eight (26, 28, 30, 50, 53, 54, 58, 66, 74, 81 (with 10), 92, 93, 101, 103, 110, 111, 117, 118), so this may be nine-syllabled also.

93-96. The dogs have more human feelings than the humans. This detail comes from the same source as the father recognizing the severed heads of his seven sons in the "Infantes de Lara" cycle, and is in just as shocking taste. It is, of course, intended to shock.

104. She was Alfonso XI's sister, and thus aunt to his children whether legitimate or not.

109-22. This version states quite unambiguously that María is the person imprisoned; this has become one of the traditional ballads in which a badly-advised King eventually comes to his senses and can tell guilt from innocence (cp. Virgil in no.24). But the original ballad cannot possibly have ended like this, and another surviving variant ends with María triumphantly gloating while Pedro is tormented by nightmare visions of a headless Fadrique riding a horse. Originally this ballad probably had the aunt imprisoned here instead; their aunt Leonor was imprisoned in 1358 shortly after Fadrique's death, and possibly even because she disapproved of it, as here. It only needs a change of dramatis personae in line 111 for this to be the sense in this ballad.

55. PEDRO AND THE SHEPHERD

2. Jerez de la Frontera, south of Seville.

8. It is not clear whether the bird that dies here is the first falcon, or (as translated here) the peregrine, whose death is then repeated in 9.

10. Pedro begins here to feel that something supernatural is afoot.

14-15. "Bulto" is a word apparently borrowed into Spanish from Latin in the fifteenth century to refer to three-dimensional religious statuary, and is thus unlikely to have been in the fourteenth-century original. Yet in general this tale has probably not changed greatly in the two centuries between the original and the printing. Ayala, in his late fourteenth-century history, included this episode; but he can hardly have believed it.

21. "Shepherd" here seems merely to mean "wild man", for he has no sheep nor shepherd-like appearance, and his hound is hardly a sheepdog. His unkempt appearance is apparently exaggerated in grotesque detail in an attempt to make his prophecy sound all the more foreboding.

25. Abrojos: "thorns".

34-35. The Spanish phrasing is unclear, but presumably it is the dog that howls and the shepherd that speaks.

36-54. Henrique had to keep hammering away at the same theme, that Pedro's cruelty made him unfit to be King; for everyone knew that Pedro was the legitimate heir and Henrique illegitimate. So the same acts return time and again into the propaganda.

41-42. This is the episode portrayed in the previous ballad.

42 and 44. The implication here is that he has been sent by God to tell Pedro this.

43-48. Blanca died in 1361; Fadrique in 1358; so this scene is set, and perhaps originally composed, between the two deaths.

49-50. Pedro had daughters, but no sons, by María de Padilla. After his death they were in exile in English Gascony; the eldest, Costanza, married John of Gaunt in 1371, and their daughter Catherine eventually married Henrique's grandson, the future Henrique III, in a settlement in 1388. Catherine was thus queen, and, after Henrique III's death in 1406, regent (1406-18). Although she was unpopular, she was hardly "wicked", and this couplet is unlikely, therefore, to have been first composed after 1388.

51-53. Henrique killed Pedro by "the blows of his dagger" in 1369, so the composition of this section probably postdates that; prophecies in literature are usually made after the composer knows whether they will be true or not, but in this case it could be that Henrique was in 1369 consciously fulfilling his own previous prophecy.

56. In another variant (M66) Pedro arrests the shepherd, the shepherd escapes, and this leads Pedro to order Blanca's death on the grounds that she has such supernatural contacts. This one ends with the atmosphere of eerie foreboding, with no explicit reaction from the King.

56. THE DEATH OF BLANCA

1.   Pedro is talking to his mistress, whose name will identify the context for an audience. María has presumably been worried that the King is really hankering after Blanca.

3.   Dos vezes: "twice". This is gilding the lily, since he only left Blanca once (unless the first time is meant to be his desertion of María for Blanca).

6.   Blanca died in 1361, for reasons that are not clear to modern historians; it could have been the plague or some other disease, or depressive misery, but it was widely assumed then that the King had had her murdered. This ballad takes that for granted and proceeds to stress the cruelty. A rival ballad (M67 and 67A) survives which supports Pedro, claiming that Fadrique (of no.54) and the Queen were lovers with a son, and scheming against Pedro. There is no historical possibility of this being true (it is in any case an obvious adaptation of historical figures into common clichés of ballad plots).

7.   Medina Sidonia is on the road from Jerez to Gibraltar, in the South-Western area where these ballads are set. Blanca´s tombstone says she actually died at Jerez, "praevalente pellice", "at the instance of the King´s mistress"; historians tend not to believe this.

8-12.   This is not a literal banner, but a symbolic representation of the planned murder. "Labor", meaning both "embroidery" and "task", is a grim pun.

14.   Alonso Ortiz; the honourable man who puts honour before political allegiance, introduced to emphasise the villainy even more.

19-20.   Ortiz skilfully phrases his refusal so as to sound respectful rather than rebellious; since this attitude would be hard to argue against, Pedro moves on to two hired killers, "maceros" (who use clubs), who will do as they´re told.

26 (and 48-50).   God, of course, is on Blanca´s side.

27-32.   She had expected this (for many years).

35-38.   Even though she is French, and the French were supporters of Henrique, she has to make it clear that her nationality has not been a higher allegiance than her duty as wife; she is in no sense a traitor.

39-40.   She can hardly have died at sixteen in the original, for the audience would know (what is not mentioned in the text) that she died eight years after the marriage (1353).

41-42.   The fact that she is a virgin makes her innocence all the
more. This could well be true. Pedro had abandoned her after three
days of marriage, to return to María, and inability or unwillingness
to make love seems a likely reason for that. That abandonment had
instigated a rebellion at the time, so her death, presumed murder, was
a sensible propaganda tool for his enemies to manipulate after 1361.

51-52.   A blunt and brutal ending to both her life and the ballad,
leaving the audience as if concussed.

57. THE DEATH OF PEDRO

The other Pedro ballads were all translated in long lines, preserving
some kind of unity of tone in the cycle; but that seems inappropriate
in as brief and pithy a ballad as this. This is an anti-lament,
celebrating Pedro´s being stabbed to death by Henrique in April 1369
(at Montiel).

18.   After the murder, Henrique is now King (Henrique II); but the
murder was not only honourably committed, "honrrado", but divinely
approved (19-22).

58. THE SIEGE OF BAEZA

The siege of Baeza happened in 1368, so chronologically this ballad is
set before the previous one (on Pedro´s death in 1369). It has been
placed here because it provides a link between the Pedro ballads and
the last category of ballads exemplified in this collection, the
"frontier" ballads set on the Late Medieval frontier between Castilian
Andalucía and Moslem Granada.

1.   Baeza (pronounced with three full syllables) is North-East of
Jaén.

2.   Audalla: Abdalla is the Moslem commander. "Mir" here is
apparently a corruption of "Emir", which he wasn´t.

5.   Pedro´s enemies strongly disliked the fact that Pedro had Moslem
allies; that appeared to be evidence of treachery, and also of
effeminacy. "Pero Gil" is a name given to Pedro by Henrique -
surviving letters of Henrique´s from 1369 use the term -: "Pero" is a
common alternative for "Pedro", and the point is that it sounds like

"perejil", "parsley", meaning the same as English "pansy". His
followers were similarly "emperogilados", "emperejilados", with the
same meaning. (The word "perejil" came from Southern France, in
probably the previous century.) Childish, but apparently effective as
a ploy. This name for Pedro did not linger, though, so the original of
this ballad is probably very close to the event.

7.   The King of Granada, Muhammad V, who reigned from 1354 to 1391.
Granada did not involve itself much in the civil wars of Pedro´s
reign, but Baeza was just over the Christian frontier, and a prize
that Granada would love to take, so an alliance was possible to
arrange for this purpose.

9.   Bedmar is a place some 25 km. south of Baeza, and the "Puerta de
Bedmar" would be the way into Baeza from the south.

11.   To scale the walls from the outside attackers would put long
ladders against them and try to climb up and over; defenders would
normally have the advantage in such circumstances.

14-16.   In line 16 of the Spanish the first person suddenly turns up:
"I saw knights come out"; rendered in English as "we" in line 14. This
unexpected development may even reflect the original composer´s being
one of the defenders, for the episode, however dramatic for the
individuals involved, is of almost no historical significance, since
the attack failed. It is not mentioned at all in Ayala´s chronicle.
Eyewitnesses composed other such occasional poems, in a tradition that
had been current from the very early Middle Ages. "We" here are
Henrique´s supporters.

15.   Calonge is a variant of "canónigo", a religious canon; a
suitable name for the gate that the Christian relief force comes
through.

17.   Ruy is the short form of Rodrigo. Ruy Fernández de Fuenmayor was
the local Lord, and his role in this event is explained by Argote in
the section before he prints this ballad. Argote´s interest is in
famous andaluz nobles, not in poetry, so his quoting this ballad
suggests that it was well known and authentically popular, rather than
his own composition, despite its not being attested elsewhere.

20.   The implication is that Pedro is unable to fight for himself, and
needs to hire Moors to do so; without them he has to run away.

59. REDUÁN

There was a brief period of frontier war from 1406 to 1410. The Moslem commander Reduán died in the attack on Jaén in October 1407, and although this narrative never reaches Jaén itself, the audience would have known that the expedition had been due to fail, so there is a sense of foreboding through the first 16 lines.

1. The King of Granada is speaking; as usual, he is not a sympathetic character in the ballad, though his frontier subjects are.

3. Jaén (pronounced with two full syllables) is a strategic city east of Córdoba and quite close to the north of Granada city itself. It had been once the capital of a separate Moslem Kingdom, and is now a provincial capital.

8-9. It is possible that "desterrar te" and "echar te" are elided futures, for "desterrar te he" and "echar te he" respectively. "Here" is the city of Granada, where the conversation is taking place.

11-14. Line 13, "si lo dije, no me acuerdo" has become famous. We are meant to assume that Reduán had never made any such rash promise, but he reckons that contradicting the King might be less dangerous than the attack. Since the audience know that it will fail, our sympathy is all meant to be with Reduán, despite the fact that he is a Moslem attacking Christians. The reason why the ballads are usually set in wartime is not that the performers and their audience gloried in blood, or that they suffered from religious or nationalistic chauvinism, but that in wartime the emotions aroused are so much stronger and more gripping.

16-17. It seems very likely that the fifteenth-century original stopped at line 16, or that if it continued the ending is not here; the rest, 17-44, may originally have been a separate ballad entirely, for it seems quite different in tone, Reduán is never mentioned again, and the King mentioned in line 34 was the King who reigned through the 1480s rather than in 1407.

17. Elvira: the Roman name for a fortress just outside Granada was ILIBERIS, of which the pronunciation eventually evolved into "Elvira". The gate is one of the Granada city gates.

19-30. Each line of the Spanish begins with the same word, which manages to be impressive rather than monotonous. The English starts each couplet with the same "so many", since there is not room in every line. These lines look like an objective literary exercise; colourful though they are, they dispel the personal tensions aroused by the first part. The clothes are essentially the bright ceremonial clothes of a display rather than the practical uniforms of a raiding party, which further suggests an origin in the post-1492 age when Granada was romanticized, its threat having gone.

34.   Rey Chico: "Little King", the nickname given to King Boabdil. If this description is of a particular expedition, it is probably of one of 1483.

36.   The Alhambra is the Moslem palace that still dominates the city, built in the fourteenth century in a conscious attempt to recapture the past glories of the (tenth-century) Moslem Caliphate. From it there is a good view, and several of these post-1492 ballads pictured women inside the palace gazing at the warriors outside, often with the warriors specifically trying to impress their female audience.

42.   Menéndez y Pelayo printed an extra couplet not in Pérez de Hita´s original text (but present in its 1876 reprint): "y te dé paz con tu tío, / señor de Guadix y Baza." These lines refer to the internal conflicts that marred the final years of Granada, and which were often later thought to have led to its fall.

60. ANTEQUERA

1.   The Castilians besieged Antequera in 1410. Antequera is still a walled town of strategic importance, where the road from Córdoba to Málaga crosses the road from Sevilla to Granada. The siege was well known and Antequera´s only claim to fame, so the opening sets the scene unambiguously (cp. any story that is initially set at Dunkirk, for example). We see nearly all of this ballad from the Moslem side, as the emotions of the besieged are stronger than those of the besiegers.

2.   The messenger going for help leaves before dawn so as not to be seen.

5-6.   Letters written in blood are a literary cliché, designed to impress the recipient and the audience with their desperation; they bring the news of Roncesvalles to Alda (no.16), and also the news of the fall of Jerusalem in 1247 in a contemporary poem in the "romancillo" metre (six-syllabled lines). It is not easy to write letters in blood, and we are at liberty to doubt if any message intended to be intelligible in detail was ever sent this way in reality.

8.   The appearance of the Moorish messenger has been embellished with details that are common in the genre and override the initial realism

of the scene, a process sometimes called "novelization". In the first couplet he was trying to be inconspicuous, but the dress wished upon him here 140 years later is anything but.

10-11.   The cliché of his aged baldness (10) is indeed contradictory with the cap he is wearing.

13-14.   Christian knights from further north tended to treat the Granada frontier as a kind of practice ground for chivalric jousting, and wear the colours of their lover there; it seems less likely that Moslems did this.

21-22.   The status of nobles is often symbolized by the number of knights in their retinue (indeed, such mathematical symbolization becomes almost obsessive in the Poema de Mío Cid). So if the nobility of this messenger is to be made clear, but he can hardly be riding with a large company, then we need to be told that he had many more at home who had not been prepared for this actual journey.

23-26.   After leaving the city, he has to get through the lines of the besiegers before he is safely in Moslem territory. The specification of "seven" ambushes is another cliché of the genre.

27.   The road from Antequera to Granada climbs quite steeply at first till the village of Archidona, which is high. The Christian besiegers seem to have been on the flanks of this hill but not to have reached Archidona at the top, so arrival at Archidona represents a safe passage to Granada.

32.   Vellida: "fine", a word almost exclusively applied to beards.

33.   Between lines 32 and 33 the messenger goes several uneventful miles to arrive outside Granada city itself.

36.   Morería: a collective noun for "moros" (as in 1.80), as well as the name for a Moorish quarter in a city (as in ballad no.40).

41.   The King recognizes his visitor as from Antequera; he calls the town "my" town, for this event too is presented in terms of a personal loss.

44.   In such tales, messengers of bad news often are killed.

52.   The King may have known of the siege already, but the desperation that the inhabitants are in seems to be news to him; the Christian troops round the walls had even prevented such news from escaping.

53.   Fernando was the brother of Henrique III, who died young in 1406.

The succeeding king was Juan II, but he was too young to rule until 1418, and till then the kingdom was under the rule of two regents: one was Fernando, and the other was the wife of Henrique III, the Catherine of Lancaster who we saw (in the notes to ballad no.55) was the daughter of John of Gaunt and Pedro I´s daughter Costanza. Fernando´s successful conduct of this siege led to him being generally known afterwards as Fernando de Antequera, even though he then left the frontier and was invited to become King of Aragon from 1412. As Fernando I of Aragon he was most influential historically, despite soon dying (in 1416), mainly as the precursor of the eventual unity of the kingdoms; in Castille he was much missed after his departure, being seen subsequently as a paragon with which nostalgically to compare the turmoil of fifteenth-century Castilian politics.

61-68. Kings would be expected to show great grief at appropriate points, so his reaction represents a sense of responsibility. (The British stiff upper lip appears to everyone else to be a mere symptom of heartlessness or hypocrisy.)

68. That is, he refuses to let anyone try to console him.

71. The "añafil" is a North African pipe, blown as a signal (as in the ballad on Baeza, no.58).

75. The Prague "pliego suelto" stops here. Ramón Menéndez Pidal suggested that the last section (75-110) was grafted onto the original ballad on the basis of an account in a prose chronicle in order to explain what happened next. This is very possible. Even so, it seems quite likely that there had been an original ballad text underlying the ending (perhaps a separate ballad rather than an alternative ending of the first one) which could have been known to the chroniclers. There is certainly a change of perspective from line 88, for then the ballad is seen from the Christian viewpoint, as the Castilians are called "nuestros" in 1.94, and the success of the siege is seen as a victory for the Virgin Mary (109-10).

76. The Moslem army is to meet at Archidona, the point within Granada closest to Antequera.

85. On the hill looking down over Antequera and the Christian army.

86-87. Real: the camps, in sight of each other.

88. Apercebirse: "get ready".

89. Dios: the Christian God, carefully distinguished from the Moslem Allah of lines 39, 47.

92. Midsummer´s Day, the Day of St John, was supposedly propitious to momentous events (cp. the discovery of Arnaldos in no.20). The battle was actually on 16th May and the surrender on 28th September, but the two are collapsed onto this day for greater drama.

94. The Christians here suddenly become "we", although there is no previous hint of such partisanship earlier; no sarcasm or gloating in the King´s distress, for example (61-68). Herida: Timoneda´s version has "reñida", "bitterly fought", which makes better sense ("herida" literally means "wounded").

99. Lombardas: cannon for firing at walls, a comparatively new practice in peninsular warfare at this time (the first use of gunpowder in Europe is said to have been at Río Salado, on the frontier, in 1340). Pertrechos: "ammunition".

100. Siege-towers were a kind of scaffolding on wheels, placed outside the walls.

101-03. The "torres" are on the encircling city walls; the "castillo" is the fortress inside the walls (which could sometimes hold out longer than the city).

104. Pleitesía: "negotiations". As was normal practice, the defeated side are acknowledging their defeat, and arrange to leave peacefully in order to avoid further bloodshed.

105-06. Spanish "haciendas" does not here mean what the modern English hispanism "haciendas" does (otherwise it was tempting to rhyme "haciendas" with "surrenders" and "defenders").

109-10. The final couplet, with its crusading perspective, jars with all the rest (the mention in 92 of St John´s Day is really a cliché), and could well be an addition of c.1550, when there was beginning a fashion to rephrase ancient literature "a lo divino", to accord with Christian values (which were often conspicuously lacking in fifteenth-century poetry).

61. THE DUKE OF ARJONA

1. Fadrique, Duke of Arjona and Count of Trastámara, great-grandson of Alfonso XI, great-nephew of Pero López de Ayala the chronicler and chancellor, was of the highest nobility, and was arrested on suspicion of treachery by King Juan II in 1429. Arjona, in the province of Jaén some 40 km. East of Córdoba up the Guadalquivir, was only made a

dukedom in 1423. Menéndez y Pelayo was unable to locate the historical event and printed this ballad with the Pedro ballads, despite the fact that the only early printed version does not so locate it, because of similarities to both the ballad on the death of the previous Fadrique de Trastámara in 1358 (no.54) and the ones on the "Prior de Sant Juan" (not printed here: M69 and M69A). Details of those traditions have become attached to this one, but the arrest was a genuine event. Although this is set in the frontier area in the fifteenth century, the relationships between the religious communities are not part of the subject matter, and it has been included in this section for chronological convenience only.

2.   The King was actually much further north, in Velamazán (see Mackay). Maybe the original had the correct setting, since that placename fits this assonance, and Gibraltar was in Moslem hands from 1333 to 1462.

7-8.   This halving of the normal travel time is a theme already current in the earlier Fadrique ballad (which we can be sure was in the tradition in 1429, although probably not in exactly the form printed in the next century)

9-10.   The Prior in the Pedro ballads (M69 and M69A) is similarly invited to a meal, although the Prior suspects a plot and the Duke does not. This present ballad lacks most of the force and piquancy of the Pedro ballads from which it seems to have derived some of the details; María de Padilla, for example, is the villain who inspires the Prior´s arrest.

15.   The complainants are presumably inhabitants of the lands of Arjona. This series of charges reflects the normal social conflicts of the age, in which the King and the peasants were often united in opposition to the nobility (both in life and in literature). Probably the original audience would have known whether these charges were true - in which case we applaud the King - or not - in which case this King is acting out of pique, like Pedro to the earlier Fadrique -.

27.   Traxisse: perhaps a variant, but probably a misprint, of "traxiesse", modern "trajese".

28.   Barjuleta: a kind of rucksack.

33.   The Duke of Arjona´s father-in-law was Diego Furtado de Mendoza, who was also the father, by a second marriage, of Íñigo López de Mendoza, the first and famous Marqués de Santillana. If this is an original detail, then, it seems as though the King is involved in a family feud, and the motivation may have been as personal as was María de Padilla´s in the model.

62. ABNÁMAR

1.   In June 1431 Juan II led an army to Granada. On the 28th he came
in sight of the city. It is the King who is speaking here at the
start, addressing his Moslem ally "Abn Ámar". Abn Almao (presumably
the same person) was a Moslem rebel briefly set up by the Castilians
as a puppet king in Granada in 1432 under the name of Yusuf IV. He
fell after a few months. At the time his name would be well known, but
the episode is of no lasting significance. The original ballad is
probably contemporary, therefore. Torres Fontes, however, has recently
argued strongly that Abn Ámar is not to be identified with the man
who became Yusuf IV.

2.   Abn Ámar is with the Castilian troops as a guide, and that is his
function here. The Castilians were genuinely dazzled by Granada, which
was more densely populated and more economically successful than
anywhere in Castille. Juan II admired its culture greatly, and his son
Henrique IV did even more, so their hearts were not usually in the
battles; in this case Juan literally falls in love with what he sees.
This scene of the view could well be reworking the actual incident.

3-4.   Seen from the North on a mid-summer´s day, with the peaks of the
Sierra Nevada still covered in snow behind, Granada is most
impressive.

5.   The castle palace and fortress known as the Alhambra was built in
the fourteenth century, and thus was still quite new. It would
naturally astonish a Castilian.

6.   Mezquita: Mosque.

7.   Alixares: the name of the King of Granada´s country residence, on
the "Cerro del Sol" ("Hill of the Sun") overlooking the river.

10.   I.e. the workmanship is of the best, a hundred doblas a day being
a large amount. The large Moslem buildings had intricately worked
decorations over most of the walls.

14.   Ballestería: another collective noun, for "crossbowmen". Abn
Ámar is not merely giving a guided tour of the view, but assessing
the military prospects.

17.   The King´s proposal of marriage to the city is a literary
representation of his admiration. This literary technique may have
been inspired by similar occasions in Arabic poetry.

19-22.   Córdoba had been the centre of Moslem culture from the eighth
to the eleventh centuries, and Sevilla from then till the thirteenth;

but Juan reckons that Granada is worth both of these cities and Jerez
as well. At the time, given the economic decline that had followed the
Christian capture of Andalucía, he might have been right. The net
effect of calling the cities a "dowry" is to reinforce the impression
that fighting over Granada is similar to the chivalric theme of
fighting over a woman.

27-30.   The city replies, representing the views of its inhabitants
(or perhaps the contents of a letter): "with respect, no thankyou".
Mackay uses this illuminatingly as an example of the wary respect that
the two sides had for each other in the usually peaceful period from
1350 to 1460; what he called "acculturation without assimilation".
Threats on Castille from Aragon, Portugal, France, England and civil
war were usually more pressing, and it was worth keeping this border
quiet.

30.   All five versions of the sixteenth-century collections contain
the whole ballad, but Pérez de Hita, at the start of the next
century, printed a version which stopped here, and which also included
at the start a section on the signs that attended Abn Ámar´s birth;
that version has thus lost touch with the original and is in the
process of becoming another of the standard love and adventure
ballads. Surprisingly, however, owing to the vagaries of scholarly
taste in our present sub-Romantic age, Pérez´s version has become in
this century the better known. The full version follows the tradition
(as with Rodrigo at Zamora, ballad no.41) of presenting a decision not
to come to peaceful terms as the result of a lover´s pique after a
jilted proposal.

34.   Sancha and Elvira are the names of the guns. Not only cities get
personified. It is hard to decide if the name "Elvira" is chosen on
purpose here; for "Elvira" is a name for Granada (the original form
being ILIBERIS).

35-36.   The couplet is ambiguous, and might well mean that if the
Alhambra is captured the city below it will give in.

37.   In fact, there was not an assault on the city at this time, but a
battle nearby at La Higueruela (cp. Bénichou´s account).

39-40.   The Moslem´s warcry, meant to terrorize the opposition, was a
famous tactic, here unsuccessful.

44-48.   Granada is not conquered, but it recognizes that it is
defeated, and adopts the time-honoured practice of paying the
Castilian invaders a large bribe (the "parias" of 1.48) to go away.

49-52.   Money is the point rather than religion or territory on this occasion; the richness of the city is what was admired at the start, and the Castilians now have some of it. Historically, the purpose of the expedition seems to have been mostly as a diversionary tactic to distract the attention of potentially rebellious nobles back north. The fact that Abn Ámar subsequently became king is not mentioned here, but if the audience know that, it gives a pleasant structure to the ballad. The practical air of the long ballad, particularly in the last half, is so out of tone with the glossy romanticization of Pérez de Hita´s version that he was probably well advised to stop at line 30.

63. ÁLORA

1.   This ballad only survives in a "pliego suelto", but it is said there to be "aquel antiguo y verdadero romance" ("that genuine old ballad"). Álora is a walled town ("bien cercada") in the hills north of Málaga, on the river Guadalhorce between Antequera and Málaga. It was unsuccessfully besieged in May 1434.

3.   Diego de Ribera was the "adelantado", the governor of the frontier area; he was acting here under the orders of the King of Castille, in a campaign that actually covered much more than this one episode.

9-16.   The Moors had brought food inside the city walls. Now that the walls are breached, they are taking it into the "castillo", the fort inside the walls, in the hope that they can hold out longer there. The implication may be that Diego should have realized that they were not planning to surrender.

16.   There is no actual honey in the Spanish, but the figs seem to be similar padding for the sake of the assonance.

19.   One of the Moors is on the city walls (that is, not in the inner fort); we may perhaps be meant to think that the flag (of line 18) was a white flag.

24.   That is, he shouts so loud that the besiegers can hear. It would be normal in a siege, once the besiegers were clearly going to win anyway, for the besieged to ask for a truce to arrange terms (as happened at Antequera, no.60); once he has shouted for a truce, Diego assumes that there is one, and lifts up his visor to speak.

29.   But it was a trick; the Moor shot him during what was thought to be a truce. This was seen and is presented as appalling treachery, comparable to the death of King Sancho II outside Zamora.

30. The arrow from the crossbow hits him in the forehead and comes out at the back of the head.

35. Maestros: "graduates", here it seems of medicine.

37. This line is ambiguous; it could mean (as translated) that as soon as the doctors tell him he´s dying he gives his will: or, that the first thing he says to them is his will.

The Castilians retreated after Diego de Ribera´s death - as the original audience would know, which is presumably why we are not told. The emotions involved in the treachery are the point, rather than the military dénouement.

64. THE DUKE OF NIEBLA

1. The speaker is either King Juan II of Castille or his Queen; the texts are not consistent, though the Silva version followed here has the speaker as the Queen.

3. Niebla is on the road from Sevilla to Huelva.

4. The Trastámara Kings were themselves descended from the Andalusian Guzmán family (Alfonso XI´s mistress was one).

5-6. The Conde de Niebla was in charge of the siege of Gibraltar in 1436.

11-12. Through much of the reign of Juan II the effective ruler was his "condestable", Álvaro de Luna. He ruled the kingdom with a strong centralizing ambition, confiscating the lands of opponents, and always winning in any civil strife. The other nobles largely disliked him, and after his death he became a symbol of autocracy that worried Spaniards for many decades.

13. The speaker is unidentified; a court noble, or perhaps a messenger from the South. The only identification of the original speaker occurs in this line, "Señora": if it were "Señor", which fits the rhythm equally, it would be the King, which might seem more plausible. The English is non-committal.

15-18. These lines explain why the Duke is "grande"; the Moslems were afraid of him.

19-30. This description of the Count´s death is probably largely true. Besieging Gibraltar had to be done by sea as well as by land, to prevent reinforcements and supplies from Africa. The currents and tides are not always predictable in the Strait, and it seems that some of the land forces were trapped by a high tide; the Count, at sea at the time, tried to come in to take some of them off, but the boat capsized and drowned. The Moslems recovered his body and hung it in a coffin over the city walls, where it stayed till the Christians captured the Rock in 1462. Juan de Mena´s poem <u>Laberinto de Fortuna</u> of 1444 recounts the incident at length (lines 1265-1480); this work was still well known in 1550, so the ballad subject was probably familiar then despite the essential unimportance of the episode.

24. The subject of "hizieron" might conceivably be the Moslems (overturning his boat).

31-36. These lines may not be meant to be part of this direct specch, but a description of the scene (there are never any inverted commas or dashes anywhere in the early texts).

36. Porque todos sabía honrrar: "he knew how to treat everyone properly".

39. Xerga (jerga): as if it were "sackcloth".

45. Medina Sidonia, an important castle North-West of Gibraltar, but (47) even so, not enough of a reward and memorial for his family.

46. Doy más: Menéndez y Pelayo interpreted this as an elided version of "de hoy más", "from today on", rather than "doy más", "I give more"; which could well be right.

65. FAJARDO

1. Chess was introduced from the East into Europe by the Moslems, so it would be expected that the King of Granada was expert.

3. Aquesse: "that", implying that Pedro Fajardo was well known and needed no further introduction. He was "adelantado", frontier-governor, of Murcia, on the Eastern end of the frontier. There may never have been a game of chess in this manner, but it seems likely that the tale is based on the breaking of some kind of gentlemen´s agreement about something, for the two were indeed friends (1.4).

5-6. Almería was an important port at the Eastern end of the Kingdom of Granada; Lorca was a strategic Christian frontier town, of less importance than Almería.

7-8. The subjects of the verbs in these lines are ambiguous. The English takes it to mean, as seems most natural in the Spanish wording, that Fajardo checks the King's king with his castle, and then the King's bishop takes Fajardo's castle, thereby winning the game; a neat to and fro (reminiscent of Roncesvalles, no.31). But the King could be the subject of both verbs; "he checked him with his rook, thereby taking the bishop". Nykl argued not only that this is the right reading but that Timoneda changed an original "alferza" ("Queen") into "orfil"; which seems unlikely. Other versions have "alférez", "knight", but "orfil" (= the more usual "alfil", both from Arabic "fil") is entirely plausible. The point remains in all versions that the Moslem wins.

13-18. Fajardo has lost, but refuses to hand over the stake. Fajardo's refusal is similar to Granada's rejection of King Juan's proposal (in no.62); the two sides respect each other, but feel they have to hold on to what is theirs.

15-16. The town is rendered as "she" rather than "it" partly on the analogy of Granada (no.62) and partly since, as Rogers pointed out, this contest is comparable to knights jousting for a lady, and some other boardgames (in stories) actually used women as wagers.

23-24. The King accepts that if Fajardo is not going to give it up, he cannot take it. Peaceful relations are maintained.

66. MORAIMA

This famous ballad is usually not regarded as a "frontier" ballad, since it deals with relations between the two communities within Christian Andalucía. The story may well have a factual origin, but if so, that is now lost.

4. From this use of "cuytada", "miserable", we can tell from the start that the outcome was unhappy for her; presumably that she was raped, and the narrative tension resides in seeing how the Christian tricked her. Aguirre, however, takes the whole ballad as Moraima's defending herself against the charge of having willingly made love with the Christian, since this is the line taken in Pinar's later "Glosa" of this ballad; yet the composer of a "Glosa" was at liberty to use the original words for any new purpose, and might well have wished to present a fellow-Christian in a less sinister light, so the original point of this ballad can probably be taken at face value as a victim's lament. The frontier spirit, in which humanity overrides any crusader bigotry, thus appears again. This poem is sympathising with a

girl tricked by an attacker, the codes of peace having been as
treacherously exploited here as the codes of war were at Álora
(no.63). This cross-religious sympathy is so normal in Southern
ballads that it is hard to agree with the argument put forward by
Mirrer-Singer, that a Spanish poem cannot express sympathy for a
Moslem and so this must represent instead a Christian denunciation of
all Moslems´ essential lawlessness (for Moraima aims to shelter a
fugitive from justice).

5.   The Christian has worked hard to deceive her, for not many of them
knew Arabic, while most Moslems (outside Granada) knew at least some
Spanish.

8.   For a Christian to invoke Allah is not only deceitful but
bordering on heresy, so it is not likely that many Christians in the
audience will have felt much solidarity with him.

9-10.   Mezquina: like "cuytada", this is an adjective agreeing with
the speaker, and hard to translate as such into English. Moraima shows
some elementary prudence; there were houses in which a Moslem girl
would always open to an insistent stranger, and the audience have to
be reassured that this is not one of those.

11-12.   The Christian pretends to be her uncle, thereby defusing any
appearance of menace. Mazote is the Hispanization of the Arabic name
Mas´ud. She must have an uncle of this name for the deception to work,
so we can see that the Christian has briefed himself in advance, and
is acting with cold calculation.

14.   After exploiting religious and family solidarity, he now exploits
the solidarity inspired by the weaker religious community´s fear of
domination. The "alcalde", though it is in origin an Arabic word, is
the name for the chief law officer, in this case a Christian.

19-20.   She has been led to omit sensible precautions and wear
something very flimsy. The same comment appears in the Melisenda
ballad (no.18, 9-10), but there it is meant to seem sexy; here it is a
sign of vulnerability.

22.   So she has opened the door and is defenceless, and since we
already know what happened next there is no need to be more explicit.

67. ALHAMA (1)

The final campaign against Granada began in 1481. This was a more serious assault than before, inspired by the international Christian community's worry that a Moslem kingdom in the West of Europe might be a fifth column at a time of Moslem Turkish advance in the East. It was to be carried out with a sense of purpose and hostility that had been lacking before.

1. The speaker is one of several envoys from the King of Granada; the addressee is the former governor ("alcaide") of Alhama.

4. A Christian attack captured Alhama on the 28th February 1482. This came as a considerable shock to Granada, for Alhama is in fact very close to the South-West of the city of Granada itself, and the Christian forces had had to cover several miles of Granadan territory to get there. The commander of the town could hardly have foreseen such an attack, since it was not on the frontier and the more serious nature of the new campaign was not yet apparent to them. In retrospect, it looks like the beginning of the end of the kingdom.

17-24. He was still responsible for the defence of the town in his absence, even though the King had given him permission to leave. He had crossed the frontier to Antequera (in Christian hands since 1410) for a social event as he would have naturally done in peacetime. This frontier ballad expresses more poignantly than most the sorrow felt by people on both sides that their previous peaceable relations were being overtaken by an inter-religious hostility alien to the frontier region itself, imported by self-conscious and militaristic commanders from elsewhere. Their frontier life was going with the wind; and was to be looked back at with nostalgia after the eventual fall of Granada (1492).

17. A shorter and probably later version has the governor going not to Antequera but to Ronda, which was still in Moslem hands, for the wedding of his cousin rather than of his sister.

20. It may be implied that the Christians in Antequera had arranged this to have him out of the way during the attack.

28. The governor reckons that he has suffered more than the King, losing his honour and his family. (This may not have been true; it seems from the next ballad that the King felt the loss very personally).

34. The Marquis of Cádiz was indeed the commander of the assault.

35.   Presumably this is meant to be a large figure, although in no.69
100 doblas seems to be the price of a slave and in no.62 the cost of
an artesan´s daily wage, so if there was a ransom offered in reality
it was probably more than this. It would have been accepted in earlier
times that prisoners were taken in war for the purpose of eventual
ransom; the shame is not so much in the capture as in the fact that
apparently she would rather remain in Christian hands. In no.62 the
point of attacking Granada (in 1431) was the extraction of money, but
now the point of the fighting (as seen on the Christian side in 1481)
is more one of religious hostility.

39-41.   María and Fátima are identifying as Christian and Moslem
names respectively. A Christian audience, for whom ballads in Spanish
were largely destined, could see the shame involved as much as he did.

43.   Granada: that is, the city itself.

50.   Islamic justice, when taken seriously, is very harsh. Losing
Moslem generals were sometimes crucified.

68. ALHAMA (2)

1.   This ballad is based on the same event as the last one, but
whereas there the King of Granada was the villain, here he is the
focus of our sympathy. Pérez de Hita published a more sentimental
version with a six-syllabled refrain inserted after every four lines,
"¡Ay de mi Alhama!", which has become more well-known than this
comparatively sober version found in all the earlier Romanceros.

5-8.   These are common reactions to bad news in the tradition.

9-10.   The horse is more business-like than the mule.

14.   The Moors are working in the "Vega", the valley below the
Alhambra.

23-32.   The gist of this section is that the loss of Alhama is some
kind of divine punishment. Pérez de Hita´s version puts the complaint
in the mouth of an "alfaquí", "fakir", a religious leader.

25.   The King (Boabdil) had been involved in civil war against these
"Bencerrajes", and it was widely thought (on both sides of the
frontier) that he had been in the wrong in the argument.

27.   In 1481 there had been persecutions of the Jewish communities in
Christian Andalucía, and several fled to Granada.

32. This seems to mean that the King has gone slightly mad, literally "because of your changed condition".

35. If Alhama was lost through the absence of its commander, it is all the more important not to leave Granada similarly undefended. Pérez de Hita´s version, composed long after 1492, includes here a prophecy of the loss of the kingdom. Such prophecies are easy to insert with hindsight after they are known to have been going to be fulfilled. This version has no such prediction, and may in origin date from close to the event.

43. Rodrigo Ponce de León, Marquis of Cádiz. (Cáliz is an alternative form of Cádiz).

49-52. Pérez de Hita´s prose history of these years suggests that this is true; the King of Granada tried, almost at once but in vain, to recapture it.

69. THE CAPTIVE

1. The participants in this tale are not public figures and it is probable that there is no reference to specific people intended. This ballad concerns relations between Christians and Moors, but it is not clear when it is set; it seems most probably set (and therefore composed) some time after the defeat of Granada. In structure it is similar to the ballad on Espinelo (no.21), as it opens with the hero´s lover asking him about his life, and the body of it concerns his adventures and how he arrived to where he is at the start. This does not mean that either ballad copied the other; they both exploited one of the structural possibilities that seem to be available to tale-tellers.

2. Esposo: this does not necessarily mean husband (as with Roldán in no.16).

7. She knows that he has been a captive, but not the details.

11. Other versions of this ballad start here. His father is from Ronda, a mountain fortress-town on the road from Málaga to Jerez; so presumably Ronda had been Christian for some time. It was taken only in 1485, so the ballad would seem to be set long after that.

14. Entre la paz y la guerra: this probably means that it was a warlike raid carried out at a time of official peace.

16. Vélez de la Gomera is an island off the coast of Morocco, much

fought over by Spaniards and Moors throughout the sixteenth century. Usually it was in Moorish hands and a base for pirates, so in a sixteenth-century context this detail makes sense whenever the singer and audience think it is meant to be set. Variants have the slave-sale at Jerez de la Frontera, which had been in Christian hands since the thirteenth century (long before either Antequera or Ronda), so it looks as though they are late compositions setting the tale at a time before the conquest; and happening to come up with a historical impossibility, although no sixteenth-century audience would mind about that even if they realized.

15. Slaves usually were prisoners of war. This happened in the late sixteenth century to, among others, Cervantes.

32. Ama; "mistress". Menéndez y Pelayo´s text misprinted this as "alma", which must have baffled hundreds of students.

35-38. Modern versions of the tale have expanded this scene into a whole conversation.

37.. Espulgava: "she took the lice out of my hair", a practical and charitable task that would also be seen as sensual.

39. This phrase is at once vague and unambiguous; were we to guess what is meant we would be right.

41-44. The translation has reversed these two couplets for practical reasons.

47-48. This is probably not meant to imply that he had been in her arms before, merely that he was back in Spain again.

70. THE CAPTURE OF BOABDIL

1. The river Genil rises in the Sierra Nevada and goes through Granada and Écija before joining the Guadalquivir; but this opening in practice unambiguously situates us near Granada.

10. This ballad adopts a cinematic technique; we see the distraught rider before we know the reason for his distress.

11. King Boabdil of Granada, known also as "Rey Chico" ("Little King"), was captured by the Christians at Lucena on the 21st April 1483.

21-23. Diego Hernández de Córdoba, "alcayde de los donzeles", was in charge of the King´s personal household.

30.   Cabra is on the road West-North-West from Granada; Lucena is very close by to the South.

39-48.   We might expect a Spanish poem to gloat over the Moslems´ distress, and of course it would be possible to perform this in such a way; but there is no hint of such an attitude in the text, where the lament seems to be meant to touch us as sincerely as that for the death of Arias Gonzalo´s son in ballad no.46.

51-56.   The ransom offered was so great that it was thought worth accepting.

57-58.   Indeed, the Moslems, with their personal affection for their King, could be made to seem to come out of this tale better than the Christians.
      This ballad is unusual for having full rhyme rather than merely assonance; every couplet ends in "-ido". Is this monotonous and obtrusive? If the audience notices it, then it is; the structure is meant to shape our appreciation of the tale, not to be an object of admiration in its own right.

71. RODRIGO TÉLLEZ DE GIRÓN

1.   The late sixteenth century saw a vogue for creating new Romanticized ballads about Granada; when the historical reality was lost, the place became part of the generalized "Romantic Orient" where exotic tales of decadent chivalry could be set. Such Romanticism survived into serious histories of even the present century. The frontier is here seen as a background for colourful jousts; fights are over a man´s reputation among the women rather than life and death for communities.

15.   A Christian could be identified by a cross, as a Moslem by a crescent.

22.   It would be possible for the Queen to see the "Vega" (riverside) of the Genil from the walls of the Alhambra.

23.   At last the colourfully-presented protagonist is identified. In the Spanish the all-purpose "Maestre" figure that turns up in several such episodes is in this case no further identified than by his title, "Maestre"; most singers and audiences might have left it at that, but Pérez de Hita makes it clear that he identifies this hero-figure as Don Rodrigo Téllez de Girón, who was Maestre ("Master") of the Military Order of Calatrava (a title explained in the notes to ballad no.54) from 1466, when he was aged 12, till his death in 1482. He was

an illegitimate twin son of the previous Maestre Pedro Girón, and in
all probability never went near Granada in his life, yet his name has
become available in the tradition for this sort of escapade. Alvar
(chapter 2, part 3, section 3) and Cirot discuss this further. The
title "Maestre" itself seemed quaint in the late sixteenth century,
since one of Isabel´s reforms (at the end of the fifteenth) had been
to concentrate all these titles of Maestre in the person of her
husband Fernando, and the "Maestres" were no longer the separate and
very powerful nobles that they had once been. As can be seen from the
fact that the illegitimate Rodrigo inherited his title from his father
at the age of twelve, the system had become open to cynical abuse.

27-82.   There is nothing in this ballad other than the events; the
emotions seem superficial and the confrontation artificial, so it is
generally thought (now) that ballads of this type are much inferior to
the genuine frontier ballads. It is, none the less, a colourful and
well told tale.

76.   This is a nice, if gruesome, touch; the Queen is expecting a
head, but not that one. But since the characters are presented as
cardboard figureheads rather than as humans, an audience will not feel
upset by this ending, as they would at the decapitation of Fadrique in
no.54, for example.

INDEX OF SPANISH FIRST LINES

More Medieval texts in the Hispanic Classics Series
General Editors: Professor Brian Tate, University of Nottingham
and Professor Joseph Snow, University of Georgia

THE POEM OF MY CID translated by Peter Such & John Hodgkinson
cloth 0 85668 321 3, limp 0 85668 322 1

Fernão Lopes THE ENGLISH IN PORTUGAL 1383-1387 translated by
Derek Lomax & Bob Oakley
cloth 0 85668 341 8, limp 0 85668 342 6

Juan Manuel EL CONDE LUCANOR translated by John England
cloth 0 85668 325 6, limp 0 85668 326 4

Fernando de Rojas CELESTINA translated by Dorothy Sherman Severin
cloth 0 85668 371 X, limp 0 85668 372 8

TEXTS OF THE RECONQUEST OF SPAIN translated by Colin Smith
cloth 0 85668 410 4, limp 0 85668 411 2

The Hispanic Classics Series also includes texts by Lope de Vega,
Calderón, Tirso de Molina, Quevedo, Lorca ..

*For full catalogues of this series and of our Classical Texts, including
medieval Latin and Arabic, please write to:*

ARIS & PHILLIPS Ltd., Teddington House, Church Street,
Warminster, BA12 8PQ